Clinician's Guide to Evidence-Based Practices

Mental Health and the Addictions

Clinician's Guide to Evidence-Based Practices

Mental Health and the Addictions

John C. Norcross, Thomas P. Hogan, & Gerald P. Koocher

OXFORD
UNIVERSITY PRESS
2008

OXFORD
UNIVERSITY PRESS

Oxford University Press, Inc., publishes works that further
Oxford University's objective of excellence
in research, scholarship, and education.

Oxford New York

Auckland   Cape Town   Dar es Salaam   Hong Kong   Karachi
Kuala Lumpur   Madrid   Melbourne   Mexico City   Nairobi
New Delhi   Shanghai   Taipei   Toronto

With offices in

Argentina   Austria   Brazil   Chile   Czech Republic   France   Greece
Guatemala   Hungary   Italy   Japan   Poland   Portugal   Singapore
South Korea   Switzerland   Thailand   Turkey   Ukraine   Vietnam

Published by Oxford University Press, Inc.
198 Madison Avenue, New York, New York 10016
www.oup.com

Oxford is a registered trademark of Oxford University Press

Library of Congress Cataloging-in-Publication Data
Norcross, John C., 1957–
Clinician's guide to evidence-based practices : mental health and the addictions/John C.
Norcross, Thomas P. Hogan, & Gerald P. Koocher.
p. ; cm.
Includes bibliographical references and index.
ISBN: 978-0-19-533532-3 (pbk.)
1. Evidence-based psychiatry. 2. Mental illness—Treatment. 3. Substance abuse—
Treatment. I. Hogan, Thomas P. II. Koocher, Gerald P. III. Title.
[DNLM: 1. Mental Disorders--therapy—Handbooks. 2. Evidence-Based Medicine—
Handbooks. 3. Substance-Related Disorders—therapy—Handbooks. WM 34 N827c 2008]
RC455.2.E94N67 2008
616.89—dc22   2007037565

1 3 5 7 9 8 6 4 2

Printed in the United States of America
on acid-free paper

Dedicated to
Veracious Evidence

Contents

▌▌▐▐ ▐
ABOUT THE AUTHORS

JOHN C. NORCROSS, PHD, ABPP, is professor of psychology and Distinguished University Fellow at the University of Scranton, editor of the *Journal of Clinical Psychology: In Session*, and a clinical psychologist in part-time practice. Author of more than 300 scholarly publications, Dr. Norcross has written or coedited 15 books. The most recent include *Evidence-Based Practices in Mental Health: Debate and Dialogue on the Fundamental Questions, Psychotherapy Relationships that Work, Leaving It at the Office: A Guide to Psychotherapist Self-Care*, the sixth edition of *Systems of Psychotherapy*, and *An Insider's Guide to Graduate Programs in Clinical and Counseling Psychology*. He is president-elect of the American Psychological Association (APA) Society of Clinical Psychology, past president of the APA Division of Psychotherapy, and Council Representative of the APA. Dr. Norcross also served on the APA Presidential Task Force on Evidence-Based Practices.

THOMAS P. HOGAN, PHD, is professor of psychology and Distinguished University Fellow at the University of Scranton, where he also served as dean of the Graduate School and director of research, as well as interim provost/academic vice president. He served previously as associate vice chancellor for Graduate and Professional Programs at the University of Wisconsin–Green

Bay. He is the author of two textbooks—*Psychological Testing: A Practical Introduction* and *Educational Assessment*—and several nationally standardized tests, including the *Survey of School Attitudes,* and coauthor of three editions of *Metropolitan Achievement Tests.* He has authored numerous articles on measurement practices in such journals as *Educational and Psychological Measurement, Mathematical Thinking and Learning,* and *Journal of Educational Measurement*; and he is a regular contributor to the *Mental Measurements Yearbook.* He is a former member of the Exercise Development Advisory Committee for the National Assessment of Educational Progress (NAEP).

GERALD P. KOOCHER, PHD, ABPP, is professor and dean of the School for Health Studies at Simmons College in Boston and editor of the journal *Ethics & Behavior.* He served as the 2006 president of the APA and, before that, as president of the Massachusetts and New England Psychological Associations as well as three APA divisions. Dr. Koocher formerly served as editor of the *Journal of Pediatric Psychology* and *The Clinical Psychologist.* He has authored or coauthored more than 175 articles and chapters, in addition to 11 books. His text (with Patricia Keith-Spiegel) *Ethics in Psychology: Professional Standards and Cases* is the bestselling textbook in its field, and his coedited *Psychologists' Desk Reference* is now in its second edition. He holds specialty certification from the American Board of Professional Psychology in five areas (clinical, child and adolescent, family, forensic, and health psychology).

▌▌▌▌▌
INTRODUCTION

We all recognize that clinical practice should be predicated on the best available research integrated with the clinician's expertise within the context of the particular patient. Practice should draw guidance from the very best research. Yet, so much of the research literature feels inaccessible and overwhelming, too removed and too large to guide what we do daily with our patients. Over the years, we also seem to have less time to retrieve the research, less capacity to understand new and complicated research designs, and, for some of us, fewer skills to electronically access the research. We have designed this book to overcome these challenges to evidence-based practice (EBP); here, we provide you with the skills to retrieve and use research in order to benefit your patients suffering from mental health and addictive disorders.

Our book is a concise, practical guide designed to assist mental health and addiction practitioners in accessing, interpreting, and applying EBPs. It is a how-to manual on EBPs.

The *Clinician's Guide to Evidence-Based Practices: Mental Health and the Addictions* is accompanied by a CD of the entire text. In addition, the CD features expanded content, interactive examples, and hyperlinked references.

Our target audience is broad and multidisciplinary. We write for busy practitioners and trainees in mental health and addictions who desire to access and apply the scientific research in order to more effectively serve their patients. Our audience includes psychologists, psychiatrists, social workers, counselors, addiction counselors, marital and family therapists, and psychiatric nurses. It also includes graduate students, interns, residents, and early career clinicians of all theoretical persuasions. As emphasized in its subtitle, the book focuses on mental health and addictions.

Although EBPs rely heavily on the scientific research, we have written this guide for practitioners and students, not for researchers. We assume that readers will have completed an introductory statistics or research methods course and thus will have familiarity with measures of central tendency, correlation coefficients, control groups, and other foundational material. At the same time, most readers will probably require a refresher, which we provide, and will enjoy many reader-friendly graphics and helpful summaries, which we also offer throughout.

The goal of EBPs is to infuse clinical work with the best scientific research, thereby guiding practice and training. In so doing, we assure that our clients will routinely receive effective, research-supported treatments. Our students will receive training in those same treatments and will commit themselves to updating their competencies throughout their professional careers. In this respect, virtually every mental health and addiction professional endorses the ethical and professional commitment to EBPs. Surely no one would advocate for the opposite: non-evidence-based practices.

While we enthusiastically support the goal of EBPs, we also harbor concerns about the reckless extrapolation of research from the lab to the consulting room and the insensitive imposition of premature EBP lists onto clinicians and their clients. The clinician's contribution and the patient's voice form a crucial foundation for establishing a successful treatment plan. In this respect, we advocate for inclusive EBPs that truly incorporate the three pillars of any EBP definition: best research evidence, clinical expertise, and patient characteristics.

The Content

The structure and contents of the *Clinician's Guide to Evidence-Based Practices: Mental Health and the Addictions* reflect the delicate balance between research-guided practice, on the one hand, and clinician and patient-informed practice, on the other. The optimal situation, of course, occurs when the extant research, clinician expertise, and patient values converge. However, we also address those situations when they do not.

In Chapter 1, we summarize the origins and definitions of EBPs. We also introduce three clinically realistic and representative clients (Jonathon, Francesco, Annique) whom we shall follow throughout the book to illustrate the real-life application of EBPs. From there, in Chapter 2, we focus on asking the right clinical questions—truly the beginning of any research-informed pursuit.

In Chapter 3, Lauren Maggio, a medical librarian specializing in health informatics, presents the skills of locating the best available research. She shows how to translate a clinical question into a targeted literature search, use search strategies, select search terms, access a wide range of information resources, and find information on tests and measures.

Then, a trio of interrelated chapters (4, 5, 6) provides a practice-friendly refresher on research designs, numbers, statistics, and the actual reports of research. Not to worry: We promise not to retraumatize any statistics-challenged practitioners. Instead, we remind you of the specialized vocabulary and appraisal skills required to dip into the research literature in order to inform your practice and, ideally, its effectiveness.

Once reacquainted with the fundamentals of reading and interpreting the research, in Chapter 7 we tackle the complexities of translating research into practice. Such translation cannot occur without carefully incorporating the patient and the clinician into the process—the aim of Chapter 8.

The closing two chapters address evaluation and education in EBPs. Chapter 9 demonstrates ways of evaluating the effectiveness and ethics of our clinical decision-making in EBPs. Chapter 10 features tips on disseminating, teaching, and implementing EBPs.

In short, the *Clinician's Guide to Evidence-Based Practices: Mental Health and the Addictions* canvasses the entire EBP process—asking the right questions, accessing the best available research, appraising the research, translating that research into practice, integrating that research with clinician expertise and patient characteristics, evaluating the entire enterprise, attending to the ethical considerations, and when done, moving the EBP process forward by teaching it to others.

The CD

The *Clinician's Guide to Evidence-Based Practices: Mental Health and the Addictions* is intentionally concise and pocket-sized. The downside of that decision was a restriction on the amount of text and the number of examples we could print in the book. We have overcome this restriction by including a mini-CD with each book.

The accompanying CD offers expanded content, interactive examples, and hyperlinked references. Look for the following box throughout the text:

These boxes alert you to additional EBP aids and practical resources on the CD. We hope you will take the time to explore and work through the CD materials.

▌▌▌▌
Instructions for Installing the CD

PC Users

To run the CD-ROM, your computer must have a CD-ROM drive, Windows XP or above, and Adobe Acrobat Reader software (version 8.0 and higher). You can obtain a free, current version of Adobe Acrobat Reader at www.adobe.com. Note: Excel files within the CD bonus material need Microsoft Office 2003 or higher to open.

1. Insert the disk into your computer's CD-ROM drive. It may open automatically. If it does not, proceed to the next step.
2. Click start, select RUN, select BROWSE, and select your CD-ROM drive.
3. Double-click the file named "CliniciansGuide.pdf " to begin.

The PDF contains the entire book text and bonus material. To access the bonus material, click the "CD Bonus" icon located throughout the text.

Macintosh Users

To run the CD-ROM, your computer must have a CD-ROM drive and Adobe Acrobat Reader software (version 8.0 and higher). You can obtain a free, current version of Adobe Acrobat Reader at www.adobe.com. Note: Excel files within the CD bonus material need Microsoft Office 2004 or higher to open.

1. Insert the disk into your computer's CD-ROM drive. It may open automatically. If it does not, proceed to the next step.
2. Open the CD-ROM icon that appears on your desktop.
3. Double-click the file named "CliniciansGuide.pdf " to begin.

The PDF contains the entire book text and bonus material. To access the bonus material, click the "CD Bonus" icon located throughout the text.

Clinician's Guide to Evidence-Based Practices

Mental Health and the Addictions

CHAPTER 1

Defining
Evidence-Based Practice

This chapter sets the stage for the book by sketching a brief history of evidence-based practice (EBP), explicating the definition and purpose of EBPs, outlining the EBP controversies, introducing three composite patients who will reappear as examples throughout the book, and identifying the core skills in conducting EBP. As befitting a how-to manual, we leave it to others (see Recommended Readings and Web Sites) to detail the history and debates surrounding EBPs in mental health and addictions.

Short History of Evidence-Based Practice

Evidence-based practice has a long past but a short history. The long past entails hundreds of years of effort to base clinical practice on the results of solid research. Starting with its separation from philosophy and Wilhelm Wundt's early laboratory experiments, psychology has always prided itself on having deep scientific roots. Similarly, from Emil Kraeplin's diagnostic scheme to Benjamin Rush's empirical efforts, psychiatry has also tried to establish itself as a science of mind (Norcross, Beutler, & Levant, 2006a). Addiction treatment was slower to embrace empirical research, having its origins in Alcoholics Anonymous and self-help traditions, but has been increasingly guided by scientific research.

The short past of EBPs in mental health traces back to the 1990s, originally in Great Britain and then gathering steam in Canada, the United States, and now around the globe. Figure 1.1 presents the annual number of citations for *evidence-based* since 1992 in three national databases: MEDLINE (medicine), CINAHL (nursing and allied health care), and PsycINFO (psychology; also see Walker, Seay, Solomon, & Spring, 2006). Since the early 1990s, we have witnessed an exponential growth in the number of articles invoking EBPs. Truly, EBP has become an international juggernaut.

In mental health, the EBP movement has become most visible (and controversial) in identifying certain "evidence-based" treatments in the form of compilations, lists, and guidelines and then publicizing these to fellow practitioners, training programs, and health-care payers. A few prominent examples follow:

♦ Task forces of several American Psychological Association (APA) divisions have published compilations of evidence-based or empirically supported treatments. These exist for children, adolescents, adults, and older adults suffering from a multitude of disorders. In addition, several APA divisions have enlarged the scope of EBPs beyond treatments to embrace evidence-based

Clinician's Guide to Evidence-Based Practices

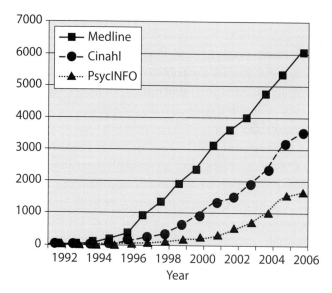

Figure 1.1 Number of articles retrieved using "evidence based" as keyword.

therapeutic relationships (Norcross, 2002a, 2002b), clinical assessments (Hunsley, Crabb, & Mash, 2004), and principles of change (Castonguay & Beutler, 2006).

♦ The American Psychiatric Association has published 15 practice guidelines on disorders ranging from schizophrenia to anorexia to nicotine dependence. Although only recently identified as explicitly "evidence-based," they and similar guidelines are identical in intent: Use the best available knowledge to compile statements of "what works" or "best practices." Literally hundreds of health-care guidelines are now widely available (see National Guideline Clearinghouse at http://www.guideline.gov).

♦ The Substance Abuse and Mental Health Services Administration (SAMHSA) has created the National Registry of Evidence-Based Programs and Practices (www.nrepp.samhsa.gov), designed to provide the public with reliable information on the scientific value and practicality of interventions that prevent and/or treat mental and substance abuse disorders.

Evidence-based practices have profound implications for practice, training, and policy. What earns the privileged designation of "evidence-based" will increasingly determine, in large part, what we practice, what we teach, and what research wins funding. The long past but short history of EBPs will increasingly require professionals to base their practice, to whatever extent possible, on research evidence. No profession can afford to sit on the sidelines; no practitioner can afford to ignore the juggernaut.

Definitions

A consensual and concrete definition of EBPs has emerged from the literature. Adapting a definition from Sackett and colleagues, the Institute of Medicine (2001, p. 147) defined **evidence-based medicine (EBM)** as "the integration of best research evidence with clinical expertise and patient values." The APA Task Force on Evidence-Based Practice (2006, p. 273), beginning with this foundation and expanding it to mental health, defined **evidence-based practice** as "the integration of the best available research with clinical expertise in the context of patient characteristics, culture, and preferences." We will use the latter as our operational definition throughout.

Several core features of EBPs are manifest in this definition. First, EBPs rest on three pillars: available research, clinician expertise, and patient characteristics, culture, and preferences. By definition, the wholesale imposition of research without attending to the clinician or patient is *not* EBP; conversely, the indiscriminate disregard of available research is *not* EBP. Second, the definition requires integrating these three evidentiary sources. The integration flows seamlessly and uncontested when the three evidentiary sources agree; the integration becomes flawed and contested when the three sources disagree (see Chapters 7 and 8). Third, not all three pillars are equal: Research assumes priority in EBP. Clinicians begin with research and then integrate with their expertise and patients' values. Fourth, compared to EBM, the patient assumes a more active, prominent position in EBPs in mental health and addictions. "Patient values" in EBM are elevated to "patient characteristics, culture, and preferences" in mental health EBPs. Fifth and finally, the treating professional performs the integration and makes the final determinations in collaboration with the patient. The practitioner makes the ultimate judgment regarding a particular intervention or treatment plan. Treatment decisions should never be made by untrained persons unfamiliar with the specifics of the case.

Part of the contention surrounding EBP revolves around the definitions of its three constituent pillars. Below we offer definitions of each of these pillars, borrowing again from the APA Task Force (2006).

- **Best available research:** clinically relevant research, often from basic health science, that will most likely yield accurate, unbiased, and relevant answers to the practice question posed for a particular patient or patient group. The research can relate to prevalence, treatment, assessment, disorders, and patient populations in laboratory and field settings. Such research evidence should be based on systematic reviews, reasonable effect sizes, statistical and clinical significance, and a body of supporting evidence.

- **Clinical expertise:** the clinician's skills and past experiences that promote positive therapeutic outcomes, including conducting assessments, developing diagnostic judgments, making clinical decisions, implementing treatments, monitoring patient progress, using interpersonal expertise, understanding cultural differences, and seeking available resources (e.g., consultation, adjunctive or alternative services) as needed. Integral to clinical expertise is an awareness of the limits of one's skills and attention to the heuristics that can hamper clinical judgment.

- **Patient characteristics, culture, and preferences:** the patient's (or patient group's) personality, strengths, sociocultural context, unique concerns, and preferences brought to a clinical encounter that must be integrated into clinical decisions to best serve the patient. Clinical decisions should evolve in collaboration with the patient and in consideration of the probable costs, benefits, and available resources. Individual patients may require unique decisions and interventions not directly addressed by the available research. The involvement of an active, informed patient will generally prove crucial to the success of mental health and addiction services. (We will occasionally use *patient characteristics* as an inclusive shorthand for the cumbersome *patient characteristics, culture, and preferences*.)

Purpose of Evidence-Based Practices

Here, we have perfect unanimity. The purpose of EBPs lies in promoting effective mental health and addiction practices. As applied to individual clinicians, EBP should increase the efficacy, efficiency, and applicability of services provided to individual patients (or patient groups). These services will include assessment, case formulation, prevention, therapeutic relationship, treatment, and consultation. As applied to society as a whole, EBP should enhance public health.

The CD contains hyperlinks to formal policy statements on EBP by several professional associations, including the APA and the American Medical Association.

The Evidence-Based Practice Controversies

As any mental health practitioner can readily attest, language has enormous power. Freud famously remarked that words were once magic. Words can diminish or privilege.

So it is with EBPs. At first blush, there is near universal agreement that we should use evidence as a guide in determining what works. It's like publicly prizing motherhood and apple pie. Can anyone seriously advocate the reverse: non-evidence-based practice?

But it is neither as simple nor as consensual as that. Deciding what qualifies as evidence, applying research to individual cases, and determining the optimal balance of research, clinical expertise, and patient values are complicated matters with deep philosophical and huge practical consequences. While unanimity exists on the purpose of EBPs, the path to that goal is crammed with contention—what some have described as the "EBP culture wars" (Messer, 2004).

By way of review, here are our top 10 controversies concerning EBPs (see Norcross et al., 2006a, for point–counterpoint arguments on each controversy).

1. *What qualifies as evidence of effective practice?* Yes, all three pillars—best available research, clinical expertise, and patient characteristics—but which should assume priority? If clinician expertise based on personal beliefs and clinical experiences stands as an equal component of "evidence" and unchecked against objective criteria, then clinical expertise may become a source of bias in judgment and the very source of error that controlled research was designed to overcome.

2. *What qualifies as research for effective practice?* The easy answer is that we should employ different research methodologies to address different clinical questions: for example, epidemiological research to ascertain prevalence rates; process–outcome research to demonstrate specific clinician behaviors that produce favorable outcome; effectiveness research to address whether a treatment works in naturalistic, real-world settings;

and **randomized clinical trials** (RCTs) to determine treatment efficacy. But the harder answer depends on the degree to which we rely on the "gold standard" of RCTs, as in medicine, to determine "what works." A spirited debate centers on the privileged status accorded to RCTs and their placement at the zenith in the hierarchy of evidence. Should case studies, qualitative designs, controlled single-participant studies, and effectiveness studies also have a role in determining effective practice?

3. *What treatment outcomes should establish EBPs?* Medicine often has physical, measurable indices of treatment outcome, such as laboratory measurements and pathology reports. By contrast, mental health and addiction have few physical indices and must rely on patient self-reports, even when reliably measured on valid self-report tests. For some outcomes, such as pain and quality of life, medicine and behavioral science struggle to find valid and reliable assessments together. Should we trust patient self-reports, which tend to be reactive and to reflect only one perspective? Should we employ more objective behavioral indices, therapist judgment, and external/societal decisions on "what works"?

4. *Does manualization improve treatment outcomes?* Outcome research requires that patients receive a similar, if not identically standardized, intervention. In medication trials, this standardization involves administering the same medication at the same dose or following a standard protocol. In mental health research, this standardization has frequently involved the use of treatment manuals and observation checks to insure fidelity. In fact, manualization has been deemed a prerequisite for inclusion in most compilations of EBPs. While treatment manuals

indisputably prove helpful for training and research, the research on their value in improving treatment outcomes shows mixed results. Should such manuals be required in practice?

5. *Do research patients and clinical trials accurately represent real-world practice?* Evidence-based practices seek to identify the most effective treatments in research studies so that we can widely implement those same treatments in practice. However, research findings do not automatically or inevitably generalize. Many hitches occur in generalizing from the lab to the clinic, in translating science to service. Just how representative are the patients in clinical trials? Can we safely extrapolate the research findings to our practice and to our patients? The degree to which we can confidently generalize remains a source of fierce debate.

6. *What should we seek to validate?* What accounts for effective treatment? In biomedical research, we traditionally credit the specific treatment method—the medication, the surgery, the discrete method applied to the patient—for successful outcomes. In mental health and addictions research, however, we often find diverse perspectives and conflicting results. Some argue that the treatment method forms the natural and inclusive target for research validation, while others argue that the psychotherapist, the therapy relationship, and the patient actually account for more of the success and, thus, should be targets for research validation and EBPs.

7. *What influences what is published as evidence?* The production, dissemination, and interpretation of research are inherently human endeavors, subject to the foibles and failings of human behavior. No purely "objective" or "unbiased" pursuit of

truth exists. As mental health professionals, we know that human behavior is influenced by a multiplicity of factors, some beyond our immediate awareness; and conducting research is no exception. Research results fall under the inevitable influence of the researcher's theoretical allegiance, funding sources, and conventional wisdom. Can we deem such research trustworthy? Should we ignore it as tainted by nonscientific biases?

8. ***Do treatments designated as EBPs produce outcomes superior to non-EBPs?*** By definition, treatments designated as evidence-based outperform no treatment and placebo treatment. We can confidently state that EBPs are superior to no treatment and sham treatments; however, we cannot state that EBPs are necessarily "best practices" or "treatments of choice" unless they outperform bona fide, structurally equivalent therapies. It remains unclear and controversial whether EBPs perform reliably better than practices not designated as evidence-based.

9. ***How well do EBPs address patient diversity?*** Neither EBPs nor treatments as usual satisfactorily address all of the dimensions of human diversity encountered in mental health and addictions. The patient's race/ethnicity, gender, sexual orientation, socioeconomic level, and disability status interacting with outcome have largely gone unstudied to date. The ensuing contention is to what degree EBPs, validated primarily on studies with majority populations, qualify as "evidence-based" for marginalized or minority clients.

10. ***Do efficacious, laboratory-validated treatments readily transport to clinical practice?*** Surely, something is lost in transport from the lab to the consulting room. Efficacious laboratory-validated treatments can transport to other practice settings and

situations but do not necessarily. The degree and predictability of transportability have become bones of contention.

Reading this top-10 list alone might lead one to conclude that there is rampant professional discord about EBPs. And there is. However, an impressive consensus also exists in the definition and purpose of EBP, and we have observed a nascent convergence on many of these contentious points. We remind readers that this process is the typical response to innovation in the professions and the normal path of science. Innovations beget conflict and engender further research. In the meantime, practitioners move forward to provide their patients—and society as a whole—with the most effective, evidence-based services at their disposal.

Three Patients

Let us introduce three composite patients who will reappear as examples throughout this book. These are hybrids of clinically realistic and representative clients we have assessed and treated over the years. Clinicians will immediately recognize these clients, complaints, and contexts.

Jonathon is an engaging and rambunctious 8-year-old white boy, "smart as a whip but a real handful" according to his mother. Jonathon's preschool and first-grade teachers both suspected that Jonathon suffered from attention-deficit/hyperactivity disorder (ADHD). He was evaluated in first grade by the school psychologist. Psychological testing, behavioral observations, and record review supported a diagnosis of ADHD (mixed type) and mild to moderate oppositional defiant disorder (ODD) accompanied by family tensions. Jonathon is the second of three children, ranging in age from 3 to 10 years, born to working parents (with health insurance) who frequently separate and reconcile. The local pediatrician treats Jonathon's asthma with albuterol and offered to prescribe a psychostimulant for the ADHD as well, but Jonathon's father firmly resists any psychotropic medication at this time. Both parents are genuinely concerned about Jonathon and willing to participate in a few family meetings. However, their demanding work schedules and marital conflicts prevent extensive outpatient treatment.

Francesco is a quiet, polite 30-year-old Hispanic man who presents at a low-income primary health-care center with diffuse and moderate anxiety (generalized anxiety disorder) due to work and relational concerns. His first marriage ended recently in a divorce, and his minimum-wage factory job seems in jeopardy due to layoffs and outsourcing. His job does not provide any health insurance, and as a single working man, Francesco does not qualify for state-funded insurance coverage. The primary-care physician saw him twice for 12-minute appointments and learned of Francesco's extensive history of alcohol dependence, including two inpatient rehabilitations. Francesco admitted his alcohol abuse but minimized its effects. The physician referred him to the clinic case manager for counseling and referral.

Annique is an emotional and insightful 51-year-old African American woman presenting for outpatient psychotherapy to a psychologist in private practice. She works full-time as a high school teacher, as does her husband of 25 years. They enjoy excellent insurance benefits and job security. Her chief complaint of chronic depression (major depressive disorder) dates back to her adolescence. Annique has successively tried a number of antidepressant medications, which "take the edge off," and sees a private psychiatrist every 3 months for medication management. This will be her third course of psychotherapy. Her family history includes many close relatives with unipolar and bipolar II mood disorders. Annique reinitiates individual psychotherapy at this time because her assertion deficits (exceeding the diagnostic threshold for dependent personality disorder) and menopausal complaints (particularly hot flashes and irritability) detract from the quality of her life and relationships.

Core EBP Skills

How, specifically, would a practitioner go about assessing, conceptualizing, and treating patients like Jonathon, Francesco, and Annique in EBP? By mastering a set of sequential, **core EBP skills**, which are taken up in the following chapters, or by following the mnemonic **AAA TIE** or **triple A TIE**:

1. *A*sking a specific, clinical question (Chapter 2)
2. *A*ccessing the best available research (Chapter 3)
3. *A*ppraising critically that research evidence (Chapters 4–6)
4. *T*ranslating that research into practice with a particular patient (Chapter 7)
5. *I*ntegrating the clinician's expertise and patient's characteristics, culture, and preferences with the research (Chapter 8)
6. *E*valuating the effectiveness of the entire process (Chapter 9)

Key Terms

AAA TIE
best available research
clinical expertise
core EBP skills

evidence-based medicine (EBM)
evidence-based practice (EBP)
patient characteristics, culture, and
   preferences

Recommended Readings and Web Sites

APA Task Force on Evidence-Based Practice. (2006). Evidence-based practice in psychology. *American Psychologist, 61,* 271–285.

Evidence-Based Behavioral Practice, www.ebbp.org

Guyatt, G., & Rennie, D. (Eds.). (2002). *Users' guides to the medical literature: Essentials of evidence-based clinical practice.* Chicago: American Medical Association.

Miller, P. M., & Kavanagh, D. J. (Eds.). (2007). *Translation of addictions science into practice.* London: Elsevier.

National Guideline Clearinghouse, www.guideline.gov

National Registry of Evidence-Based Programs and Practices, www.nrepp.samhsa.gov

Norcross, J. C., Beutler, L. E., & Levant, R. F. (Eds.). (2006). *Evidence-based practices in mental health: Debate and dialogue on the fundamental questions.* Washington, DC: American Psychological Association.

Straus, S. E., Richardson, W. S., Glasziou, P., & Haynes, R .B. (2005). *Evidence-based medicine: How to practice and teach EBM* (3rd ed.). London: Elsevier.

Thyer, B. A., & Wodarski, J. S. (Eds.). (2007). *Social work in mental health: An evidence-based approach.* New York: Wiley.

▌▌▌▌▌
CHAPTER 2

Asking the Right Questions

Formulating a specific, answerable question constitutes the first core evidence-based practice (EBP) skill and lies at the heart of accessing the best available research. Not all clinical questions can be answered by the research, nor do all research projects answer specific, clinical questions. This chapter focuses on asking the right questions.

Clinicians have an average of one to four questions for each 10 patients they care for. However, they either do not pursue or do not find answers to two-thirds of their questions (Huang et al., 2006). Subsequent analyses show that most unanswered questions could be answered through improved query formulation. Thus, this chapter also focuses on asking answerable questions.

Why Bother Formulating Specific Questions?

Our students and colleagues frequently complain that this first skill feels tedious and unnecessary; they want to "jump right into the research literature" to secure answers. After a few hours of frustration and incomplete searches, they begrudgingly return to us and request our assistance. You must form an answerable clinical question before beginning a literature search; otherwise, you will probably incur frustration and waste time.

Authors of the venerable *Evidence-Based Medicine*, now in its third edition (Straus et al., 2005, p. 23), argue that using well-formulated questions helps in these ways (beyond preventing frustration and saving time):

- increases the probability of locating evidence that is directly relevant to our patient's needs
- helps focus on evidence that directly addresses our particular knowledge needs
- directs us to high-yield search strategies (see Chapter 3)
- improves our communication with colleagues in discussing cases, sending referrals, and receiving new patients
- suggests the forms that useful answers might take
- enhances our satisfaction with EBPs by virtue of having our questions answered, our knowledge augmented, and our curiosity reinforced

We believe—but have no controlled research to support our belief—that mental health and addictions practice leads to a greater number and complexity of clinical questions than medicine. Mental health practice entails many types of interventions, in multiple settings, for a wide variety of potential patients. We work in hospitals, outpatient clinics, day programs, independent practices, schools, military posts, public health programs, rehabilitation institutes, primary-care facilities, legal settings, prisons, counseling centers, and nursing homes. We assess, diagnose, prevent, treat, supervise, research, write, and consult. Our multiple activities and varied work settings provide all the more reason for formulating specific clinical questions that yield answers directly addressing our knowledge needs as they relate to specific patients.

Questions that Research Cannot Answer

As we marvel at the glories of scientific research, we should simultaneously acknowledge the outer limits of its applicability. Empirical research can inform but can never answer some of life's fundamental questions: What is the good life? How do you define quality of life for yourself? What does it mean to be a good person? What ethical principles should guide my life?

Research can generate crucial information on the incidence, effectiveness, and consequences of our moral and philosophical positions. It can tell us about the incidence of, say, rational suicide, the effectiveness of sexual abstinence programs, and the consequences of gun-control laws. But research cannot directly determine personal values.

A Good Question Is Like a Beautiful Painting

In posing specific clinical questions, visualize patients as you might visualize a beautiful painting or photograph (Walker et al., 2006). Questions will naturally arise in both foreground and background. Foreground questions concern the immediate and specific case, whereas background questions ask about the general situation or setting.

Take the cases of Jonathon, Francesco, and Annique (presented in Chapter 1). Ask yourself (or your students and colleagues): What specific pieces of knowledge would you like to have in order to render them effective care?

Background questions concern general knowledge about disorders, tests, treatments, and any other health-care matter. They usually begin with the words *who, what, where, how, why,* and *is/are,* followed by a particular condition or situation (Walker et al., 2006). Representative background questions for our three patients include the following:

> What are the effective psychological treatments for attention-deficit/hyperactivity disorder (ADHD, Jonathon)?
>
> Why would parents be opposed to stimulant medication that might help their kid (Jonathon)?
>
> What is effective for patients who minimize their substance dependence (Francesco)?
>
> What causes dependent personality disorder (Annique)?
>
> How does depression relate to dependent personality disorder (Annique)?

In each case, note that the background questions specify two components: a question root (with a verb) and a disorder, treatment, or other health-care matter. Questions not written in this format should be rewritten before proceeding further (Straus et al., 2005). Ask the questions you want answered, but do so in a format that is answerable by sophisticated searches.

Foreground questions have greater specificity and, when formulated well in searchable terms, possess five components: the patient, population, or problem of interest; the intervention broadly defined to include tests and treatments; the comparison intervention; the outcomes of interest; and the type of question you are asking. Foreground questions are thus written in a searchable format known as **PICO**: the *p*atient, *i*ntervention, *c*omparison, and *o*utcome. The format is sometimes known as *PICOT*, adding the *t*ype of question you wish to answer.

Practitioners are interested in both background and foreground questions. The relative proportion of each seems dependent upon familiarity and experience with the particular disorder. In medicine, for example, beginning clinicians pose more background (general) questions than foreground (specific) questions, whereas more experienced clinicians ask more foreground than background questions (Straus et al., 2005). Novices want and need different information from what experts want; our knowledge needs depend upon our experience with a particular disorder or condition. But none of us ever becomes so expert as to ignore background knowledge.

PICO Format

Today, most people search electronic resources using natural language, which usually consists of putting long phrases (or even complete questions) into a search box. Many popular Web sites, especially search engines like Google, accept such searches. However, as you begin to use more specialized interfaces, you will find that natural language searches will not always yield the desired results. When this happens, it becomes important to break searches down into the PICO formats that are identifiable by all search systems.

Table 2.1. **Questions to Ask for PICO**

	Ask yourself...	**Information to possibly include in your question**
P **Patient**	Who is your patient? What is the patient population of interest?	Your patient's primary complaint, sex, age, race, history (any factors that will influence your search)
I **Intervention**	What are you planning to do for your patient?	Specifics of your planned assessment or treatment (any therapies you are considering)
C **Comparison**	Is there an alternative to the treatment? (Sometimes there is no comparison.)	The alternative treatments, if any
O **Outcome**	What do you think will occur after applying the treatment?	Your desired or hypothesized outcomes

Table 2.1 features the salient questions to ask yourself for each of the PICO ingredients.

In this book, as throughout most of health care, we use the term *patient* for *P* to refer to the child, adolescent, adult, older adult, couple, family, group, organization, community, or other population receiving psychological services. However, we recognize that in many situations there are important reasons for using such terms as *client*, *patient population*, or *person* in place of *patient* to describe the recipients of services.

The optional *T* in PICOT is useful for determining the type of question you seek to answer. The most common types of clinical questions pertain to diagnosis and therapy, but we can ask many more: etiology, prevalence, comorbidity, assessments, prevention, therapy relationship, relapse potential, and so forth.

Clinician's Guide to Evidence-Based Practices

Determining the type of clinical question helps you anticipate the particular kinds of studies to look for while searching.

For example, Francesco, your 30-year-old patient with an extensive history of alcohol dependence, returns to your office. He feels further stressed by his job instability and admits to drinking more heavily. You wonder if evidence indicates that another round of inpatient alcohol rehabilitation would prove effective. This scenario raises a therapy question; therefore, you would likely seek a randomized clinical (or controlled) trial (RCT) or a summary review of RCTs. On the other hand, if your concern rests principally with an etiology question—like "Does Francesco's job stress contribute to his alcohol abuse?"— then you may find a cohort study more interesting.

Here is another, full example of the PICO strategy. You meet with Jonathon, your 8-year-old patient with ADHD (mixed type) and mild to moderate oppositional defiant disorder (ODD) accompanied by family tensions. Concerned about Jonathon but mindful of their time, his parents ask about the effectiveness of family therapy and refer to an article that they found online. They turn to you for evidence that family therapy is worth the time and effort. Your initial instinct may be to dive into the literature, but you should first formulate a solid, specific question using PICO (see Table 2.2). It might take the form: For an 8-year-old with ADHD (mixed type), ODD, and family tension, would family therapy versus individual therapy improve the ADHD and ODD conditions?

Not all clinical questions will contain all of the PICO components. In fact, only 37% of questions involve both intervention and outcome. The research reveals that the PICO format centers

Table 2.2. **A Specific Clinical Question Using PICO**

P **Patient**	8-year-old male with ADHD (mixed type), ODD, and family tensions
I **Intervention**	Family therapy
C **Comparison**	Individual therapy
O **Outcome**	Improved ADHD, ODD, and family functioning

ADHD, attention-deficit/hyperactivity disorder; ODD, oppositional defiant disorder.

primarily on therapy questions and proves less suited for representing other types of information needs, such as prognosis and etiology questions (Huang et al., 2006).

Using PICO may not always seem immediately relevant to a particular clinical question. If you find yourself struggling with creating a PICO, take a step back and simply divide your question into meaningful key components. That will increase the specificity of your question and, thus, the probability of securing useful answers.

Our advice to increase the specificity of your questions via the PICO format in EBPs is, happily, evidence-based itself. Using PICO or PICOT increases the proportion of specific questions asked (e.g., Villanueva et al., 2001) and the level of precision in the answers retrieved (e.g., Schardt et al., 2007).

Asking Patients the Right Questions

A well-formulated, PICO-formatted question assumes that you have already acquired a fair amount of information about the particular patient. You will gather such information by conducting an assessment, making diagnoses, and identifying patient strengths. In addition, we urge you to ask patients (and their significant others) a series of questions that will enable you to narrow your searchable PICO. These questions include the following:

- What are your preferences about potential treatments?
- Are there any types of services you would *not* accept at this time?
- Do you have strong preferences for practitioners in terms of profession, gender, ethnicity, language, religion, or sexual orientation?
- What have you tried in the past that seemed helpful?
- What have you tried in the past that was ineffective?
- What is your insurance status and financial ability to pay for services?
- What are your time constraints and work/home schedule?
- What are your family and social supports?
- What other professionals are involved in your health care?
- As we collaborate on a treatment plan, what else should I know about you and your situation?

The best-laid plans and the most evidence-based treatments often go awry because practitioners simply do not acquire (or consider) the individuality of the patient and the singularity of the situation. None of this should imply, of course, that we prematurely settle for a suboptimal treatment plan; it is merely to say that forewarned is forearmed. Ask early and avoid later surprises and disappointments.

Prioritizing Searchable Questions

In a typical day of practice, the curious clinician will wonder briefly about dozens of questions—prevalence and comorbidity of disorders, validity of assessment tools, effectiveness of treatments, appropriateness of therapeutic relationships, applicability to patient characteristics, probability of reoccurrence, and so forth. However, very few of us have the luxury to immediately conduct an electronic search on the run or during practice hours. Instead, we must temporarily shelve our questions and then prioritize them for those brief periods we have to search the literature.

Deciding which of your many questions to pursue requires judicious prioritizing. Try this sequence of filters to prioritize (Straus et al., 2005):

- ◆ the urgency of the question to your patient's well-being
- ◆ the relevance to your learning and knowledge needs
- ◆ the feasibility of answering the question in the available time
- ◆ the prevalence of the question in your practice
- ◆ the personal interest the question holds for you

Urgent, relevant, feasible, prevalent, and personally interesting questions should get your precious time. A moment of reflection will usually allow you to select from the multitude.

To answer clinical questions, practitioners must systematically formulate answerable questions in an efficient manner. The next core EBP skill involves locating and accessing research-based answers. That is the topic of Chapter 3.

Key Terms

background questions   PICO
foreground questions

Recommended Readings and Web Sites

BMC Medical Informatics and Decision Making, www.biomedcentral.com/
    bmcmedinformdecismak (an open-access journal publishing original peer-
    reviewed articles in information management, health-care technology, and
    medical decision making).

Forming a Clinical Question, medlib.bu.edu/tutorials/ebm/pico/index.cfm

PICO Maker, www.library.ualberta.ca/pdazone/pico/ (a free application that
    lets users create and store queries in the PICO format for educational
    purposes and later reference).

PICO Tutorials at healthlinks.washington.edu/ebp/pico.html (University of
    Washington) and www.urmc.rochester.edu/hslt/miner/resources/evidence
    (University of Rochester).

Straus, S. E., Richardson, W. S., Glasziou, P., & Haynes, R. B. (2005).
    Evidence-based medicine: How to practice and teach EBM (3rd ed.). London:
    Elsevier.

| | | | |
CHAPTER 3

Locating the Best
Available Research

Lauren A. Maggio

This chapter is designed to provide evidence-based practitioners with working knowledge of:

- ♦ Translating a clinical question into a targeted literature search
- ♦ Utilizing search strategies
- ♦ Selecting search terms
- ♦ Using efficiently a wide range of information resources
- ♦ Accessing information on tests and measures

The Search Process

After formulating a clinical question using **PICO**, it is time to search for evidence-based answers. But *where* should you begin? Should you look for a Cochrane Systematic Review, search Google, call a colleague, or consult a textbook? These are all viable search options, but you will probably be better served by beginning with a sound search strategy.

Librarians and experienced searchers recommend beginning by searching background information, which provides an overview of your topic; then moving on to filtered information, which provides access to time-saving synthesized information; and finally (if necessary) looking into unfiltered information, which provides access to primary sources, such as individual studies.

For example, say you begin a search on a professional organization's Web site (background information) where, after boning up on your topic's main concepts and keywords, you search the Cochrane Database of Systematic Reviews (filtered resource, defined in a few moments). After consulting related Cochrane Reviews, you track down a promising original study in PubMed or PsycINFO (unfiltered), which you then analyze and apply.

Here are the three principal types of information sources—background information, filtered information, and unfiltered information—with a few introductory words on each.

Background Information
Background information provides a general understanding of a topic and sometimes also an overview of the available evidence. Background information is available from textbooks, topic review services like UpToDate, Web sites, and practice guidelines. At first, consulting background information may seem inefficient, but in the long run it can prevent frustrating and time-consuming false starts due to a searcher's lack of familiarity with the topic. Background information can help a searcher

identify a topic's specialized vocabulary or key researchers, both of which can be integrated into a subsequent filtered information search. A quick background search can also provide a sense of a topic's scope in the literature. For example, if you are having difficulty finding background information on your topic, it may be an indication that there will be even less filtered information available. In this case, you know that it may be necessary to broaden your search as you move through the process.

Filtered Information

Filtered information sources are designed to save busy practitioners time and effort by providing expert analysis, removing the burden of reading and synthesizing dozens, if not hundreds, of individual studies. Another benefit of filtered information sources is that, in many cases, they pull together a wide range of evidence that would otherwise be difficult to locate in one convenient resource. Filtered information sources include systematic reviews, and enhanced critical abstracts.

The major downside of filtered information sources is that there are fewer of them available simply due to the fact that filtered information takes longer to create, often making it difficult to find filtered information on current topics or rare conditions. Despite this drawback, the majority of information resources introduced in this chapter are filtered because they are the most practical resources for most practitioners.

Unfiltered Information

Unfiltered information sources are the more traditional sources, like PubMed or PsycINFO, that you may have been inclined to search first in the past. Unfiltered information can be found in a wide variety of bibliographic databases and is generally the basis for all other kinds of evidence. The primary weakness of unfiltered information is that it needs to be analyzed and synthesized, which can be time-consuming. Also, because there is so much unfiltered information available, it can be quite difficult to search and isolate the key evidence related to a topic.

Now that you have a general understanding of the three major types of information resources, it is important to learn how to best use them. Fortunately, these information sources are all usually governed by the same basic search concepts, so a strong grasp of the following search basics will make approaching any database less frustrating and time-consuming.

Basic Search Concepts

Boolean Operators

Boolean operators are search commands used to logically connect search terms. The most common Boolean operators are AND and OR, although some search systems also allow for the use of the less common Boolean operator NOT.

AND narrows a search, making it more precise. For example, "depression AND alcoholism" retrieves information about both depression and alcoholism. A search using AND ensures that all retrieved citations contain information about both search terms. Figure 3.1 presents a Venn diagram of the conceptual relationship of AND.

By contrast, the Boolean operator OR broadens a search, making it more comprehensive. For example, "depression OR alcoholism" retrieves information about either depression or

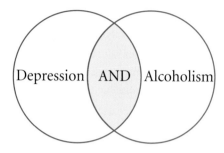

Figure 3.1 Venn diagram of the conceptual relationship of AND in electronic searches.

alcoholism. Figure 3.2 portrays the logical relationship of OR in the form of a Venn diagram.

OR can be helpful for stringing together synonyms. For example, to locate information on depression, it would also be useful to search for synonyms such as "mood disorders," "dysthymia," and "affective disorders." Therefore, to be inclusive, search for "depression OR mood disorders OR dysthymia."

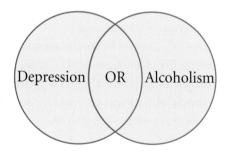

Figure 3.2 Venn diagram of the conceptual relationship of OR in electronic searches.

The Boolean operator NOT excludes information from a search. To continue with our example, "depression NOT alcoholism" retrieves only information about depression and excludes information about alcoholism. Use caution when applying NOT as it can exclude potentially valuable information relevant to both concepts.

Boolean tips:

♦ Boolean operators can be notated in different ways. For example, some databases may use "&" to represent AND. OR is sometimes represented as "or /" Be sure to check each information resource's search tips.

♦ Boolean operators sometimes need to be capitalized to be recognized. Always capitalize Boolean operators, thereby ensuring compatibility with databases that require capitalization; those that do not will not be affected.

♦ Some search systems automatically insert Boolean operators between search terms. For example, Google automatically inserts AND between two or more search terms.

♦ Boolean operators can generally be used together in a single search thanks to a technique called "nesting." Nesting is generally notated by parentheses, for example, "(depression OR alcoholism) AND obesity." In this case the parentheses command the search system to first isolate and search the information inside the parentheses, then combine it with the search command outside.

Wildcards/Truncation

Wildcards, or **truncation**, broaden searches by automatically searching for variations on search terms. Wildcards, sometimes

Clinician's Guide to Evidence-Based Practice

notated as *, ?, $, or !, can generally be applied to any part of the search term, prompting the search system to identify possible alternate letters. In some cases, a wildcard may retrieve a string of letters; in others, it may only substitute a single letter.

Here are three wildcard examples:

- "Wom!n" retrieves "women" and "woman"
- "P$diatrics" retrieves "pediatrics" and "paediatrics"
- "Diabet?" retrieves "diabetes" and "diabetic" and "diabetics"

The last example above, the one that searches for alternate endings, is also known as "truncation." Truncation adds variations to the end of search terms and can be helpful when searching for plural forms of search terms. Some sophisticated search systems now search automatically for plurals of terms.

Medical Subject Headings

While searching the mental health and addiction literature, you will most likely encounter **Medical Subject Headings** (MeSH). This is the National Library of Medicine's subject heading system or controlled vocabulary that helps searchers generate comprehensive targeted searches in MEDLINE. Similar controlled vocabularies, offshoots of MeSH, have been adopted by other search systems such as CINAHL and Psyc-INFO. Bearing this in mind, a good grasp of MeSH fundamentals will help you to understand and use other controlled vocabularies.

One of the major benefits of searching with MeSH (or any controlled vocabulary) is its ability to provide a standardized way of describing a resource. A search with MeSH for "antidepressive agents," for example, will automatically retrieve information about the related terms "thymoleptics" and "antidepressant medications," therefore making it unnecessary to string synonyms together with OR. This is unlike keyword searching, which only searches for the phrase "antidepressive agents" and may miss relevant citations due to divergent vocabulary. Additionally, the above keyword search may also retrieve citations not specifically related to "antidepressive agents."

Remember: A keyword search generally only scans for the inputted string of letters, which does not guarantee that the citations retrieved will focus on your topic. For example, a keyword search of "antidepressive agents" might retrieve articles that simply state "this article is not about antidepressive agents." Searching with MeSH helps avoid this problem thanks to the efforts of professional indexers, who scan each article and assign relevant MeSH terms based on the article's major concepts. Therefore, when you search using MeSH, you are retrieving articles in which the MeSH term has been specifically selected as a major concept in that article, which helps to ensure an extremely targeted retrieval.

Indexers are only human, and there may be times when you do not agree with their indexing decisions. Thus, if you are having difficulty searching with MeSH, it is also advisable to try a keyword search to ensure that you are not losing any relevant citations. Lastly, MeSH is updated annually. However, in between updates new treatments and conditions emerge and new medications are launched. Because these new concepts will not be introduced until the annual update, it is important to search these concepts as keywords.

Information Resources

We now return in more detail to the three principal types of information resources—background information, filtered information, and unfiltered information—and present the frequent sources for each. These are illustrative, not exhaustive, sources in common use among mental health and addiction practitioners.

Background Information

The most common sources under this category are textbooks (including e-texts), ACP PIER, eMedicine, Web sites, and practice guidelines. We consider each briefly in turn.

Textbooks

Textbooks are a common source of background information; they tend, however, toward obsolescence rather quickly, gradually losing their value as evidence resources. To combat this, publishers are insisting on frequent revisions and are creating e-texts which can be updated more rapidly. In some cases, e-texts are simply online versions of traditional textbooks; conversely, some publishers are constantly creating new, value-added evidence components. For example, *Goodman and Gilman's Pharmacological Basis of Therapeutics* (Brunton, 2006), which has always been available in print, is now also available electronically by subscription through McGraw-Hill's Access Medicine collection at www.accessmedicine.com/. As an e-text, this title is updated frequently based on emerging evidence, and these references are also directly linked to the full PubMed citation, providing instantaneous access to primary evidence, ultimately saving a practitioner time and effort.

E-texts, which are available both online and for PDAs, are still a relatively new trend, and the quality of e-texts varies. Not all e-texts automatically update or include evidence features. Most e-texts are available by subscription only, and you may want to investigate access options to e-texts through your library.

Physicians' Information and Education Resource

Created and maintained by the American College of Physicians, the Physicians' Information and Education Resource (ACP PIER) is a topic overview resource (updated monthly) promoted as an evidence-based decision clinical support for point-of-care use. In this resource, over 300 diseases and conditions are addressed in terms of their diagnosis, therapy (including complementary and alternative medicine), prevention and screening, and related legal and ethical issues. These informative overviews are tied directly to current evidence when possible and then linked directly to related PubMed citations, allowing for immediate access to primary evidence. The ACP PIER contains a psychiatry module, which covers drug and alcohol abuse, depression, and eating disorders, as well as other mental health topics. The main strength of ACP PIER is its ability to provide succinct background information with the immediate option of reviewing the primary literature. Members of the ACP have free online access to ACP PIER through pier.acponline.org/. Nonmembers can subscribe to ACP PIER through Stat!Ref at www.statref.com.

eMedicine Clinical Knowledge Database

The eMedicine Clinical Knowledge Database is a continually updated evidence-based resource that provides background information for over 59 medical specialties, including psychiatry, which includes specific modules relating to addictions. This resource consists of the work of approximately 10,000 health-care professionals who have written or reviewed articles on over 6,500 conditions. This resource's articles are dense but easily navigable, providing a general introduction to the condition and then progressing into more detail regarding potential therapies (including specific information on drug therapy), prognosis, and differential diagnosis. A "miscellaneous" section is also some-times included, which varies by topic. In addition, all sections include a bibliography, which allows users to immediately link, when possible, to the complete PubMed citation for the reference.

eMedicine is a product of the company WebMD and is available free of charge at www.emedicine.com/. Although free, the site does push users toward trying WebMD's continuing education products. There is also a small, unobtrusive section on the home page clearly labeled "InfoCenters: Information from Industry," which features drug information from pharmaceutical companies.

Web Sites

As evidence-based practice (EBP) continues to raise its profile in health care, its presence on the Internet increases. For example, many professional and government organizations are creating EBP sites and adding evidence-based information to existing Web sites. The Internet's instantaneous nature and flexible publishing policies also allow for the immediate publication of research that is in press or that would never appear in print. For example, in relation to Francesco, your patient with an extensive history of alcohol dependence, beginning the search process at the Substance Abuse and Mental Health Services Association (SAMHSA) at www.samhsa.gov website would be recommended. This U.S. government Web site features extensive statistical data on the national and state levels and a wide variety of valuable reports, including surgeon general reports. Importantly, SAMHSA features the National Registry of Evidence-Based Programs and Practices (NREPP).

The NREPP is a database of mental health and substance abuse treatments freely available at www.nrepp.samhsa.gov/find.asp. This full-text database provides intervention summaries, which describe each intervention and its targeted outcomes, comment on the research on which the intervention is based, report the intervention's references, and identify the individuals who developed the intervention. Two ratings are provided for each intervention: a quality of research rating and a readiness for dissemination rating. Currently, this database contains 69 interventions, which can be quickly browsed by clicking "view all." However, in the future NREPP is expected to grow exponentially. In anticipation of this growth, NREPP features a user-friendly search platform that allows a user to search by keyword with the option of limiting to various topics, areas of interest, evaluations/study designs, or population groups.

As always, when using information from the Internet (or from any source for that matter), be a cautious consumer. Keep the following questions in mind when you are using the Internet as a source of health-care information:

♦ When was the site last updated? How current is the information?

- ◆ Who claims responsibility for the site? Is it a pharmaceutical company, a government agency, an academic institution?
- ◆ What is the motive behind the site? Is it asking you to purchase products or services?
- ◆ Are there any references to scholarly sources?
- ◆ Do I trust the information on this site? Trust your instincts: If the information does not feel right, move on. There is plenty of good, reputable information elsewhere.

No section on Web sites would be complete without a word on Google (www.google.com/). Google, the most popular Internet search engine, is a great resource; for many of us it is the first place we look for information on just about anything. However, when using Google for mental health and addiction information, you may find it helpful to limit a search to a specific domain. By using a certain command or the advanced search option it is possible to limit a search to only those Web sites in a specific domain. This can limit a search to just government, nonprofit, or educational Web sites, weeding out commercial (.com) sites.

Using the Google Advanced Search feature, look for the "domain" search option and enter the domain range you seek. If you choose to do this using the standard Google search box, simply input your search terms and the word *site* followed by a colon and then your specified domain range, e.g., .gov, .com, or .org. If

A screen shot of Google.

seeking noncommercial sites on bipolar disorder, for example, you would enter "bipolar disorder site: .org." This search will retrieve sites on bipolar disorder only from those sites ending in .org. You could also search for sites with .edu and .gov domains.

Practice Guidelines

Practice guidelines are another source of background information and have been defined as "user-friendly statements that bring together the best external evidence and other knowledge necessary for decision-making about a specific health problem"

Box 3.1. **Featured Background Information Resources**

- ◆ E-Texts
    - ◆ *Goodman and Gilman's: The Pharmacological Basis of Therapeutics*: www.accessmedicine.com
    - ◆ National Library of Medicine's free e-texts: www.ncbi.nlm.nih.gov/entrez/query.fcgi?db=Books
- ◆ ACP PIER: pier.acponline.org
- ◆ UpToDate: www.uptodate.com
- ◆ Web Sites
    - ◆ Substance Abuse and Mental Health Services Association (SAMHSA): www.samhsa.gov
    - ◆ National Registry of Evidence-Based Programs and Practices (NREPP): http: www.nice.org.uk/
    - ◆ Google: www.google.com
- ◆ Practice Guidelines
    - ◆ The National Guideline Clearinghouse: www.guideline.gov
    - ◆ The National Institute for Health and Clinical Excellence: www.nice.org.uk/

(Sackett et al., 1997, p. 112). In addition to providing background information, many guidelines are increasingly providing direct links to current evidence. Many guidelines can be found on professional association Web sites or through clearinghouse sites such as The National Guideline Clearinghouse (www.guideline.gov) and the UK-based National Institute for Health and Clinical Excellence (NICE). Both of these sites are searchable and provide access to the full text of EBP guidelines. For mental health and addictions, for example, The National Guideline Clearinghouse features over 160 specific mental health guidelines from relevant professional organizations such as the American Academy of Child and Adolescent Psychiatry and SAMHSA.

Filtered Information Resources
Here, we consider several of the most frequently used and, in our opinion, the most helpful filtered information resources for mental health and addiction professionals.

- ◆ Cochrane Database of Systematic Reviews
- ◆ Campbell Collaboration Reviews
- ◆ Database of Abstracts of Reviews of Effects
- ◆ *BMJ Clinical Evidence*
- ◆ Evidence-based journals

Cochrane Database of Systematic Reviews

The **Cochrane** is a database within the Cochrane Library comprised of systematic reviews which identify and expertly synthesize available randomized clinical trials (RCTs) on a given health-care topic. Considered to be a "gold standard" of EBP in mental health, the Cochrane Database of Systematic Reviews

(CDSR) is a great place to start searching filtered information. The Cochrane is especially useful when searching for therapy information but less helpful when searching for other types of clinical questions (although some diagnosis-focused reviews are available). When searching the CDSR, it is important to remember that its reviews are time-consuming to produce, so if a topic is fairly new, it may not yet be covered. Also, because Cochrane reviews synthesize a number of related RCTs, a substantial number of RCTs must be available before a review can be undertaken. This makes the Cochrane a solid resource for established topics that have been investigated in the health-care literature, but it may be hit or miss when it comes to new or rare topics.

The CDSR was created and is maintained by volunteer health-care practitioners, biomedical researchers, expert searchers, and consumers who comprise the Cochrane Collaboration, an international nonprofit organization. The CDSR is updated quarterly; Cochrane reviewers are encouraged to update their specific reviews at least once every 2 years. Figure 3.3 presents the opening page of the Cochrane Web site.

Cochrane reviews are dense documents divided into user-friendly sections. Reviews may include the following sections: implications for practice and research, author's conclusions, and descriptions and an analysis of the RCTs examined. The full text of the CDSR is available either on CD-ROM or online by subscription. Abstracts and plain language summaries of Cochrane reviews, which contain substantial and conclusive information, can also be accessed freely through the Cochrane Library at thecochranelibrary.com and at PubMed.

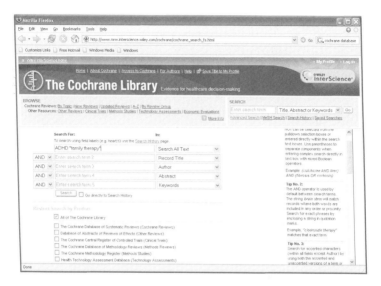

Figure 3.3 A screen shot of Cochrane Library home page.

Although the CDSR is available directly and through several other access points, we focus on Wiley InterScience. This interface simultaneously searches the entire Cochrane Library, which also includes other EBP resources as discussed later in this chapter.

Consider our question of whether family therapy or individual therapy is best supported by the evidence for our 8-year-old patient with ADHD, ODD, and family tension In this case, ADHD, ODD, family tension, family therapy, and individual therapy are the main ideas. In beginning our search, "ADHD" is chosen because of its prevalence in the health-care literature and "family therapy" is selected because it is the main therapy. A viable search could look like: ADHD "family therapy."

This interface automatically inserts AND between terms, so AND does not need to be included. "Family therapy" was placed in quotes to alert the database that it was to be searched as a phrase. This relatively simple search yielded a highly relevant Cochrane review: "Family Therapy for Attention-Deficit Disorder or Attention-Deficit/Hyperactivity Disorder in Children and Adolescents" (Bjorstad & Montgomery, 2005).

Not all clinical questions are so easily searched, so you may want to explore the Cochrane Library's advanced search option. This resource is also easily browsed as it is divided into approximately 50 major topic areas, including schizophrenia, drugs and alcohol, tobacco addiction and depression, anxiety, and neurosis. Stymied searchers can also use the contents of the CDSR, which include the citations of the RCTs examined and the review's expert search strategy, for tackling tough questions. For example, if your search does not locate a Cochrane review that specifically answers your question but you did find a review that is closely related, take a look at the original research and the review's search strategy with plans of incorporating these expert search terms and citations into your own searches.

As mentioned previously, the Cochrane Library simultaneously searches EBP databases in addition to the CDSR; one of these related resources is the Cochrane Central Register of Controlled Trials (CENTRAL). This is an unfiltered information resource, which means that any information you find needs to be evaluated. CENTRAL currently contains over 489,000 citations for controlled clinical trials and studies of health-care interventions that are gathered by search professionals from biomedical databases, specialized registers, and conference proceedings. Citations include each study's title, where and when it was published, and in some cases a short summary; full text is not included. This database is primarily used for compiling systematic reviews for the CDSR, but it can also be useful for finding citations of studies which you could then investigate further to answer your question.

Campbell Collaboration Reviews of Interventions and Policy Evaluations

Established in 2000, the Campbell Collaboration (C2) is a relatively new nonprofit group patterned on the Cochrane Collaboration. Like the Cochrane Collaboration, the C2 creates and maintains systematic reviews focused on, but not limited to, behavioral science evidence in the areas of education, social justice, and crime. These reviews are contained in the Reviews of Interventions and Policy Evaluations (C2-RIPE) database. The C2 reviews feature expert meta-analysis of topics, providing a convenient gateway into literature which could otherwise be difficult and time-consuming. The C2 is similar to Cochrane in that it maintains a register of trials called C2 SPECTR, which contains over 11,000 records that can be searched free of charge at geb9101.gse.upenn.edu/. Bear in mind, though, that the full text of these records needs to be tracked down in other databases and then analyzed. Although the C2 is similar in many ways to the Cochrane Collaboration, it is not yet as developed in terms of search capability and the availability of reviews. Improvements are expected in the near future.

The C2 reviews are written by policy makers, service providers, and consumers. Reviewers are urged to update their reviews at least every 24 months. Access to the C2-RIPE is available freely online at www.campbellcollaboration.org and includes access to PDF versions of the full text of systematic reviews. Once at this site, C2 Library searchers can simply browse reviews by three subdivisions: education, crime and justice, and social welfare. This is a manageable task at the moment due to the limited number of reviews.

Database of Abstracts of Reviews of Effects

The Database of Abstracts of Reviews of Effects (DARE), established in 1994, is produced by the UK National Health Service Centre for Reviews and Dissemination. It currently contains over 4000 structured abstracts that critically analyze systematic reviews culled from major biomedical databases, select journals, and a wide range of other literature. The DARE reviews focus on investigating the impact of various health and social care interventions, making it an effective resource for mental health and addiction questions; a few DARE abstracts also investigate diagnostic systematic reviews. The DARE reviews are written by two reviewers who critically appraise each selected systematic review, providing a concise summary of the systematic review, including its funding sources, study design, results, and author conclusions. Reviewers also provide critical analysis of the strengths and weaknesses of the selected systematic review; this is intended to help busy practitioners in making educated decisions about whether or not the particular systematic review is worth the time and effort to review in full. For practitioners interested in pursuing the original systematic review, DARE provides a direct link to the original review's citation in PubMed, which saves time.

The database is updated monthly and currently available full-text without charge at www.crd.york.ac.uk/crdweb/. Note that DARE can also be simultaneously searched through the Cochrane Library. You must, however, have a subscription to search and retrieve DARE records from the Cochrane Library through Wiley InterScience.

Searching DARE using the free CRD Web site is straightforward as the page features a single search box with the sole option of limiting by date. Instructions to the left of the search box prompt users to select "all these words," which is akin to connecting terms with the narrowing Boolean operator AND, or "any of these words," which is analogous to the broadening Boolean operator OR. By choosing one of these options, the user applies either AND or OR across the entire search. This is fine for the majority of searches; however, for more complicated searches that require multiple Boolean operators, it is possible for users to override these two default options by manually inputting either of the Boolean operators.

Consider the 51-year-old patient Annique who visits your office. She mentions that her hot flashes are driving her crazy and that her friend suggested that soy may help. She asks your opinion. You promise to do some research and get back to her. Your clinical question is as follows: For a 51-year-old with hot flashes would treatment with soy improve her symptoms?

 A screen shot of DARE.

A viable search could look like "(hot flashes OR hot flushes) AND soy."

Because *hot flashes* can also be called *hot flushes*, this search includes both terms and they are connected with OR. Notice that the Boolean operators AND and OR were both included in this somewhat sophisticated search to override the generic search commands that only allow for a single Boolean operator. This search takes advantage of nesting by enclosing the synonyms in parentheses, which tells the search system to isolate the enclosed search term and process the operation inside the parentheses first—much like the order of operations in algebra. This search interface also offers the option of restricting a search to certain fields. This search returned five related DARE reviews and one abstract from another source.

BMJ Clinical Evidence

This tool is designed to aid evidence-based practitioners in making treatment decisions based on a summary of available evidence regarding the benefits and harms of a therapy. *BMJ Clinical Evidence* is available online, for PDAs, and as a print book, though this format will soon be discontinued. This resource provides evidence for over 2000 treatments and preventative measures for more than 200 common health conditions, including mental health. Available by subscription at www.clinicalevidence.com, this resource is updated continuously.

Health conditions and their interventions are thoroughly analyzed by clinicians or epidemiologists with significant EBP experience. Each condition is presented as an easy-to-use comprehensive module; this is one of its major advantages. Each module contains the authors' systematic review of the health condition, which succinctly summarizes the benefits or disadvantages of the various related interventions. These systematic reviews are based on current RCTs, observational studies, and other systematic reviews. Figure 3.4 presents a screen shot of the *BMJ Clinical Evidence* home page.

A major strength of *BMJ Clinical Evidence* is how it compiles all of this key information into one easy-to-access location. It also benefits by being a BMJ resource, meaning that it is connected to the wide range of BMJ journals and evidence resources. This extensive connectivity allows users to quickly access additional information with minimal effort. Be aware, though, that

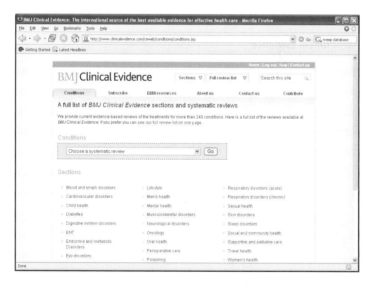

Figure 3.4 A screen shot of *BMJ Clinical Evidence* home page.

access to full text of these BMJ resources is governed by a user's subscription access. One of the drawbacks of *BMJ Clinical Evidence* is its focus on therapy, which makes it less useful for other types of clinical questions.

Each Web page of *BMJ Clinical Evidence* features a standard search box, which is relatively user-friendly as long as you remember that OR is automatically inserted between all terms and that the Boolean operators AND and NOT must be capitalized. This resource does feature search help pages. In addition to searching via its search box, *BMJ Clinical Evidence* is easily browsed by section or health condition arranged alphabetically.

Evidence-Based Journals

Journals specifically dedicated to facilitating EBP have become a recent trend in publishing. Examples include *Evidence-Based Complementary and Alternative Medicine*, *Evidence-Based Nursing*, *Journal of Family Practice*, and, most relevant for our purposes, *Evidence-Based Mental Health*.

Evidence-Based Mental Health began in 1998 as a quarterly journal of structured abstracts that summarizes and analyzes mental health articles; these include original studies and review articles from over 50 international medical journals and the Cochrane Library. Each structured abstract focuses on an individual article and succinctly presents its methods, main results, and conclusions. A mental health expert also provides a short critical analysis of the main article and makes recommendations for its use in clinical practice. A strength is its value-added commentary, which can influence a practitioner's decision whether or not to pursue the original article for further examination. This resource is useful due to its mental health focus and the ability to conveniently pull together a wide range of key journal articles that would otherwise be difficult for a single practitioner to access and effectively analyze.

Evidence-Based Mental Health is accessible by subscription in print or online at ebmh.bmj.com/. This resource is best accessed electronically because it provides the option of browsing by issue or topic.

Besides browsing *Evidence-Based Mental Health*, it is also possible to run a keyword or title word search of the journal. To access these search options, click on "advanced search." This search assumes OR between your search terms, but you can also use AND or NOT to narrow a search. This resource is also searchable by inputting the citation of an original article to see if it has been appraised by *Evidence-Based Mental Health*. This feature can be helpful if you are having difficulty tracking down the full text of a promising original article since it always provides a summary and a recommendation for practice.

In addition to EBP journals, many other titles across a wide range of specialties also now include evidence sections, including meta-analyses of articles, systematic reviews, or an evidence-based approach to a particular topic. For example, the *American Journal of Psychiatry* includes a monthly series called "New Treatment in Psychiatry," which features a hypothetical clinical case that presents a common problem in patient care, summarizes the relevant literature, and includes expert recommendations for treatment and diagnosis. For another example, you could also consult the journal *Psychiatric Services*, which often includes the column "Best Practices" that introduces a best practice based on evidence and then provides commentary.

Unfiltered Information

As you will recall, unfiltered information is the "raw data" of original research studies that have not yet been synthesized or aggregated. Among the most popular for mental health and addiction practitioners are MEDLINE, PubMed Clinical Queries, CINAHL, Social Services Abstracts, PsycINFO, LexisNexis, the Cork Database, and Google Scholar.

MEDLINE

The premier database of the National Library of Medicine currently contains over 15 million biomedical citations dating back to 1950. Currently, MEDLINE indexes approximately 5000

Box 3.2. **Featured Filtered Information Resources**

♦ Cochrane Database of Systematic Reviews (CDSR): www. thecochranelibrary.com

♦ Campbell Collaboration Reviews of Interventions and Policy Evaluations (C2-RIPE): www.campbellcollaboration.org

♦ Database of Abstracts of Reviews of Effects (DARE): www.crd. york.ac.uk/crdweb/

♦ National Institute for Health and Clinical Evidence (NICE): guidance.nice.org.uk/

♦ *BMJ Clinical Evidence*: www.clinicalevidence.com

♦ Evidence-Based Journals

♦ *Evidence-Based Mental Health*: ebmh.bmj.com

Clinician's Guide to Evidence-Based Practice

biomedical journals published in the United States and in over 80 other countries. The strength of MEDLINE is its massive size and scope as well as its expert indexing with MeSH. It is freely searchable online or by PDA through PubMed, a larger database at www.pubmed.gov. By searching MEDLINE through PubMed your search also retrieves these "PubMed-only" citations. At first glance this broader retrieval may seem counterproductive, but because you are seeking the most current information, MED-LINE in-process citations can be crucial. In-process MEDLINE citations generally consist of the most current research which is simply waiting to be added to MEDLINE; part of this delay is the time it takes for MeSH terms to be assigned to each citation. Conversely, there have been instances when older citations have also proved critical (Perkins, 2001), so it is a good idea to incorporate all of PubMed's citations into a search.

At first glance, the PubMed search box appears standard, as shown in Figure 3.5. Behind the scenes, however, PubMed is shaping your search. For example, you have already found a couple of excellent Cochrane reviews (filtered information on your clinical question of family therapy vs. individual therapy for a child with ADHD, ODD, and family tension). Unfortunately, the filtered information you found simply did not answer your specific question. You decide to move to the final phase and search the larger unfiltered literature.

A viable search could look like "ADHD AND family therapy." This search query seems straightforward; however, PubMed is actually creating a search that comprehensively combines MeSH and text words. For example, "ADHD" is searched as a keyword as well as by its proper MeSH "attention deficit disorder with

Figure 3.5 A screen shot of PubMed's home page.

hyperactivity." "Family therapy" is similarly searched. This search produced 89 results, which is normally a reasonable number of citations; when searching for a quick EBP answer, though, this is simply too many. Using the "Limits" tab, this search can be limited by age group, date, language, article types (including RCTs), and a host of other options. Remember to apply limits one at a time and to be careful when selecting PubMed limits because limits remain in effect until deselected. For example, if in the above search you had limited by age group to "child: 6–12" and subsequently decided to research your adult patient Francesco's condition, then the child age limit would need to be deselected or your search would retrieve only citations applicable to children.

Clinician's Guide to Evidence-Based Practice

It is possible, using the previous example where a Cochrane review was found, for a searcher to also identify several original studies within that review worth investigating further. For easy tracking of citations for these original articles and full text (when available), PubMed has a tool called the "Single Citation Matcher." This tool is located in PubMed's left navigation bar, and it allows users to input full or partial citations in order to pull up the full record, which in some cases may include the article's abstract or even full text. Note, however, because Cochrane reviewers also select information that is outside of PubMed, it is not always possible to locate a citation for the original study in PubMed.

PubMed Clinical Queries

This resource is a PubMed option geared specifically for practitioners seeking EBP answers. "Clinical Queries" is available in PubMed's left navigation bar or at www.ncbi.nlm.nih.gov/entrez/query/static/clinical.shtml. "Clinical Queries" provides three search options: clinical study categories, systematic reviews, or medical genetics citations.

You will primarily be interested in searching by clinical study type, which is featured first. This search option applies specialized search filters to your search. These filters can be seen in their entirety at www.ncbi.nlm.nih.gov/entrez/query/static/clini caltable.html. Searches are basically conducted as they would be in PubMed, except that searchers are also prompted to select a search category, which includes etiology, diagnosis, therapy, prognosis, or clinical prediction guides. Lastly, users select to run either a "broad, sensitive search" or a "narrow, specific search." A broad, sensitive search returns more results (some of which may be off-topic), whereas a narrow, specific search locates fewer, more relevant citations. "Clinical Queries" is not intended to search the literature comprehensively but, rather, to offer a quick portal into clinically relevant citations.

One last note regarding PubMed: The National Library of Medicine provides a great deal of high-quality online support for all of its resources, including interactive online tutorials, frequently asked questions pages, and help manuals. Also, face-to-face PubMed trainings are offered on occasion. Training schedules are available at nnlm.gov/ntcc/index.html.

 Screen shot of Clinical Queries.

Cumulative Index to Nursing and Allied Health Literature

The subscription database Cumulative Index to Nursing and Allied Health Literature (CINAHL) contains over 1 million citations from 2500 nursing and allied health journals, some dating back to 1982. This database's strength is its extensive coverage of nursing literature as it includes the majority of English-language nursing journals and publications. Although some of its content overlaps with MEDLINE, this is definitely the key resource for nursing literature. Also, CINAHL provides citations for books, book chapters, conference proceedings, dissertations, newsletters, standards of practice, and research instruments, all of which would be extremely difficult to find elsewhere. Although primarily a bibliographic database, CINAHL does offer some full-text articles. It is available as a print index, on CD-ROM, or by online subscription through several library vendors including Ovid Technologies.

The following search example was performed using Ovid's search platform; however, the key concepts are applicable across other search interfaces. Through Ovid, CINAHL can be accessed by subscription through www.ovid.com/.

After searching the filtered information, you have not answered your clinical question: For a 51-year-old with hot flashes would treatment with soy vs. no therapy improve her symptoms? You decide to try CINAHL.

A viable search could look like: "hot flashes AND soy." This simple keyword search looked for the specified terms in the following fields: title, subject heading, abstract, and instrumentation, returning 37 citations. This is a manageable number of citations to scan; however, you could limit your search by applying a wide range of limits, including age group, publication type, date range, and language. Another way to further target this search is by searching by subject heading only; this is easy to do using Ovid's interface as it allows users to automatically map the search terms to the appropriate subject heading contained in the CINAHL thesaurus. The CINAHL thesaurus contains over 11,000 subject headings, which, although similar to MeSH, does have 2000 unique terms specific to nursing and allied health.

To take advantage of Ovid's subject heading feature, it is necessary to input each search concept individually; this allows the system to match each term to the appropriate subject heading. The addition of search terms in this way is called *set searching* because you are building individual sets to be combined later. For example, the steps of a viable search would look like:

1. Hot flashes
2. Soybeans (soybeans, the appropriate heading for soy, was selected)

 Screen shot of CINAHL.

3. 1 and 2 (to combine sets, enter the set numbers you wish to combine with the appropriate Boolean operator)

Using this set searching technique, which searched specifically for the subject headings of each search term, five on-target results were retrieved. Set searching may take slightly more time and effort; however, in the case of searching a major topic such as schizophrenia, which has nearly 5000 citations when searched as a keyword, a more targeted approach using the CINAHL thesaurus would be useful. Further information on set searching is available at ovid.com.

Social Services Abstracts

Geared toward professionals in the field of social work, human services, and community development, this database is available by subscription online through Proquest at www.proquest.com/. This database provides access to bibliographic citations and abstracts from over 100,000 journal articles, dissertations, and book reviews dating back to 1979. Citations are added monthly. Coverage highlights the following topics: social services and addictions, social and health policy, community and mental health services, family and social welfare, social work practice, and crisis intervention.

Social Services Abstracts is searchable using the Proquest search interface, which presents you with a user-friendly search box. The search box accepts Boolean operators and allows for truncation. Directly under the search box there is a link to additional search tips. Additionally, there is a "Search Tools" tab, which allows you to browse the database's thesaurus and add terms to your search.

PsycINFO

This subscription database is produced by the American Psychological Association (APA) and provides access to mental and behavioral health information, including journal articles, books, dissertations, and technical reports. PsycINFO contains over 2.3 million citations, many from peer-reviewed journals that are international in scope and, in some cases, date back to the 1800s. PsycINFO's major strength is its mental health focus in a wide variety of indexed resources. PsycINFO primarily features citations and abstracts only, thus requiring valuable time to track down full-text resources. PsycINFO is available by subscription at www.PsycINFO.com or through vendors, including EBSCO. The following search examples are based on the subscription EBSCO interface, which is used by many libraries (along with Ovid).

The EBSCO search platform defaults to a basic search, which is fine for the majority of searches. This simple search interface allows the use of the three major Boolean operators (AND, OR, NOT) and the application of key limits, such as publication type, age group, population group, and publication date. Remember:

Apply limits with care and try to apply them one by one so that you are able to better track your search results.

After searching for filtered information regarding Annique's question about soy as a potential therapy for hot flashes, you are still not satisfied with your findings, and you decide to try the unfiltered evidence. You start with PsycINFO.

A viable search could look like "hot fl?shes AND soy." In addition to Boolean operators, this search utilizes wildcards, as indicated by "?." In this case, "?" would retrieve citations for both *hot flashes* and *hot flushes*. In PsycINFO, this search retrieved only two articles. Despite this small retrieval, a search need not stop here thanks to the database's cited reference feature; this links the user to information about articles cited by the articles retrieved. PsycINFO currently contains more than 23 million cited references; this allows you to connect to related citations and (in some cases) full text that may otherwise be difficult to find. This cited reference feature often serendipitously leads you to great evidence.

 Screen shot of PsycINFO.

To aid in your selection of search terms and to better target your search, PsycINFO uses the specialized Thesaurus of Psychological Index Terms; this consists of 8000 standard and cross-referenced terms which are added to PsycINFO citations by APA's expert indexers. The EBSCO interface allows for both browsing and searching of the thesaurus. Once an appropriate index term is found, it can be manually inputted into the search box to be searched as a keyword. Users also have the option of specifically selecting index terms to be searched as descriptors. When searched as a descriptor, the database will only retrieve citations that the APA indexers have specifically tagged with that particular term. This hand indexing allows for a more targeted search.

For example, "schizophrenia" searched as keyword retrieves 68,557 citations. "Schizophrenia" searched as a descriptor retrieves 46,220 citations. Even when searched as the more targeted descriptor, this topic is still too large for you to realistically search. Therefore, it is useful to take advantage of the option "Narrow results by subject" found in the resource's left navigation bar, which presents related subjects, narrowing results to a subset of topics. For the example of schizophrenia, drug therapy and etiology are two of the narrowing options.

LexisNexis

Available by subscription at www.lexisnexis.com/, LexisNexis provides access to over 5800 full-text publications. These publications include more than 1000 world newspapers, magazines, and broadcast transcripts; a wide variety of legal information sources, including court decisions, federal regulations, and international legislation; and medical journals. LexisNexis is an extremely powerful search tool that is especially useful because it aggregates and makes searchable materials that would otherwise be extremely difficult to locate and search. This is especially true in the case of locating information from the media. For example, if in passing a colleague mentions that she had recently viewed a short television news segment on soy as a treatment for hot flashes, without LexisNexis, which maintains full-text records for these types of transcripts, it would be an arduous task to find the specific segment. Additionally, LexisNexis is invaluable for locating legal information because it brings together in a single resource many disparate legal resources, such as codes and regulations, case law, and information from law reviews and legal magazines and newspapers.

When searching LexisNexis, you can choose to search news, legal, medical, or business information. Note that the default search interface is generally set to search news information. However, if you are specifically interested in searching legal, medical, or business news, you must select from the database's left navigation bar which of these major topics you would like to search. Although each of these major topics has its own search interface tailored to the discipline that it represents, all are fundamentally searched using the same techniques. This text will focus on searching for legal information.

For example, you practice in Massachusetts and are interested in recent legal cases dealing with the civil commitment of patients. Because you are interested in legal information for Massachusetts, you would select the legal research link from the LexisNexis home page and then click the link "state case law," which will search for state high court and appellate decisions. Next, you would select "Massachusetts," which will limit your search to that particular state. At this point you have finally reached the basic search box, which allows full-text searching of each case. An appropriate search string could be "civil commitment!"

Notice that the Boolean operator AND does not need to be included because it is automatically inserted between all search terms and that the wildcard "!" was added to capture the plural form of commitment. OR is also acceptable to this database, but it must be included between the appropriate terms. This search returned six relevant full-text cases from the past 6 months. By default LexisNexis generally searches only the last 6 months of information, however, from the main search page you are able to easily extend or shorten this date range. In this case, the database retrieved only six citations; however, in many cases due to the database's size it will return many more citations than you can handle. Therefore, there is a "Focus search" box in the top left corner of every results page, which allows you to enter additional search terms to hone your retrieval.

Cork Database

Originally begun as a medical education initiative at the Dartmouth School of Medicine, this database is freely accessible at www.projectcork.org and provides access to over 69,000 citations on substance abuse, which are pulled from professional journals, books, and reports from federal and state agencies. This database is updated quarterly and contains materials going back to 1978, with some additional retrospective coverage. The Cork Database's major strength is that it provides access to information from the social sciences and life sciences as well as from clinical settings. Additionally, special attention is paid to coverage of attitudes toward substance abuse, college and university campuses, treatment methods, and the impact of substance abuse on society.

The Cork Database features a straightforward search interface, which allows you to select either a basic or an advanced search. Similar to MEDLINE, this database's citations are also indexed using a controlled vocabulary, which features over 400 terms. It is recommended that before beginning your searches you quickly familiarize yourself with the database's thesaurus, which is linked directly from the database's main page. For example, in the case that you are looking for information on "Al-Anon," it is helpful to know that it is indexed as "Alcoholics Anonymous." This database also provides user-friendly help pages, which are worth browsing before undertaking a search.

Google Scholar

Accessible free of cost at www.scholar.google.com, this Google product searches "scholarly sources" including journal articles, book chapters, theses, and conference proceedings across many disciplines including the health sciences. Google Scholar provides access to citations and, in some cases, full text of unrestricted publications. Of course, additional access to full text may be available through your affiliated library.

Google Scholar is now (as of 2008) in the beta, or testing, phase, which can mean frequent changes to the interface and search options; Google does, however, provide numerous help pages. The most attractive feature of Google Scholar is its ease of use and its ability to provide lots of citations (perhaps too many citations) almost immediately. However, there are several cautions to keep in mind when using Google Scholar:

- Google Scholar does not specify which resources it includes, nor does it define what criteria are used when labeling a resource "scholarly." This could mean that information that is not generally considered scholarly may be included or that scholarly sources may be excluded.

♦ While Google Scholar does include PubMed records, it has been found that citations from PubMed retrieved by Google Scholar searches tend to be "approximately one year out-of-date" (Giustini & Barski, 2005, p. 85). For evidence-based practitioners seeking the best current evidence, this may be a shortcoming.

♦ It is unknown when or how often Google Scholar is updated, which could negatively impact search retrieval in terms of timeliness and comprehensiveness.

Despite these shortcomings, Google Scholar is definitely worth keeping on your radar, as it evolves.

Let's work a search example on Francesco and a potential relationship between his lack of medical insurance and his recurring depression. Out of curiosity you run a Google Scholar Search. A viable search could be: Can not having medical insurance cause depression?

Unlike the other information resources discussed thus far, the basic search feature of Google Scholar allows for the use of natural language. By default, Google Scholar automatically inserts the Boolean operator AND between all search terms. To use OR, you must type OR in capital letters for it to be recognized.

Although the basic Google Scholar interface is useful, it may be more beneficial to search using the advanced search feature accessed by clicking on the "Advanced Scholar Search" to the left of the search box. In the advanced search mode it is possible to limit to subject areas including medicine and pharmacology and by date, author, or publication title.

Box 3.3. **Featured Unfiltered Information Resources**

- PubMed (MEDLINE): www.pubmed.gov
- PubMed Clinical Queries: www.ncbi.nlm.nih.gov/entrez/query/static/clinical.shtml
- Cumulative Index to Nursing and Allied Health Literature (CINAHL): www.cinahl.com/ or at www.ovid.com
- PsycINFO: /www.PsycINFO.com or www.ebsco.com
- LexisNexis: www.lexisnexis.com/
- Social Services Abstracts: www.proquest.com/
- Cork Database: www.projectcork.org
- Campbell Social, Psychological, Education, and Criminological Trials Registry (C2 SPECTR): geb9101.gse.upenn.edu/
- Google Scholar: /www.scholar.google.com
- Cochrane Central Register of Controlled Trials (CENTRAL) www.thecochranelibrary.com

Evidence-Based Medicine Search Engines

There is a final type of information resource that does not fall gracefully into any of the categories of background, filtered, or unfiltered information since it is a combination of all three. The EBP search engines simultaneously present access to background, filtered, and unfiltered resources. The now freely available Turning Research into Practice (TRIP) Database (www.tripdatabase.com) is an excellent example of an EBP search engine because it quickly retrieves practice guidelines, Web sites, Cochrane reviews, and journal citations in a single search. It tries to be one-stop shopping for EBP resources.

The TRIP Database is updated monthly and contains evidence-based synopses resources, like *BMJ Clinical Evidence*, clinical guidelines, systematic reviews, core medical journals such as the *New England Journal of Medicine*, and links to "canned" searches in PubMed, which allow users to run PubMed Clinical Queries designed for their research topic. Keep in mind, however, that even though the TRIP Database may list citations from certain subscription resources, it is still necessary to have subscription access in order to obtain the full text of these restricted resources. The TRIP Database is a commercial site featuring advertising, which raises the possibility of external influence by its advertisers, prominently including the pharmaceutical industry.

The TRIP Database is easy to use. However, unlike general Web searching, you will need to think more carefully about your search terms, once again isolating the key concepts you wish to search.

Imagine that you are approaching the following question for the first time: "For an 8-year-old with ADHD, ODD, and family tension would family therapy vs. individual therapy be the treatment of choice?" A viable search for this search engine would be as follows: ADHD and "Family Therapy."

In TRIP, it is unnecessary to include multiple synonyms to ensure comprehensiveness because the database automatically utilizes a synonym dictionary to include related synonyms. In the search described above, "ADHD" will be searched along with "attention-deficit/hyperactivity disorder" and several other synonyms. You are also able to view the synonyms used from the results page. Notice that quotes were used to alert the system to search "family therapy" as a phrase during this search.

The TRIP Database displays the title, the source of the information, and its dates. In the right navigation bar the results are broken up into several key filter areas including evidence-based synopses, guidelines (broken out by region), systematic reviews, e-textbooks, and clinical questions. The MEDLINE results are also broken out by the main question types (e.g., diagnosis, therapy, prognosis). Clicking on these topics dumps you into the PubMed search interface for that search, which appears to simply be the search run in PubMed Clinical Queries.

Because this resource connects users with various types of evidence that all use different search systems, you are sacrificing precision and control over the search when using TRIP. In some cases, this will mean getting inundated by too many resources. Although these resources aim to be extremely comprehensive, there will be several gaps and some specialty journals may not be covered that could be found using other more specialized resources.

Accessing Information on Tests and Measures

Last but not least, we turn to the more specialized matter of locating evidence on tests and measures. Virtually all research studies in the mental health field utilize tests or measures. Most importantly, tests often define the dependent variable(s) in a study. For example, tests may operationalize levels of depression, ADHD, alcoholism, and hot flashes. Tests may also be used to describe characteristics of the participants in a study, for example, levels of academic achievement. Because of the central role played by tests and measures, thoughtful evaluation of the research requires accessing information about them.

Some research reports provide detailed information about the tests employed in the study, for example, regarding their development, reliability, and validity. However, this is often not the case. It is not unusual for a research report to provide little information beyond the name of the test and reference to its manual. In fact, sometimes a test is referred to only by its acronym or initials. Even when researchers provide test information regarding such matters as reliability and validity, you need to think critically about the test. The researchers are not an unbiased source of information. Having used the test as a measure of their dependent variable, they are certainly inclined to say that the test is a reliable and valid measure rather than a test with limitations, which all tests are. In many cases, then, you need to secure additional information about the test or measure.

We identify here the most immediately helpful sources and then provide reference to additional sources.

Test Information Databases

The Educational Testing Service **(ETS) Test Collection**, Web-accessible at sydneyplus.ets.org, provides basic, descriptive information for approximately 20,000 tests. The Test Collection is searchable by test title, author, and even acronym (e.g., "BDI" will locate the Beck Depression Inventory as well as several other tests with BDI initials in their titles, "STAI" will locate the State Trait Anxiety Inventory). The search first returns a simple description of the test, including its purpose, administration time, and target groups. Clicking on the test title link brings up more information, including authors and publisher or other source (e.g., a journal article where the test first appeared). Knowing the publisher is crucial for using another source of information, the publisher's catalog, as described later.

The major strengths of the ETS Test Collection are its comprehensiveness—it attempts to capture every test available in English—and its immediate accessibility on the Internet. The principal drawback for the Test Collection is that it does not provide evaluative information about the test. The best and the worst get equal coverage and are indistinguishable in terms of quality. Another drawback is its currency. It does not always have information about the latest versions of tests.

A source somewhat similar to the ETS Test Collection is the Health and Psychosocial Instruments (HaPI) Database, a product of Behavioral Measurement Database Services. It is available online and on CD-ROM from Ovid Technologies. However, the product must be purchased separately and is not freely available on the Internet.

Two hard-copy counterparts to the ETS Test Collection are *Tests in Print* (TIP) and *Tests*. TIP (Murphy, Spies, & Plake, 2006), now in its seventh edition with new editions appearing about every 3 years, attempts to list all tests that are regularly published and in English. *Tests: A Comprehensive Reference for Assessments in Psychology, Education, and Business* (Maddox, 2003), now in its fifth edition, with new editions appearing about every 6 years, attempts to provide similar coverage but only for tests in the areas identified in the title. TIP has approximately 3000 entries, and *Tests* has approximately 2000. Like the ETS Test Collection, these hard-copy sources provide only basic information about tests: purpose, scores, publisher, target audience, administrative format, and so on. They do not provide evaluations of quality. These sources are quite comprehensive for regularly published tests, but they do not include unpublished tests. For regularly published tests they tend to be more up-to-date than the ETS Test Collection. The major drawback to these hard-copy sources is simply the fact that they are hard copy and, hence, must be found in a library (most academic libraries will have copies) and must be searched by hand.

Test Reviews

None of the aforementioned sources provides evaluative information about tests. There are two premier sources specifically devoted to providing such professional evaluation. The first is the ***Mental Measurements Yearbook*** (Geisinger, Spies, Carlson & Plake, 2007), now in its seventeenth edition with new editions appearing about every 3 years. This source is often referred to by its initials **MMY** or as **"Buros"** after its originator, Oscar Buros. The second is ***Test Critiques*** (Keyser, 2004), now in its eleventh volume with new volumes appearing periodically. In both sources, experts in the field review evidence about a test's quality, defined primarily in terms of validity, reliability, norms, and practicality. Both sources limit entries to regularly published tests. Both sources have helpful indexes, permitting searches by test title, test author, constructs, and names of scores. *Test Critiques* considers fewer tests than does MMY, concentrating on the more widely used tests and providing only one review per test. Each volume of MMY covers approximately 400 tests and provides two independent reviews for most entries. For a sample review in MMY, go to www.unl.edu/buros/bimm/html/reviewsample.html. *Test*

Critiques is available only in hard copy, but MMY is available in several modes, which we describe next.

All volumes of MMY are available in hard copy; major academic libraries have these volumes. The earliest volumes were available only in hard copy. Reviews appearing in the tenth edition of MMY (1989) and onward are available electronically in two forms. First, a review may be purchased via the Internet from the Buros Institute of Mental Measurements (www.unl. edu/buros). This is much like shopping at the Amazon or L. L. Bean Web site. The current cost is $15 per review. Second, many academic libraries subscribe to an Ovid Technologies service that provides full MMY reviews at no cost to the user. An odd feature of searching within this database is that even when an exact test title is entered as the search term, the database returns not only that test but a host of related tests.

The major strength of MMY and *Test Critiques*, obviously, is their provision of professional reviews of test quality. Their major weakness is that they do not cover all tests. In addition, one must remember that the reviews are only opinions and are usually directed at the ordinary use of the tests, whereas in a particular research study the test might be used in a somewhat different way. Finally, the reviewing process, understandably, takes some time to complete; thus, reviews are not always as up-to-date as one might hope.

Test Publishers

Most, but not all, of the tests used in research are available from a publisher, which is a valuable source of information. The test information is available in catalogs issued periodically in hard copy and on publisher's Web sites updated continuously. These sites are easily located with any common search engine. Once located, these sites usually allow for easy searching to get to the test of interest.

Publishers' Web sites (or hard-copy catalogs) are the preferred sources of information about practical matters such as current costs, new editions, recent technical manuals, types of response formats available, and so on. Previously listed sources often have outdated information on these matters. However, the publisher is definitely *not* a preferred source of information about the quality of a test since the publisher has a vested interest in marketing and selling the test.

An Example

While working with Annique and her chronic depression, you come across in the unfiltered information an abstract of an article that presents relevant treatment research. The abstract contains reference to the RHRSD as the crucial outcome measure in the study. The initials do not ring a bell. You go to the Buros website (www.unl.edu/buros/), click on Test Reviews Online, enter "RHRSD" under keywords, check the box for acronym search, and then click "Find." You learn that RHRSD stands for Revised Hamilton Rating Scale for Depression and that the MMY contains two reviews of the RHRSD, which you can purchase online or access free through a university library. You also check the ETS Test Collection (sydneyplus.ets.org), entering the name of the test, and find that there are actually two versions of the RHRSD: the Clinician Rating Form and the Self-Report Problem Inventory. Both the Buros site and the ETS Test Collection give Western

Psychological Services as the RHRSD publisher. You search Western Psychological Services, bring up its Web site (portal.wpspublish.com/), use the publisher's search function to locate the test, and get the publisher's information about scores, scoring services, and so on. Altogether, you have invested about 15 minutes getting a pretty good idea of what the RHRSD is all about.

More Expert Assistance

This chapter has introduced you to a wide variety of popular information resources for mental health, addictions, and health care and provided you with the fundamental skills to approach these resources as a searcher. Even with these skills and the increasing ease of scholarly searches, there will probably be times when you will come up against a clinical question that is difficult to answer. Specialized searching methods or niche resources may be required. When this happens, your best bet is to contact a librarian, one at your local university or at your regional health-care library.

Key Terms

Boolean operators	*Mental Measurements Yearbook* (MMY)
Buros	PICO
Cochrane	*Test Critiques*
ETS Test Collection	wildcards
Medical Subject Headings	truncation

Recommended Readings and Web Sites

Boston University interactive tutorial, Introduction to Evidence Based
    Medicine, medlib.bu.edu/tutorials/ebm/intro/index.cfm.

Center for Evidence-Based Medicine, www.cebm.net.

Centre for Evidence-Based Mental Health, www.cebmh.com.

Centre for Health Evidence, www.cche.net.

ETS Test Collection, sydneyplus.ets.org.

Evidence-Based Behavioral Practice, www.ebbp.org.

Evidence-Based Resources for the PDA (Dartmouth Medical School), www. dartmouth.edu/~biomed/resources.htmld/guides/ebm_pda.shtml.

Hogan, T. P. (2005). Sources of information about psychological tests. In G. P. Koocher, J. C. Norcross, & S. S. Hill (Eds.), *Psychologist's desk reference* (2nd ed., pp. 105–107). New York: Oxford University Press.

University of Hertfordshire EBM Resources, www.herts.ac.uk/lis/subjects/ health/ebm.htm.

University of Sheffield. Netting the evidence, www.shef.ac.uk/scharr/ir/ netting/.

▌▌▌▌▌
CHAPTER 4

Reading and Interpreting the Research: Research Designs

Evidence-based practice depends on research. The research follows one of several designs, each with its own strengths and weaknesses. Each research study typically pursues one or more hypotheses. In order to understand and apply the research, we must focus on the way in which hypotheses are stated and on the characteristics of the research design. This chapter treats these topics.

Hypotheses: Research, Statistical, and Null Hypothesis Significance Testing

Most empirical studies include explicit hypotheses. They can be a source of great confusion, specifically because the typical study includes two distinctly different, even opposite, hypotheses. First comes the **research hypothesis**, also sometimes called the "scientific hypothesis." The research hypothesis states what the researcher hopes or expects to show. In clinical contexts, a research hypothesis might read that "this new psychotherapy will benefit clients, specifically by reducing their depression." Second comes the **statistical hypothesis**. The statistical hypothesis will virtually always state some version of the **null hypothesis** (described next). In our clinical example, the null hypothesis asserts that the new therapy does *not* work. In effect, the researcher hopes to reject the null hypothesis, thus confirming the research hypothesis (at a certain level of probability). A "statistically significant" result constitutes rejection of the null hypothesis. A nonsignificant result means we must retain the null hypothesis, thus disconfirming the research hypothesis. Because the phrasing of the research hypothesis and the statistical hypothesis typically "go in opposite directions," you must remain especially alert when reading research reports as to what hypothesis is referenced when the report makes statements such as "the hypothesis was confirmed" or "the hypothesis was rejected."

In rare instances, the research hypothesis may be the same as the statistical hypothesis. This would occur if the researcher, skeptical about the claims for the efficacy of a treatment, actually set out to demonstrate the ineffectiveness of the treatment. In the case of correlation, the null hypothesis states that the correlation in the population (ρ, rho) equals 0: no correlation exists between the two variables. For example, a study investigates the correlation between severity of attention-deficit/hyperactivity disorder (ADHD) as rated by teachers and as rated by mothers. The research hypothesis posits a noticeable, positive correlation between teachers' and mothers' ratings. The statistical hypothesis states that $\rho = .00$. Obtaining a "significant correlation" means rejection of the null hypothesis ($\rho = .00$). A nonsignificant correlation means retention of the null hypothesis. Once again, the research hypothesis and statistical hypothesis "go in opposite directions." And, once again, in rare instances, the research hypothesis and statistical hypothesis may coincide, for example, if the researcher wants to demonstrate that teachers' and mothers' ratings are *not* correlated.

Null Hypothesis Significance Tests

After descriptive statistics (especially the mean, standard deviation, and correlation coefficient), the **null hypothesis significance test (NHST)** is the most common statistical technique encountered in the research literature. Despite numerous calls for curtailment or elimination of the NHST (e.g., Kirk, 1996; Thompson, 1996), it remains a prominent feature of mental health research. There are many specific NHSTs (e.g., t, F, χ^2), but they all share a few key properties, which we outline here.

First, as suggested by their title, all NHSTs start with some version of the null hypothesis.

Second, the hypothesis focuses on parameters of the population. We do not make hypotheses about statistics based on samples. We know these statistics: Just calculate them. In the language of inferential statistics, we customarily designate parameters with Greek letters. These parameters include μ (mu, or mean), σ (sigma, or standard deviation), and ρ (rho, or correlation coefficient). Note that in most typographical fonts the Greek letter ρ looks like the English lowercase "p." Greek ρ is not a "p," and you should not confuse it with the ubiquitous "*p*" used for probability statements in inferential statistics. When referencing more than one population, subscripts distinguish the respective parameters; for example, μ_1 and μ_2 refer to the means of population 1 and population 2, respectively. Alternatively, English letters as initials for words describing the populations may be used as subscripts; for example, μ_T and μ_C may designate population means for treatment and control groups, respectively.

As a third feature of NHSTs, evidence-based research typically pits one condition against another (e.g., a psychotherapy condition against a control or no-treatment condition) or several conditions against one another (e.g., behavior therapy vs. medication vs. control). A typical expression of a null hypothesis in these contexts is $\mu_1 = \mu_2$. That is, if we tested everyone in populations 1 and 2, we would find the population means to be equal. By a simple rearrangement of terms, $\mu_1 = \mu_2$ becomes $\mu_1 - \mu_2 = 0$, a very pure expression of the null (zero) hypothesis. Some other examples of null hypotheses include:

- The correlation between anxiety and depression is the same (no difference) in males and females: $\rho_M = \rho_F$ (or $\rho_M - \rho_F = 0$).
- The variance in attention span is the same (no difference) in boys and girls: $\sigma^2_B = \sigma^2_G$ (or $\sigma^2_B - \sigma^2_G = 0$).
- Using a solution-focused therapy, there is no difference in outcome whether there are one, two, three, or four therapy sessions: $\mu_1 = \mu_2 = \mu_3 = \mu_4$.

A fourth feature of NHSTs is that they all involve examination of statistics. The relevant statistics correspond to the parameters in the hypothesis. Thus, if the hypothesis involves population means, the relevant statistics are sample means. If the

Clinician's Guide to Evidence-Based Practices

hypothesis involves a population correlation coefficient, the relevant statistic is a sample correlation coefficient.

Fifth, the statistics have a certain degree of instability due to the fact that they originate with samples drawn from the population and each sample will likely differ somewhat from each other sample. We call this *sampling fluctuation* or *sampling variability*.

Sixth, a key part of any NHST is the **standard error of a statistic**. The standard error of a statistic is the standard deviation of a distribution of sample statistics around its parent population parameter. The distribution of these statistics is called the *sampling distribution*. For an illustration of a sampling distribution, see Figure 5.3.

Seventh, we have convenient, well-known formulas for most of the standard errors of statistics we use in hypothesis tests. An extremely important feature of the standard errors of statistics is that sample size(s), usually notated as n or n_1, n_2, etc., always enters into the denominator of the standard error. Thus, as sample size (n) increases, the standard error decreases; and when sample size is small, the standard error increases.

Finally, NHST involves setting an **alpha level (α)**, also known as a **significance level**. The most common levels are .05 and .01. One also occasionally encounters .10 and .001 levels. Selection of any particular alpha level arises purely from historical convention. A researcher may use any alpha level. Whatever alpha level we adopt, if the result of the NHST exceeds the designated alpha level, we declare the result "significant" and reject the null hypothesis. Alternatively, we may express the result as an **exact p value**, which expresses the probability of obtaining the result by chance (due to random sampling variability) under the assumption that the null hypothesis is true. This matter of alpha levels reminds us that NHST methodology always results in statements of probability, not certainty. We can say that a hypothesis proved "probably true" or "probably not true." We cannot say the hypothesis is "true" or "false."

Objections to Null Hypothesis Significance Testing and Recommendations

Statistical experts have voiced numerous (and often passionate) objections to NHST (see Kirk, 1996; Wilkinson & APA Task Force on Statistical Inference, 1999). We note here only the two most prominent objections.

First, almost certainly, every null hypothesis is false. Consider the hypothesis from above: $\rho_M = \rho_F$ (i.e., the correlation between anxiety and depression is the same in males and females). ρ_M may be .46 and ρ_F may be .47. So, in fact, the null hypothesis proves false, albeit trivially so. We could make a similar case for any null hypothesis.

The second objection to NHST is that its result (reject or do not reject, significant or nonsignificant) depends excessively on sample size(s). With very large samples, you can rather easily get "significant" or "highly significant" results. In contrast, small sample sizes will usually yield results of "no significant difference."

Two recommendations usually accompany the objections to NHST. The first suggests using **confidence intervals** (for statistics) either in place of or as an adjunct to NHST. The second suggests reporting measures of **effect size**. We cover both of these topics elsewhere (Chapter 5).

Clinician's Guide to Evidence-Based Practices

Types of Error in Hypothesis Testing

Research studies make frequent reference to types of error (Type I and Type II) and to power in hypothesis testing in the context of NHST. Figure 4.1 defines types of errors in hypothesis testing. Constructing this figure requires us to play a mind game, pretending that we "really know the true state of nature." We use the term *mind game* because (in the context of research) we never know the true state of nature. After all, if we did, we would not have to conduct the research. In the top row of Figure 4.1, we will assume that we really do know the true state of nature, specifically that we know the truth or falsity of the null hypothesis.

Let us use this scenario to develop the figure. We wish to determine if behavioral training in impulse control (B) will prove useful for treating ADHD cases in elementary school children. We have a pool of 100 boys identified as ADHD in one school system. We randomly assign 50 cases to the behavioral training (B) group and assign the other 50 to the control condition (C). We measure improvement with the ADHD Index of the *Conners' Rating Scale for Teachers* (CRS-T).

We begin with the usual null hypothesis: $\mu_B = \mu_C$ or $\mu_B - \mu_C = 0$, where the subscripts B and C stand for behavioral training and control, respectively. Examine each quadrant in Figure 4.1. The upper right quadrant represents the situation where the null hypothesis proved false (behavioral training really is effective), and our statistical test led to rejecting the null hypothesis, a correct conclusion. The upper left quadrant represents the situation where the null hypothesis proved true (behavioral training really is not effective), but our statistical test rejected the null hypothesis, yielding a "significant" result and declaring behavioral

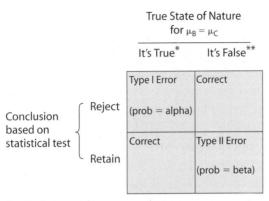

True State of Nature
for $\mu_B = \mu_C$

	It's True[*]	It's False[**]
Reject	Type I Error (prob = alpha)	Correct
Retain	Correct	Type II Error (prob = beta)

Conclusion based on statistical test

[*] μ_B really is equal to μ_C, that is, behavioral training is not effective.

[**] μ_B really is not equal to μ_C, that is, behavioral training is effective.

Figure 4.1 Types of errors in hypothesis testing.

training effective, no doubt followed by recommendations for its adoption. But the conclusion is in error, specifically a **Type I** error. One of the nice things about the NHST apparatus is that we know the probability of making a Type I error. It is precisely alpha (e.g., $\alpha = .05$). We know that if we set $\alpha = .05$, there is a 5% chance that we will incorrectly reject the null hypothesis, even if exactly true.

We can, of course, reduce the chance of making a Type I error by setting alpha at a lower value, moving it, say, from .05 to .01. As shown later, a drawback exists to this strategy. Probably the more important antidote to making a Type I error involves replicating the study several times before issuing treatment recommendations based on the results.

The Type I error rate applies to a single hypothesis test in a study. If testing hypotheses on more than one variable (as commonly happens in the context of a study), the chances of making a Type I error on at least one of the hypothesis tests increase. For example, if conducting two tests with alpha set at .05, the probability of making a Type I error on the first test equals .05. The probability of making a Type I error on either the first test or the second test or on both tests is higher than .05. This compounding of probabilities gets progressively worse as we conduct more hypothesis tests; it becomes particularly severe when conducting a great many separate tests. For example, if we conduct 15 separate hypothesis tests with alpha at .05, a 50–50 chance of making a Type I error somewhere among the entire set of tests exists.

The **Bonferroni correction** adjusts the alpha value so that it truly reflects the probability of making a Type I error. The correction involves simply dividing the original alpha level by the number of tests to be conducted and using the result as the adjusted or corrected alpha level. For example, if you want to work at alpha .05 but you are conducting 10 independent hypothesis tests, set alpha at .05/10 = .005; if you are conducting 20 statistical hypothesis tests, set alpha at .05/20 = .0025.

The CD contains a worksheet giving Bonferroni corrections for α = .05 and .01 for 1–20 hypothesis tests. The formulas built into the worksheet may be used to substitute other alpha values and different numbers of statistical tests.

Now consider the lower left quadrant in Figure 4.1. This represents the situation where the null hypothesis proves true (behavioral training is not effective), and the statistical test results in retaining (some prefer to say "not rejecting") the null hypothesis. This is a correct decision.

Finally, consider the lower right quadrant. The null hypothesis proves false: Behavioral training really is effective. However, our statistical test failed to reject the null hypothesis. We failed to detect a real difference. In fact, we may abandon this approach and tell others that we tried it and it did not work. This is a **Type II error**: failing to reject the null hypothesis when we should reject it.

The probability of making a Type I error simply equals alpha. We designate the probability of making a Type II error as beta (β). Furthermore, we define the **power** of the statistical test as $1 - \beta$. This is the probability of *avoiding* a Type II error. The conventional goal for power is .80 (i.e., with power of .80, we have an 80% chance of correctly rejecting a false null hypothesis). In our example, it means an 80% chance of correctly identifying behavioral training as having a positive effect.

The Type II error constitutes one of the most pernicious in research studies. It may occur for many different reasons. We noted above that we can adjust the probability of making a Type I error by changing alpha. We can also adjust the probability of making a Type II error, but that adjustment involves many factors, which we now consider.

Power and Factors Affecting It
The power of a statistical test corresponds to reducing the probability of making a Type II error. Numerous ways exist to

increase the power of a statistical test (i.e., to reduce the probability of making a Type II error).

We continue with the example of contrasting behavioral training with a control condition for ADHD using 50 patients in each group. The null hypothesis states that no difference exists between the behavioral training and control groups. We ask: What factors in the structure of the statistical test (e.g., a t test) will lead to rejecting the null hypothesis? We describe eight ways to increase the power of a statistical test.

1. Increasing sample sizes magnifies the statistical test (e.g., t or F). Increasing the numbers of cases decreases the standard error in the test, which in turn drives up t or F. The size of samples typically becomes the most common concern in discussions of statistical power. Cohen's (1988) tables remain the classic hard-copy reference on matters of power. However, a host of algorithms now available on the Internet can help to determine the number of cases needed in each group to achieve a certain degree of power for a given effect size and alpha level or to determine power with a given number of cases, alpha level, and effect size.

 The CD contains hyperlinks to several Internet sites that provide calculations for power and sample size.

2. Increasing the difference between the two conditions, for example, between behavioral training and control, magnifies t or F. You might wonder how to influence the difference

between means of the two groups. In our study of the effectiveness of behavioral training, we have to ensure that the treatment has sufficient potency. We might call this the "wallop" or dosing factor. A treatment may prove effective if applied regularly over a 6-month period but ineffective if applied over a 6-day period.

3. Increasing the alpha level increases the likelihood that the statistical test will prove significant, yielding a more powerful test. For example, changing the alpha level from .01 to .05 makes it easier to find significance. Of course, this also increases the chance of making a Type I error. Setting the alpha level always involves a trade-off between Type I and Type II errors.

4. A related factor concerns use of a one-tailed, rather than a two-tailed, test. A one-tailed test (provided the result occurs in the predicted direction) provides greater power. However, two theoretical reasons suggest eschewing a one-tailed test. For example, to use a one-tailed test in a treatment study, one needs to make the gratuitous assumption that the treatment could only prove beneficial and has no chance of causing harm.

5. Reducing the size of the standard deviations increases the likelihood that the statistical test will prove significant, thus making for a more powerful test. We can reduce the size of the standard deviations by using more homogeneous groups, for example, restricting the age levels in the study and controlling other such variables. Of course, such restriction reduces the generalizability of the results, but it does increase power.

6. Using equal numbers of cases in the two groups (assuming equal or approximately equal standard deviations) yields a

smaller standard error than using groups of unequal size. Since our attention focuses on the treatment, one might think it wise to split the 100 available cases into, say, 70 in the treatment group and 30 in the control group. That would be unwise because it would yield a less powerful test. The optimal split of 50–50 minimizes the standard error.

7. Using more reliable tests for the dependent variable increases power. In this example, we use a test of ADHD. The more reliable the test we use, the more powerful the statistical test we obtain. Reliability of the dependent measure has a substantial impact on power. In this regard, one must pay particular attention to tests of significance on subscales, which often have substantially less reliability than the full scales in which they reside. Researchers often overlook the effect of reliability when discussing power and effect size.

8. Use of parametric versus nonparametric statistical tests affects power. When the assumptions required for a parametric test are met, it will yield more powerful results than its nonparametric counterpart (e.g., the independent-samples t test vs. its nonparametric counterpart, the Mann-Whitney U test). When the assumptions required for a parametric test are seriously violated, the nonparametric test will prove more powerful.

All of these matters related to power are important for the researcher planning a study. However, they also have importance for the person evaluating and applying research. Lack of appropriate power in research evaluating treatments may mean that a potentially effective treatment goes undetected.

Test Statistics Commonly Used in
Null Hypothesis Significance Testing

Null hypothesis significance tests commonly use three types of test statistics: t, F, and χ^2. When the NHST involves comparing one sample with a population or comparing two samples with one another (e.g., a treatment vs. a control), the most typical procedure is the *t* **test**. When comparing more than two groups (e.g., treatment 1, treatment 2, and treatment 3), the *F* **test** is typically used. The F test uses the **analysis of variance (ANOVA)**. The F test may also be used instead of the t test when comparing two groups, in which case $F = t^2$.

The ANOVA and its accompanying F test is a remarkably flexible family of techniques, used for the one-way design as well as the factorial designs described next. It can also provide a test for equivalence of variances ($\sigma^2_B = \sigma^2_G$) and for significant increments in multiple regression (see "Multiple Regression" later in this chapter). Thus, F tests pop up in many research studies for a variety of purposes.

In the one-way and factorial designs, we analyze only one dependent variable at a time. For example, the dependent variable may be scores on a depression inventory. Hence, we call these "univariate designs." The *uni* refers to the number of dependent variables—here only one, even though there may be more than one independent variable, as in the case of a factorial design.

Many studies have more than one dependent variable. For example, a study may use scores on tests of depression, anxiety, and treatment satisfaction. In such a study, the researcher may use three separate F tests to analyze these three dependent variables. However, the preferred procedure involves using multivariate analysis of variance (MANOVA), which analyzes all three dependent variables at once. In the process of doing so, MANOVA takes into account the degree of relationship among the dependent variables and helps to protect against the compounding of probabilities when conducting multiple tests (see earlier discussion of Type I error). Note that MANOVA deals with multiple dependent variables, whereas a factorial design deals with multiple independent variables. Researchers frequently use MANOVAs with factorial designs, that is, where the study has both multiple independent variables and multiple dependent variables.

A third type of test statistic is χ^2 (chi-square). The t and F test statistics apply most often when measurement of the dependent variable occurs on a continuous scale, for example, score on a depression inventory. The χ^2 statistic is used when data are on a nominal scale, for example, classification of persons by a category such as gender (male, female) or diagnosis (e.g., anxiety disorder, mood disorder, substance disorder). However, like the F test, χ^2 is a remarkably flexible tool and pops up in a surprising array of applications. All three of the tests (t, F, and χ^2) use the mechanisms of NHST as described above: alpha levels, null hypotheses, and so on.

Research Designs

A research study typically follows one of several basic designs. Each design has its strengths and weaknesses. In this section, we briefly describe the common designs and "what to watch out for" when evaluating a study using that design. When first encountering a research study, identifying its basic design will help alert you to its shortcomings.

True Experimental Design

The "gold standard" for empirical research in mental health and addictions is the **true experimental design**. In clinical contexts, we call this design **randomized clinical trials** (RCTs) or randomized controlled trials. We must exercise care using the words *experiment* and *experimental*. In ordinary conversation, they can simply mean new or different. In the world of research, the term *experiment* has a much more specific meaning, as we describe here.

The true experimental design has five key features. Figure 4.2 illustrates these features for the two-group case, comparing a treatment group with a control group.

1. The design starts with a participant pool. The pool may contain all children identified with ADHD in a school system or all postmenopausal women self-referred to a particular clinic.

2. The researcher assigns members of the participant pool at **random** to one of the two groups, in this case to the treatment (experimental) group or to the control group. Random assignment is *essential* and is the most defining characteristic of the true experimental design. Common methods of random assignment to groups include using tables of random numbers, flipping a coin, or drawing names from a hat. Any nonrandom method of assignment destroys the experimental design. For example, placing all ADHD cases from one school building into the treatment group and cases from another school building into the control group is *not* random assignment.

Placing the more severe cases of depression into the treatment group and using less severe cases as controls is *not* random assignment.

3. An **independent variable** is applied. In the clinical context, the independent variable is usually a treatment, for example, psychodynamic therapy or medication. The experimental group receives the treatment and the control group does not. Or the design may involve two types of treatment, for example, a psychodynamic therapy for one group and pharmacotherapy for the other group. All circumstances other than the independent variable remain constant or vary at random between the two groups.

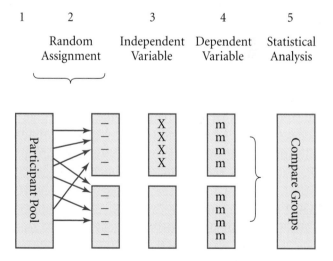

Figure 4.2 Illustration of key features of a randomized clinical trial for a two-group case.

4. Following application of the independent variable, the researchers measure the **dependent variable**. The dependent variable defines the behavior or outcome of interest in the research. It may include scores on a test, clinicians' judgment of improvement, clients' self-report of change, or some type of behavioral counts. Very often, the design includes several dependent variables. For example, the study may include all four of the variables just mentioned: a test score, clinicians' judgment, self-report, and behavioral count.

5. Finally, the investigator applies statistical analysis to the dependent variable in order to compare the two groups. The result typically employs a **significance test**, such as a t test, F test, or chi-square (χ^2), accompanied by a declaration of significant or nonsignificant difference between the groups and, preferably, a measure of effect size.

Why Is It the Gold Standard?

We consider the RCT as the gold standard among research designs because it is the only one that allows for drawing a causal conclusion: that the variation in the independent variable causes the difference in the dependent variable. More specifically, the only possible differences between the groups are (1) the independent variable and (2) random differences. The statistical test accounts for the random differences. If the difference between groups exceeds what we can attribute to random sampling variation, then the independent variable remains as the only possible explanation for the difference. In effect, the RCT allows us to make causal statements regarding the efficacy of the treatment.

Random Assignment versus Random Sampling

A key feature of the RCT design is random assignment of participants to the different groups or conditions. We must carefully distinguish between such random assignment and the notion of **random sampling** from a population. Random sampling from a population is the model used in elementary statistical inference. We start with a well-defined population, for example, all children with ADHD or all men with cocaine dependence. Then, we take a random sample from this population. Research studies rarely operate with this model because investigators seldom have access to large populations from which to easily conscript randomly selected participants. Rather, research studies usually start with some ad hoc or convenience group of individuals and then randomly assign the members of such a group to conditions in the study. With random assignment to conditions, the true experimental design works. However, that does not mean that the results will generalize to some well-defined population. In fact, this constitutes one of the major problems with research studies even when they do use random assignment. To what population do the results generalize? The answer usually becomes very much a judgment call not subject to careful statistical reasoning and procedures.

We must also make a distinction between a random sample and a representative sample. A representative sample accurately reflects important characteristics of the population, where the meaning of *important* varies depending on the topic being studied. One can draw a simple random sample in such a way that each element of the population has an equal chance of entering into the sample. A random sample is *not* necessarily representative, as many people incorrectly suppose. Any particular random sample may prove quite unrepresentative of the larger population. The value of using a random sample lies in the fact that rules of probability define the likelihood that the random sample will prove representative.

The greatest shortcoming of the RCT design is that it cannot be used to address many questions precisely because we cannot use random assignment to conditions for many topics of interest. For ethical and/or simple physical reasons, we cannot randomly assign people to their gender, their socioeconomic level, their degree of depression, their history of substance abuse, their age, and so on. For these, we must rely on other types of research designs, all of which prevent drawing firm causal conclusions.

Factorial Designs

The RCT typically has one independent variable and, therefore, we sometimes call it a one-way design. A **factorial design** has more than one independent variable operating at the same time. For example, one independent variable may consist of the type of treatment (control, medication, integrative therapy) and the other may involve duration of the intervention (6 weeks, 12 weeks). Figure 4.3 outlines this design. Participants are assigned at random to each of the cells in this design. Each *m* is a measure on a participant in the study, say, a measure of self-reported improvement.

The factorial design allows for analyzing the effect of type of treatment and the effect of length of treatment (time) within the same study. We call each of these variables a **main effect** in the study. The unique feature of the factorial design allows for the study of possible **interaction** between the two independent variables. An interaction might occur if the effectiveness of the

Clinician's Guide to Evidence-Based Practices

	Treatment		
Time	Control	Medication	Therapy
6 wks	m m m m m m m m	m m m m m m m m	m m m m m m m m
12 wks	m m m m m m m m	m m m m m m m m	m m m m m m m m

Figure 4.3 An example of a 3 x 2 factorial design.

type of treatment differed depending on length of treatment. We designate the interaction as "treatment x time," read as "treatment by time." For example, the medication may prove more effective than the integrative therapy for the 6-week duration but the integrative therapy treatment might prove more effective than the medication for the 12-week duration. We can only identify such interactions if we use a factorial design. Hence, such designs are a powerful addition to the researcher's tool kit.

Simply identifying a significant interaction does not reveal exactly what is happening. Understanding an interaction in a factorial design requires examination of cell means (i.e., calculate the mean for all cases within each cell). Then, a graph of the cell means "tells the story" of the interaction. Figure 4.4 shows the cell means for the treatment x time design in Figure 4.3. We have used self-reported improvement as the measure (dependent variable), on which we consider a high score favorable.

	Treatment		
Time	Control	Medication	Therapy
6 wks	10	20	15
12 wks	12	14	22

Figure 4.4 Cell means in a 3 x 2 factorial design.

To interpret these cell means, many researchers prepare a graph (see Fig. 4.5). They put the dependent variable on the y (vertical) axis. Pick *either one* of the independent variables and place it on the x (horizontal) axis. We have chosen treatment for the x axis. Then, for the other independent variable (in this case, time), plot the cell means, connect the plotted means with straight lines, and label each line. The plot tells the story of the interaction between treatment and time.

We described a two-way factorial design above. We might have more than two independent variables, resulting in a three-way or four-way design. In fact, there is no limit to the number of independent variables, although we rarely encounter more than three in any one study. Many variations on the assignment of participants in factorial designs also exist.

In the example just given, both independent variables were true, manipulated variables. Hence, we can draw causal conclusions about both of them. We often find that a factorial design

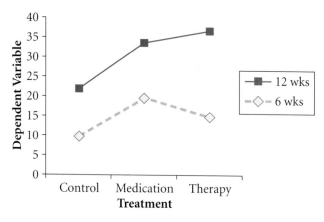

Figure 4.5 Plot of interaction revealed by cell means.

has one (or both) variables that are natural group variables (see later discussion of natural group contrasts, under "Quasi-experimental Designs"). When that occurs, we cannot draw causal conclusions about the natural group variable(s). For example, in Figure 4.3, substitute gender (men, women) for the time (6 weeks, 12 weeks) variable. Gender qualifies as a natural group variable. We do not assign cases at random to gender categories. Thus, use of a factorial design does not automatically mean that the design qualifies as a true experimental design. We must examine the nature of the independent variables and the method of assigning cases to groups to determine whether we can draw causal conclusions.

Quasi-experimental Designs

Quasi-experimental designs comprise a whole family of research designs, all of which try to approximate the RCT, as described above. The crucial issue is random assignment to conditions. None of the quasi-experimental designs features random assignment. Campbell and Stanley (1963) introduced the concept of quasi-experimental designs, and their book remains the classic reference on such designs.

Quasi-experimental designs fall into three broad categories. The first category includes **natural group contrasts**. For example, we may compare ADHD and non-ADHD children or severely depressed and moderately depressed women. The natural group contrast easily extends to comparisons among more than two groups, for example, nondepressed, moderately depressed, and severely depressed women. Such natural group contrasts look very much like experimental designs. Figure 4.6 outlines a natural group contrast study. Notice how similar it seems to the true experimental design in Figure 4.2. Both designs have contrasting groups, an independent variable, and a dependent variable. The statistical analysis proceeds in *exactly* the same manner whether the design follows an experimental or a quasi-experimental model. The difference involves random assignment of patients to conditions in the experimental design but not in the quasi-experimental design. Natural groups in the quasi-experimental design may (and probably do) differ in numerous ways in addition to the nominal basis for their grouping.

For example, consider the nominal classification of gender: men and women. Subjects likely differ not only in gender but also in average height, arm strength, interests, socialization, hormonal levels, and numerous other variables. Thus, if we find a difference between men and women, it may, at the root, result from a difference between people of varying heights. We call these other variables **confounds**. They become confounded or mixed up with

Clinician's Guide to Evidence-Based Practices

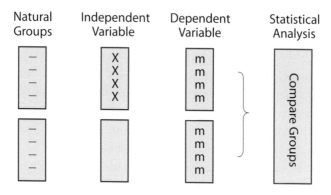

Figure 4.6 The common natural groups contrast quasi-experimental design.

the nominal basis for classification and quite literally confound our interpretation of results from natural group contrasts.

Research very often involves natural group contrasts yielding results often subject to misinterpretation. People seem to have an irresistible urge to attribute causality to the nominal basis for the classification without taking into account the many confounding variables.

A second broad category in the quasi-experimental family includes **time series**. The simplest case involves an Off–On (or AB) design. A group of participants is measured for, say, alcohol abuse before the introduction of an independent variable (treatment). This is the Off condition. Then the treatment switches "On" and we again measure participants' alcohol abuse. If alcohol abuse decreases, one could reason that the treatment worked. The design is very weak because a host of factors might have affected the participants in addition to the treatment, including the fact that we monitored their alcohol abuse twice. Thus, a strengthened design would flow as Off–On–Off–On–Off–On (or ABAB). Many variations of time series designs exist, but all variations attempt to find the elusive causal connection between independent and dependent variables. All suffer from lack of random assignment.

A third broad category of quasi-experimental designs includes techniques that rely strictly on statistical analysis. The most common of these is **analysis of covariance (ANCOVA).** The essence of ANCOVA focuses on adjusting the results of comparison between groups on the dependent variable for possible differences in confounding variables. These analyses give rise to conclusions such as "the groups differed in ability even after accounting for differences in socioeconomic level" or "the groups differed in levels of depression even after equating them on anxiety." Such expressions signal that ANCOVA was employed. However, one never knows whether another confounding variable might still be operating. The independent variable of interest (say, a psychotherapy) may become confounded with a host of other variables. For example, using the natural groups contrast, we may compare outcomes for a group of ADHD boys receiving a behavioral treatment at Lincoln School with a group of ADHD boys not receiving the treatment at Washington School. We determine that the outcomes are favorable for the boys receiving the treatment in comparison with those not receiving the treatment. We would like to conclude that the treatment proved effective. But we remain stuck with the possibility that many other differences may exist between the two groups besides the treatment variable. Perhaps Lincoln School has facilities or teachers that

Clinician's Guide to Evidence-Based Practices

make it a nicer place. Perhaps one of the schools recently changed principals. Perhaps the root of the differences in outcomes lies in the neighborhoods for the two schools. We can make the same type of argument for any of the quasi-experimental designs. Even when ANCOVA "equates" the groups on some extraneous variables, the possibility always exists that some other variable, not captured in the covariance, influenced the outcome.

Identifying Causal Words

A truism of research design holds that one cannot draw causal conclusions from any quasi-experimental design. When examining quasi-experimental research, remain alert to inappropriate use of the words *cause* and *causal*. However, the English language contains many words that imply causation, and you should be equally alert to inappropriate use of such words. Here is a partial list of such words, the words on the left suggesting a positive causal impact and words on the right suggesting a negative causal impact:

Leads to	Undermines
Produces	Weakens
Increases	Undercuts
Raises	Reduces
Enhances	Lowers
Improves	Decreases
Boosts	Eases
Develops	Damages

Beware of any of these terms suggesting a causal link. They apply appropriately only when the research design is adequate to the task.

Survey Designs

Mental health and addictions research makes wide use of surveys. Such surveys comprise the principal source of information about prevalence rates (see "Prevalence Rates and Related Ratios" in Chapter 5). We also use surveys routinely to solicit people's reactions to policies, practices, programs, and procedures. A **survey design** includes the population we want to sample, the method of participant selection, the method of contact, the survey questions, and the method of analysis and reporting.

An important issue in sampling from a population is the definition of the sampling frame. The **sampling frame** lists specific elements in the population and becomes the operational definition of the population. We need to stay alert to possible mismatching between the sampling frame and the population of real interest. For example, a population of interest may be residents of a particular city, and the sampling frame may focus on the telephone directory for that city. However, some residents of the city do not have a telephone, have unlisted numbers, or use only a cell phone. Other residents of the city have more than one entry in the telephone directory. Thus, the sampling frame in this instance does not align as a perfect match with the population of interest.

Some surveys do not involve sampling from a population. Rather, an entire group, albeit a small one, forms the desired respondent group. For example, we may aim a survey at all 300 persons currently under care in a psychiatric hospital or all adolescents attending a partial hospitalization program where these groups precisely represent our interest. In such cases, methods of sampling become irrelevant and we do not need inferential statistics (e.g., standard errors).

A second important issue for survey designs involves sample size. Surveys usually report the margin of error for the results. The **margin of error** is the standard error of a percentage, the percentage being the most common metric used for reporting survey results. Sample size (N) enters the equation for this standard error. Thus, a report may say "The margin of error for the survey was ±3 points." The CD gives values of the standard error of a percentage (SE_p) for simple random samples with selected values of N from 10 to 1000, along with confidence intervals. In the language of survey methods, these confidence intervals are the survey's margin of error.

The CD contains a file that shows confidence intervals for $p = .50$ at different levels of N. You can enter any value for N and see the resulting confidence intervals.

Another crucial aspect of any survey is the nonresponse rate. Many surveys have substantial nonresponse rates. When this occurs, the nonresponse rate is a far greater potential source of error than the official margin of error. Suppose the target sample contains 500 people; 40% (200) respond, and 60% (300) do not respond. Among respondents, 75% answer "Yes" to a certain question. Theoretically, anywhere from 0 to 300 of the nonrespondents might have answered "Yes" to this question. Thus, the final percentage answering "Yes" could range anywhere from 30% to 90%. The margin of error based on nonresponse in this example is 60%, whereas the official margin of error is only 6% (a 95% confidence interval). Reporting a margin of error at only 6% would grossly mislead readers. The best one can hope for in such circumstances would involve the researchers demonstrating that the nonrespondent group presented as highly similar to the respondent group on a host of variables relevant to the survey topics.

The wording of survey questions is another crucial aspect of any survey design. Even subtle differences in wording (e.g., "a" rather than "the") may have a major effect on results. When reviewing a study employing the survey method, carefully examine the exact wording of questions. The influence of question wording is a matter of judgment rather than statistical analysis.

A final source of difficulty for interpretation of survey results involves the manner in which the investigator summarizes results. A simple example makes the point. Take this question: "Do you think your treatment was effective?" Responses are distributed as follows: Yes 45%, No 25%, Unsure 30%. This array of responses supports all of these assertions, which give very different impressions of the results. (1) Only a minority of respondents felt the treatment was effective. (2) Only a minority of the respondents felt the treatment was ineffective. (3) Of those who reached a conclusion about the treatment, a majority felt the treatment was effective. Our point: One must examine actual response data in order to interpret conclusions. This matter of how we summarize the data stands quite apart from the problem of question wording.

Observational Studies

Observational studies concentrate on obtaining an accurate description of some phenomenon. They may attempt to provide an overall description; for example, observe and describe what Jonathon, our 8-year old ADHD patient, does during a 1-hr period in his classroom. Or, it may focus on observations concentrating on a specific, operationalized behavior. For example, again for Jonathon, how frequently does he engage in off-task behavior during a 5-min period? Investigators often report results from such focused observations in the form of counts or checklists.

All scientific investigations begin with observations; observations form the original "stuff" of science. However, observational studies result chiefly in descriptions. They lack explanatory power. They may suggest avenues for later work leading to explanations, but they do not themselves provide explanations and causal connections; thus, we rarely see them considered in evidence-based compilations.

Case Studies

The **case study method** involves detailed descriptions of individual cases or small numbers of similar cases. Some case studies limit themselves to pure description, but researchers often attempt to suggest causes of behavior(s) manifest in the cases. The case study method can prove particularly valuable when attempting to understand new or rare conditions for which insufficient numbers of cases exist to conduct any other type of study. The case study method does not allow for drawing strong conclusions simply because it involves only one or a few cases. Well-written case studies, such as those by Freud, can sound very persuasive regarding suggested causal connections, so one must exercise exceptional caution in drawing conclusions from such reports.

Multivariate Techniques

Mental health and addictions research has become replete with reports using multivariate statistics. However, the typical report using one of these techniques relies on a few basic mechanisms summarized below to enhance your interpretation and application of such studies.

Multiple Regression

Multiple regression is a set of techniques to express the relationship between one variable (the criterion) and a composite of other variables, with the composite constructed so as to apply optimal weights to each entry in the composite. "Optimal" weights maximize the relationship between the criterion and the composite of predictor variables. For example, we may predict suicidal ideation (the criterion) from three predictors: level of depression, self-reported quality of life, and age.

A multiple regression provides a correlation between the criterion and the composite. We call this a **multiple correlation**, designated by R. Subscripts on R indicate the predicted variable and which variables fall in the composite of predictors. For example, the designation $R_{Y.123}$ indicates the multiple correlation of Y (the criterion) with the optimal composite of variables 1, 2, and 3.

An outcome of a multiple regression analysis is a **multiple regression equation**. Research reports often present the equation. It may look like this: $Y = b_1X_1 + b_2X_2 + b_3X_3 + c$, where b shows the weight given to each predictor. In one version, b appears as beta weight (the Greek letter β). They help us understand the contribution each variable makes to the prediction.

Here is perhaps the most crucial point about the weights applied in the regression equation: They depend not only on the correlation of each predictor with the criterion but also on the correlations among the predictor variables. A predictor may have a reasonably high correlation with the criterion, but if it also has a high correlation with other predictors, then it will not receive a large weight and, in fact, may be eliminated completely.

A common analysis developed from a multiple regression involves examining the increase in R as we add different variables to or delete them from the regression equation. This type of analysis introduces the terms R^2 and $\Delta\mathbf{R}^2$ (read delta R^2). The delta represents the *difference* (increase or decrease) in R^2 as we add or remove variables. Does adding a variable to the equation significantly increase R^2? To follow our example from above, would adding a measure of hopelessness improve our prediction of suicidal ideation? If it does, we want to add that variable to the equation. If adding the variable to the equation does not significantly increase R^2 (i.e., ΔR^2 is small), then we have no good reason to add the variable. Similarly, we ask "Does deleting a variable lead to little change in R^2?" If so, we can eliminate the variable with no significant loss in predictive power.

A researcher has several options for conducting a multiple regression analysis. The options relate to such matters as the method for entering variables into the analysis and rules for when to stop entering or removing variables. However, all of the points made above apply to interpreting results regardless of the options chosen by the researcher.

The **stepwise method** is a common approach to entering variables into a multiple regression equation. In this method, we examine each variable in turn. First, we enter the variable accounting for the most variance. Next, we select the variable that accounts for the most remaining variance after partialling out (see "Partial Correlation") the first variable. Entry of new variables stops when adding new variables no longer accounts for significant amounts of variance (i.e., ΔR^2 is small).

Another common application is **hierarchical regression**. In this method, the researcher specifies the order in which variables will enter and may specify that certain groups of variables (e.g., all demographics) will enter as a block. The order of entry originates with some theoretical consideration or hypothesis being tested. As with the stepwise method, increments in variance accounted for, as indicated by ΔR^2, constitute important considerations in the interpretation of a hierarchical model.

Partial Correlation

Partial correlation is a procedure for expressing the degree of relationship between two variables (A and B) with a third variable (C) "held constant" or "partialled out." We accomplish the "holding constant" by predicting A and B from C. Figure 4.7 shows the sequence of steps involved in determining the partial r of variables A and B with C partialled out. We express the result as $r_{AB.C}$, read as the correlation between A and B with C held constant or partialled out. We also say we have "removed the effect of C."

Consider this example. In a group of children aged 8–13, we find the correlations among chronological age (C), mental age (M), and shoe size (S) computed as follows:

$$r_{CM} = .65 \qquad r_{CS} = .75 \qquad r_{MS} = .50$$

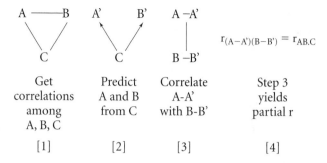

Figure 4.7 Sequence of steps for partialling out a third variable.

What happens to the correlation between mental ability and shoe size with age held constant ($r_{MS.C}$)? The partial r for the latter data is .02! Hence, with chronological age held constant, the correlation between mental age and shoe size (originally .50) approximates 0.

We can sometimes hold a third variable constant by the way we collect data. In the latter example, we could accomplish this by collecting data only on children within a 1-year age span, say, age 8. However, frequently it is inconvenient or impossible to hold the third variable constant in the data collection stage. Partial correlation proves particularly useful in those circumstances.

Note that we can hold constant or partial out more than one variable. In fact, researchers frequently do so. For example, $r_{AB.CDE}$ indicates the correlation between *A* and *B* with *C*, *D*, and *E* partialled out or held constant.

Here is an important point about partial correlations: We do not find them reported frequently in the research literature.

CD BONUS

The CD has a worksheet with sample values used to calculate partial *r*. You can substitute other values to note the effect of partialling out a third variable.

However, they underlie much of the work carried out with other multivariate techniques.

Logistic Regression

Logistic regression is similar to multiple regression in that it aims to predict one variable (the criterion) from an optimal combination of several other variables. Logistic regression differs from multiple regression mainly in the nature of the variables involved in the analysis. Most typically in multiple regression we focus only on continuous variables. In logistic regression criterion variables will usually take dichotomous form, with at least some discrete predictor variables. Examples of dichotomous variables are ADHD/non-ADHD, depressed/not depressed, and dead/alive. Thus, we may use logistic regression to predict membership in the ADHD group from a combination of variables including gender, score above a cut-point on an ADHD scale, and teacher nomination. The logistic regression provides the optimal weighting of the three predictor variables to predict membership in the ADHD group (or, conversely, in the non-ADHD group). It is possible to have discrete categories with more than two groups (e.g., severely depressed, mildly depressed, not depressed), but these categories get converted into sets of dichotomies in the analysis.

Because of the dichotomous criterion variable in logistic regression, researchers will generally interpret the final result of the analysis as a probability or some transformation of a probability. For example, given a set of predictor variables, with their optimal weights, what is the probability that a child belongs to the ADHD group? A common transformation of the probability from logistic regression is the **odds ratio** (see "Odds Ratio and Relative Risk" in Chapter 5).

Two statistical procedures similar to logistic regression in their purpose and in at least some of their procedures are discriminant analysis and cluster analysis. However, we do not see these analyses used as much as logistic regression in the mental health research literature.

Factor Analysis

Factor analysis is a family of data reduction techniques designed to identify basic dimensions (factors) among a multiplicity of variables. We start with many specific variables, for example, scores on 20 personality measures, and then determine the correlations among these measures. Factor analytic techniques operate with these correlations. As variables we may use scores on entire tests or single items within tests. The reasoning, which actually operates in the form of mathematical functions, proceeds as follows. If we find that two variables correlate very highly (say, $r = .90$), we can think of these two variables as if they fall along a single dimension. Similarly, say that four of the original variables correlated highly, we could then collapse these four variables into a single dimension or factor. Variables that do not correlate highly cannot be so collapsed. Factor analysis techniques analyze all the relationships among the original variables to determine how many factors are needed to account for the relationships.

Research reports tend to concentrate on four outcomes:

- ◆ the factor matrix
- ◆ the percent of variance accounted for by factors
- ◆ rules for when to stop extracting factors
- ◆ the naming of the factors

Figure 4.8 presents an example of a factor matrix. In this case, the factor analysis yields four factors for the 15 items, using one of the standard criteria for extracting factors. We call entries in the body of the table **loadings**. They express the relationship between each theoretical factor and each item. Loadings of .40 or higher are shown in bold. It is customary, although not required, to highlight high loadings (say, over .30 or over .40) with bold, italics, or underlining. These highlighted items best represent the apparent underlying dimension. Entries below the table show the percent of the total variance for the 15 items accounted for by each factor and the percent of variance accounted for by each factor among the variance covered by the four factors.

As you read, stay alert to when to stop extracting factors. The mathematical routines will continue to extract factors up to the limit of the number of variables in the analysis. However, factors extracted later in the process will prove meaningless, precisely because they account for so little variance. A research report will usually identify the criterion for stopping the extraction process, and ordinarily one can accept the researcher's choice of criterion.

The analysis displayed in Figure 4.8 shows one dominant factor, accounting for over half of the variance covered by the

Item	Factor			
	1	2	3	4
1	−.006	**.439**	.177	**.737**
2	.073	.343	−.038	.035
3	.177	.097	**.644**	.183
4	.113	.092	**.747**	.188
5	**.467**	.193	.240	−.006
6	.393	.328	**.426**	−.042
7	.156	−.149	.216	**.431**
8	**.442**	.006	.215	.099
9	**.755**	.139	.016	.101
10	**.809**	.099	.035	.133
11	.307	**.583**	.202	−.091
12	.371	**.504**	.319	.165
13	**.678**	.293	.226	−.047
14	.311	.295	.085	−.012
15	.031	**.597**	.109	.053
Percent of total variance accounted for	31	10	10	7
Percent of variance accounted for by the 4 factors	53	17	17	12

Figure 4.8 Example of factor analysis results.

four factors, although covering somewhat less than one-third of the total variance. Then, we have three weaker factors, with the fourth one of marginal utility. Naming the factors calls for judgment and insight: It is not a mechanical or mathematical operation. One examines the variables with highest loadings on each factor to see what they seem to have in common and then develops a word or a few words that capture the essence of the factor.

We described above what is called *exploratory factor analysis* (EFA): It explores the underlying factor structure. *Confirmatory factor analysis* (CFA), by contrast, begins with a theory about the underlying factor structure and then attempts to show that the factor data fit the theory. For example, we may hypothesize that the correlations among the Wechsler intelligence subtests best fit a four-factor model. We use CFA to test the fit of this model. We encounter EFA more frequently in the research literature, but CFA occurs with increasing frequency. Actually, CFA is a subcategory of structural equation modeling, which we take up next.

Structural Equation Modeling

Structural equation modeling attempts to infer causal connections among many interrelated variables. Structural equation modeling starts with correlations among the variables. As every statistics textbook emphasizes, one cannot infer causation from correlation coefficients. The modeling techniques suspend this truism. Essentially, they say: Let us suppose that causal directions do exist among these intercorrelated variables and that we can surmise these directions based on theory or research so as to build a model showing these causal directions.

As with all multivariate techniques, structural equation modeling, sometimes called *causal modeling* precisely because it imputes causality, includes a variety of specific approaches. One example is **path analysis**, aptly named because it shows paths (with causal directions) among a number of variables.

The most distinctive feature of a structural equation model is the diagram showing relationships among variables and the causal directions. The presence of such a diagram signals that the investigator has used structural equation modeling. Text accompanying the diagram provides verbal descriptions of relationships depicted in the diagram. Figure 4.9 shows a path model, adapted and simplified from Holahan, Moos, Holahan, Brennan, and Schutte (2005). The model attempts to "explain" 10-Year Depressive Symptoms (on the far right in the figure). Single-headed arrows show implied causal direction. The double-headed arrow between Baseline Avoidance Coping and Baseline Depressive Symptoms shows that they mutually influence one another. Baseline Avoidance Coping directly influences status on 4-Year Life Stressors. Notice that, in this model, Baseline Avoidance Coping does not directly influence 10-Year Depressive Symptoms but 4-Year Life Stressors mediates the influence of Baseline Avoidance Coping on 10-Year Depressive Symptoms. In contrast, Baseline Depressive Symptoms has a direct influence on 10-Year Depressive Symptoms, as well as an indirect effect through Baseline Depressive Symptoms' influence on 4-Year Life Stressors. Coefficients on each arrow indicate the strength of relationships.

A structural equation model begins its analysis with a correlation matrix (or covariance matrix). It then applies multiple

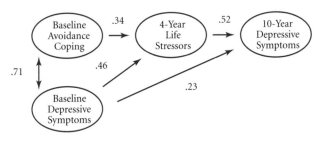

Figure 4.9 Example of a path model. Adapted from Holahan et al. (2005).

regression procedures and partial correlation procedures to the many possible relationships among the variables; it may also use factor analysis to form composite variables, often called *latent* variables. Most importantly, before the analysis begins, the researcher must have a theory about the causal connections among variables. This theory guides the specific analyses used to trace paths through the network of relationships. Finally, it customarily provides some measure of "fit" which tells how well the theoretical model agrees with the actual data, that is, the original set of correlations. Very often, two or more models will be "fit" and the researcher hopes to show that the proposed model provides the best fit. Importantly, one must remember that the model, no matter how good the fit, flows from correlations that do not themselves point in causal directions. For more on structural equation modeling, see Klem (1995), Kline (1998), and Ullman (2007).

For all of the multivariate techniques, remember this important point: If the variables entering the multivariate analysis do not represent the relevant or important facets for the topic, then the multivariate technique will not and cannot identify them. Multivariate analysis can only reveal relationships among the entered variables; it cannot tell us what is missing or what may be more important than the variables entered. For example, if you omit anxiety measures in a study, then you will not get an anxiety factor in your factor analysis. If no information about genetic or family history enters your structural equation model attempting to predict depression, then family genetics will not show up as an important mediator. Whenever interpreting results of multivariate analyses, always ask yourself this question: What important information might be missing from the mix?

The purpose of this chapter was to highlight important features of research designs frequently used in mental health and addictions research. Most of the research falls into recognizably distinct categories. Each category has its special strengths and weaknesses. Spotting the basic design and being alert to its strengths and weaknesses should help you to use the research literature effectively to inform your evidence-based practice.

Key Terms

alpha level (α)
analysis of covariance (ANCOVA)
analysis of variance (ANOVA)
Bonferroni correction
case study method
chi-square (χ^2)
confidence interval
confound
ΔR^2
dependent variable

effect size
exact p value
factor analysis
factorial design
F test
hierarchical regression
independent variable
interaction
loadings
logistic regression

main effect
margin of error
multiple correlation
multiple regression
multiple regression equation
multivariate analysis of variance
   (MANOVA)
natural group contrasts
null hypothesis
null hypothesis significance test
   (NHST)
observational study
odds ratio
partial correlation
path analysis
power
quasi-experimental design

random
random sampling
randomized clinical trial (RCT)
research hypothesis
sampling frame
significance level
significance test
standard error of a statistic
statistical hypothesis
stepwise method
structural equation modeling
survey design
time series
true experimental design
t test
Type I error
Type II error

Recommended Readings and Web Sites

Campbell, D. T., & Stanley, J. C. (1963). *Experimental and quasi-experimental designs for research.* Chicago: Rand-McNally.

Center for Bioinformatics and Molecular Biostatistics, University of California–San Francisco (2006). Power and sample size programs [computer software], www.biostat.ucsf.edu/sampsize.html

Cohen, J. (1988). *Statistical power analysis for the behavioral sciences* (2nd ed.). Hillsdale, NJ: Erlbaum.

Grimm, L. G., & Yarnold, P. R. (Eds.). (1996). *Reading and understanding multivariate statistics.* Washington, DC: American Psychological Association.

Kirk, R. E. (1995). *Experimental design: Procedures for the behavioral sciences* (3rd ed.). Pacific Grove, CA: Brooks/Cole.

Kirk, R. E. (1996). Practical significance: A concept whose time has come. *Educational and Psychological Measurement, 56,* 746–759.

Lenth, R. V. (2006). Java Applets for Power and Sample Size [computer software], www.stat.uiowa.edu/~rlenth/Power

Pedhazur, E. J. (1997). *Multiple regression in behavioral research: Explanation and prediction* (3rd ed.). Fort Worth, TX: Harcourt Brace.

Tabachnick, B. G., & Fidell, L. S. (2007). *Using multivariate statistics* (5th ed.). Boston: Pearson.

▮ ▮▮ ▮
CHAPTER 5

Reading and Interpreting the Research: Numbers and Measures

Not surprisingly, the research that fuels evidence-based practice is filled with numbers. In order to make sense of the research, you will need a degree of familiarity with the kinds of numbers most frequently employed. This chapter covers these frequently used numbers, defining each and giving examples typical of those encountered in mental health and addictions research. We have made a judicious selection from among the plethora of choices, based primarily on frequency of usage and utility in informing clinical practice.

The Normal Curve

Research literature often refers to the "normal curve," "assumptions of normality," "departures from normality," and "common benchmarks within the normal curve," for example, z-scores and cutoff points. Figure 5.1 presents a graph of the normal curve. Reference points within the curve shown on the bottom include z-scores, percentiles, *T*-scores, deviation IQs, and the familiar SAT score scale. Each of these last three reference systems is a standard score system, with means and standard deviations (*SDs*) of 50 and 10, 100 and 15, 500 and 100, respectively.

We refer to the theoretical normal curve as *unimodal* (i.e., it has one "hump," reaching its maximum at the center of the distribution). The curve flows in a symmetrical shape about its

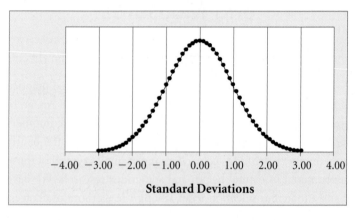

z-scores		-3	-2	-1	0	$+1$	$+2$	$+3$
Percentiles		<1	2	16	50	84	98	>99
T-scores		20	30	40	50	60	70	80
Deviation IQ		55	70	85	100	115	130	145
SAT		200	300	400	500	600	700	800

Figure 5.1 The normal curve with selected reference points.

center. At that center lie the mean, the median, and the mode. The tails of the distribution flow in an *asymptotic* manner with respect to the base (i.e., approaching but never touching the baseline). Of course, in any actual distribution, the data set does have finite limits. The theoretical normal curve also has a certain relationship between its height and width. We can best describe this characteristic as the curve's "shoulder" width, formally known as *kurtosis*.

Common departures from normality refer to the characteristics of modality and symmetry. There may be more than one mode (hump); for example, a bimodal distribution has two humps. This does not happen very often in mental health data. Many people assume that a bimodal distribution will result if we combine two distributions with different means (e.g., the heights of adult males and females). However, we can demonstrate that the two means must differ by at least 2 *SD*s for bimodality to result (Schilling, Watkins, & Watkins, 2002). Two *SD*s represents a whopping big difference. Consider the fact that mean heights for adult males and females—a very noticeable difference in daily life—differ by less than 2 *SD*s.

A second departure from normality deals with the symmetry property of the normal curve. We call departures from symmetry *skewness*. When data "pile up" at the low end of the curve, with a long tail to the right, we have *positive skewness* or *skewness to the right*. We refer to piling up at the high end with a long tail to the left as *negative skewness* or *skewness to the left*. Many distributions in the behavioral sciences exhibit abnormal skewness in one direction or the other, sometimes wreaking havoc with assumptions made in statistical analyses.

Confidence Intervals and Standard Errors

In mental health and addictions research, we often refer to *confidence intervals* and *standard errors*, intimately related issues. Two main types of standard errors and resulting **confidence intervals (CIs)** demand our attention. Although the terminology used for these two types seems similar, the terms refer to two quite different issues. We take them up in turn, first for test scores and then for statistics.

Confidence Interval for a Test Score

Construction of a CI for a test score depends on reliability within the context of classical test theory, specifically from the notions of **obtained score**, **true score**, and **error score**. An *obtained score* indicates what we actually get for an individual on one occasion. The person's *true score* represents what we really want to know—but never have. We can think of it as the score a person would receive if we had a perfectly reliable test (i.e., with a standard error of zero). Alternatively, we may think of the true score as the average of an infinite number of obtained scores for an individual (assuming no fatigue from taking an infinite number of tests, no recollection of content from earlier administrations, and so on). The *error score* represents the difference between the true score and the obtained score. We commonly represent the relationship as:

$$O = T \pm E \quad \text{or} \quad T = O \pm E$$

where T is the true score, O is the obtained score, and E is the error score. Thus, the obtained score equals the true score plus or minus error due to unreliability. Conversely, the true score would equal the obtained score contaminated by unreliable error.

If we had an infinite number of obtained scores, we would assume that the obtained scores would be normally distributed around the true score, which equals the mean or expected value for the entire distribution. Figure 5.2 illustrates this theoretical distribution of many obtained scores around a true score. Of course, we never get an infinite number of obtained scores. We get just one obtained score, but this model predicts how an infinite number of obtained scores would distribute themselves. We use this model to reason about the one obtained score.

The *SD* of this theoretical distribution is the **standard error of measurement *(SEM)*.** The most common formula for the *SEM* is:

$$SEM = SD\sqrt{1 - r}$$

where *r* is the test's reliability and *SD* is the test's standard deviation for the group on which the *r* was determined. Thus, if a test's reliability stands at .85 and the *SD* equals 15, we would calculate the *SEM* for that test as 5.8, or approximately 6 points.

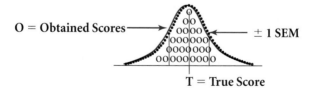

Figure 5.2 Hypothetical distribution of many obtained scores around the true score for an individual.

We can use the *SEM* to construct a CI around the obtained score. We can then state, with a certain degree of probability, that the person's true score lies within this CI. Note that the CI falls around the obtained score (*O* in the model), not around the true score (*T*) because we never know *T*.

To construct a CI for a test score, we need the test's *SD* and a reliability coefficient (which together yield the *SEM*, as indicated in the formula above) and a multiplier based on the probability for the width of the interval. The most common levels of confidence use a multiplier of 1.0, yielding a 68% CI; a multiplier of 1.96, yielding a 95% CI; and a multiplier of 2.58, yielding a 99% CI.

Let us define these CIs for Jonathon, our rambunctious 8-year-old boy with a diagnosis of attention-deficit/hyperactivity disorder (ADHD). Jonathon's evaluation included an assessment of his intellectual ability, let us assume, with the Wechsler Intelligence Scale for Children, 4th edition (WISC-IV). The *SD* for the WISC-IV Perceptual Reasoning Index score is 15. The manual gives the internal consistency reliability for Jonathon's age group as .93. Thus, *SEM* = 3.97, which we will round to 4. Jonathon's index score is 110. Let us apply CIs to Jonathon's score.

- We have a 68% certainty that Jonathon's *true* score is $110 \pm (1.00 \times SEM) = 110 \pm 4$ or 106–114.
- We have a 95% certainty that Jonathon's *true* score is $110 \pm (1.96 \times SEM) = 110 \pm 8$ or 102–118.
- We have a 99% certainty that Jonathon's *true* score is $110 \pm (2.58 \times SEM) = 110 \pm 10$ or 100–120.

These are the most commonly used CIs. You can construct any width interval by using different multipliers, which in turn refer to different areas in the normal distribution. For example, a multiplier of 1.65 yields a 90% CI. When referencing the CI for a test score, we will find it important to know whether the interval covers 68%, 95%, 99%, or, perhaps, some other percentage interval.

The examples presented for Jonathon's CIs make these handy generalizations clear:

- The more confidence you want to have about capturing the true score, the wider the interval you will want to use.
- The narrower the interval, the lower your confidence in capturing the true score.
- The lower the test's reliability, the wider the interval you will want to use.
- The higher the reliability, the narrower the interval you will need.

What Reliability Do We Capture with the Confidence Interval?
Talking about *the* reliability of a test will prove misleading. Several sources of unreliability exist, and most reliability coefficients capture only one or a few of these sources. For example, *test–retest reliability* captures unreliability due to temporal fluctuations, but it does not capture unreliability due to differences in test content. *Internal consistency reliability* captures unreliability due to differences in test content, but it does not capture unreliability due to temporal fluctuations. *Generalizability theory* (Brennan, 2001) allows for examining multiple sources of unreliability. However, despite its elegance, generalizability coefficients simply do not exist for most tests. Reliability capturing only one source of

unreliability will prove greater than reliability covering several sources of unreliability. Since the *SEM* incorporates the reliability information (see the formula for *SEM*) and the *SEM*, in turn, enters the CI, most CIs for test scores presented in test manuals are smaller than they really should be for practical applications. No simple formula exists to correct for this underestimation.

Confidence Intervals for Statistics

We call a descriptive measure (e.g., the mean or a correlation coefficient) on a sample a **statistic**. We call a descriptive measure on an entire population a **parameter**. We use a statistic to estimate a parameter. For example, we use the mean of a sample to estimate the mean of a population; we use a correlation based on a sample to estimate the correlation in the population. The common practice involves designating statistics with ordinary italicized English characters (e.g., *M*, *S*, *r*) and designating parameters with Greek letters (e.g., μ [mu], σ [sigma], ρ [rho]). It is certainly confusing to call a sample's descriptor a "statistic" because we refer to the entire field as "statistics." Nevertheless, statisticians use these as common terminology.

Recognize three facts about this situation. First, we almost always want to know what is true for a population. For example, we want to know the mean score on the Beck Depression Inventory–II for all postmenopausal women or the correlation between anxiety and depression if we tested everyone in the population. Second, we nearly always have only the information on a sample—in this instance, the sample mean. Third, we use the sample statistic (e.g., *M*) to estimate or draw an inference about the population parameter (e.g., μ).

Clinician's Guide to Evidence-Based Practices

The **standard error of a statistic** provides an index of precision with which the statistic estimates its corresponding parameter. Think of many random samples drawn from the population. On each sample, we calculate the statistic of interest. These statistics will form a distribution around the parameter. The distribution may follow the normal curve, as in Figure 5.3. Let us assume for the moment that the parameter lies at the center of this distribution and that we can determine the distribution's *SD*. We call the *SD* of this distribution the *standard error* (SE) *of the statistic*. Note that the *SE* is an *SD*, but it is not the *SD* of the original measures (e.g., people's test scores). It is an *SD* of the means of many samples. With the *SE* in hand, we can use the properties of the normal curve to make statements about the likelihood that a particular statistic (the one we got for our sample) lies within a certain distance of the parameter. Figure 5.3 uses a distribution of sample means around the population parameter μ.

A CI creates a region around a statistic with the expectation that the parameter corresponding to the statistic falls within that region, with a certain degree of probability. As was the case for the CI for a test score, as described above, we will often find CIs for statistics given for the 68%, 95%, and 99% levels. For many

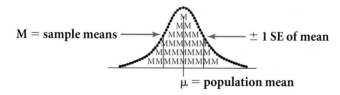

Figure 5.3 Distribution of sample means (*M*) around the population parameter *μ*.

statistics, these levels correspond to multiplying the *SE* of the statistic by 1.00, 1.96, and 2.58, respectively. One exception to this rule is use of varying *t* values from Student's *t* distributions for small sample statistics. However, the concept remains the same.

Figure 5.4 shows a graphic presentation of CIs for a mean (*M*) of 19 and *SE* of 2. Confidence intervals suggest how much "wobble" might occur in using the statistic to estimate a parameter.

We have illustrated the concept of an *SE* and its corresponding CI with the sample mean and the population mean. The same concepts apply to any statistic and its corresponding parameter. However, not all statistics yield a normal or even a symmetrical sampling distribution. We must investigate the nature of the sampling distribution for each statistic. Once we have handled this matter, the concepts of *SE* and CI apply.

Two Important Features of Standard Errors and Confidence Intervals

Sample size (*N*) enters the denominator of the formula for *SE*. Hence, the larger the *N*, the smaller the *SE* we will obtain. This is a general feature of all *SE* formulas. It agrees with common

```
       [     M     ]     2.58 SE = 99% CI   (14-24)

        [     M     ]     1.96 SE = 95% CI   (15-23)

           [ M ]          1.00 SE = 68% CI   (17-21)

+++++++++++++++++++++++++++++++++++++++++++
```

2 4 6 8 10 12 14 16 18 20 22 24 26 28 30 32 34 36 38 40

Figure 5.4 Illustration of a confidence interval for a mean (*M* = 19, *SE* = 2).

Clinician's Guide to Evidence-Based Practices

sense: The larger the sample, the better we expect the sample statistic to approximate its corresponding parameter. This feature of *SE*s has a direct impact on CIs: The larger the *N*, the narrower the CI will be.

A second important feature of CIs for statistics corresponds to one of the generalizations identified for CIs for test scores. The more confidence we want to have that we have captured the parameter within the interval, the wider the interval we must have. This results from the multiplier (e.g., 1.96 or 2.58) applied to the *SE* of the statistic.

Effect Size

Measures of Effect Size Are Important

The results of tests of statistical significance, as outlined in Chapter 4, are heavily dependent on the size of the samples (*N* or N_1 and N_2). Given sufficiently large *N*s, almost any difference in means or any degree of correlation will qualify as "significant." Beware of such declarations as "significant" and "highly significant" when very large or unspecified *N*s exist.

Consider this hypothetical example involving the comparison of two groups of alcohol abusers (men = 1 and women = 2) with means, $M_1 = 50$ and $M_2 = 52$, and with $SD = 10$ for each group. If N_1 and N_2 were each 25, the *t* test would yield $t = .70$, a clearly nonsignificant difference. However, if N_1 and N_2 were each 1000, the *t* test would yield $t = 4.47$, a clearly significant difference, with $p < .001$. We must temper our interpretation of this "highly significant" result by the observation that a 2-point difference may be of little practical importance. This illustrates the oft-cited difference between "statistically significant" and "clinically significant."

We can observe the same kinds of results when working with other hypothesis tests. Large Ns may produce statistically significant results that may not have much practical meaning. For this reason, we like to supplement a hypothesis test with some measure of effect size. Measures of **effect size (ES)** aim to express the degree of difference between group means or the degree of correlation between variables *independent of the sample size* (N). Although many journals have policies encouraging use of ES measures, the editors do not always enforce such policies consistently. Furthermore, even when an original article reports measures of ES, they often become lost when others summarize the results from the article elsewhere. Intelligent interpretation of results always requires application of the notion of ES—if not formally, at least informally.

Two Common Measures of Effect Size

Researchers commonly use two measures of ES along with a host of others. We first describe the two most common measures. The first is *d*, sometimes called **Cohen's *d***, although variations on Cohen's version exist with other names attached. We present here the simplest case of *d*:

$$d = \frac{M_T - M_C}{SD}$$

where M_T and M_C are the means of the treatment and control groups, respectively, and SD is the pooled standard deviation for the two groups (or, in one version of *d*, simply the *SD* of the control group). For example, if $M_T = 25$ and $M_C = 20$ and $SD = 10$, then $d = .5$. We provide further examples of d below.

The second common measure of ES is simply the correlation coefficient (r), a number confined to the range -1.00 to $+1.00$, constituting a self-defining measure of ES. For example, an r of .95 is very high; an r of .10 is very low. However, N affects the statistical significance of r. Note that N (sample size) enters into the formula for determining the SE of r; which in turn enters into the hypothesis test. As above, a very large N can yield a "highly significant r" that does not have much practical importance. For example, $r = .04$ attains significance at the .001 level when based on $N = 10,000$. But $r = .04$ will prove worthless, for practical purposes. Also, $r = .15$ based on 500 cases rates as significant at the .001 level but is of little practical value.

Benchmarks for the Two Common Measures of Effect Size

Cohen (1988) offered a series of **effect size benchmarks** for the interpretation of d and r. Often, researchers refer to these as "Cohen's benchmarks." Although intended as informal (in the sense of arising from common sense rather than from statistical theory), these designations have struck a resonant chord in the research community and have won adoption with surprising consensus. Figure 5.5 lists these benchmarks.

Graphic Illustrations of Effect Size

Keeping these benchmark figures in mind for measures of ES will prove useful, but you will find it even more useful to draw the measures of ES and keep the drawings in mind when interpreting research results. Figure 5.6 illustrates the three benchmark measures for d. As shown there, $d = .20$ has almost

	Small	Medium	Large
d	.20	.50	.80
r	.10	.30	.50

Figure 5.5 Summary of Cohen's benchmarks for *d* and *r* as effect size.

complete overlap between the two distributions, for example, between a treatment and a control group. Even with $d = .8$, there is quite a bit of overlap. To achieve almost complete separation between the two distributions requires a d of approximately 6, an ES almost never found in mental health and addictions research. For example, when reading about an "evidence-based" treatment for which the investigator claims much more effectiveness than a control or waiting list, one might expect an ES (d) of .80, a large ES according to the customary benchmarks; remember that patients overlap in the outcome measures of, say, depression or alcohol abuse.

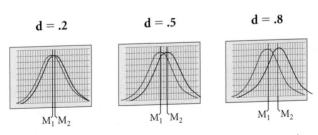

Figure 5.6 Overlapping distributions illustrating Cohen's benchmarks for *d*.

Clinician's Guide to Evidence-Based Practices

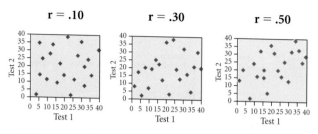

Figure 5.7 Scattergrams illustrating Cohen's benchmarks for *r*.

Figure 5.7 shows examples of correlation scattergrams for the three benchmarks for *r*. For *r* = .10, a relationship between the two variables is barely detectable by the naked eye. For *r* = .50, one can clearly detect the drift of points from lower left to upper right, although it is far from perfect. Note that the verbal descriptions for these benchmarks for *r* do not apply to measures of reliability. We have much higher standards for reliability. For example, we would consider a reliability of .50 very low.

Other Descriptors of Effect Size

Table 5.1 presents additional ways to interpret measures of ES. The left-hand column contains the traditional measure of effect size, *d*, as described above, for treated versus untreated or wait-list patients. The second column shows the percentile rank of the average treated patient in comparison with untreated patients for each level of ES. For example, with an ES of .60 in favor of a treatment, the average patient in the treatment group would stand at the 73rd percentile in the untreated group. The third column shows the success rate of treated patients in comparison

Table 5.1. **Alternative Frameworks for Interpreting Measures of Effect Size**

Effect Size (ES or *d*)	Percentile of Treated Patients	Success Rate of Treated Patients	Type of Effect	Cohen's Standard
1.00	84	72%	Beneficial	
.90	82	70%	Beneficial	
.80	79	69%	Beneficial	Large
.70	76	66%	Beneficial	
.60	73	64%	Beneficial	
.50	69	62%	Beneficial	Medium
.40	66	60%	Beneficial	
.30	62	57%	Beneficial	
.20	58	55%	Beneficial	Small
.10	54	52%	No Effect	
.00	50	50%	No Effect	
−.10	46	<50%	No Effect	
−.20	42	<50%	Detrimental	
−.30	38	<50%	Detrimental	

with untreated patients. The fourth column provides a "common sense" descriptive label for the numerical indicators. The right-hand column applies the Cohen benchmarks.

Other Measures of Effect Size

We presented above the two most commonly used measures of ES. Researchers use a host of other measures, each developed to accompany a particular type of statistical analysis; and we see new measures of effect being developed steadily. The intent of each of these other measures is the same as that for the two

Clinician's Guide to Evidence-Based Practices

common measures (*d* and *r*), that is, to give some sense of the meaningfulness of results apart from tests of statistical significance, which are overly dependent on *N*.

Simple formulas allow for conversion between many of the measures of ES. For example, we can convert Cohen's *d*, expressing the difference between two group means, to a *point biserial correlation* (a variation of the usual Pearson correlation where one variable, in this case group membership, has a value of 0 or 1). Such conversions prove helpful when comparing results from different studies. For example, one study may express its results as correlation coefficients while another study presents *t* tests. Thus, these conversions frequently appear in meta-analyses, which combine results from many different studies. The various conversion formulas are scattered throughout books and journal articles. For convenience, we have gathered many of the formulas together on the accompanying CD, drawing on Cohen (1988), Glass and Hopkins (1996), Grissom and Kim (2005), Wolf (1986), and some of our own algebraic conversions.

 The CD contains a list of many measures of effect size and formulas for converting between them.

Interpreting Results as Proportion of Variance in Common
A popular way to interpret a variety of research results involves focusing on the **proportion of variance in common**. When results appear as correlation coefficients (*r*, *R*, etc.), the square of

the coefficient (r^2, R^2) tells the proportion of variance in common between the variables. For example, with $r = .50$ between a measure of anxiety and a measure of depression, we say that the two measures have 25% (i.e., $.50^2$) of their variance in common. We can translate results of t tests, F tests, and χ^2 tests into correlation form to use this same method of interpretation (see CD Bonus, Measures of Effect Size). It is useful to think about this method of interpretation graphically. Figure 5.8 shows how to do this in the case of r; or substitute R (multiple correlation) for r and it works equally well.

In the left-hand panel of Figure 5.8, the two variables overlap very substantially, in fact, almost completely. We find little that is unique to either variable outside of the other. In the middle panel, the two variables overlap about one-half. In the right-hand panel, not very much exists in common between the two variables, corresponding to a very modest r of roughly .30.

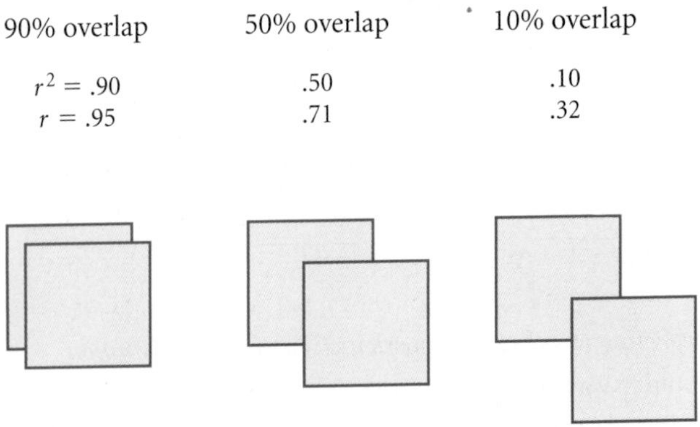

90% overlap	50% overlap	10% overlap
$r^2 = .90$	.50	.10
$r = .95$	.71	.32

Figure 5.8 Illustration of percent overlap in the variance for two variables.

Clinician's Guide to Evidence-Based Practices

Using proportion variance in common as a method of interpretation often gives rise to conflicting viewpoints on an issue. Consider the case of $r = .30$, which is "moderate" according to Cohen's benchmarks for r but corresponds to only 9% variance in common, which sounds almost negligible. Or consider $r = .50$, which seems, on the face of it, a respectable correlation and, in fact, qualifies as "large" according to Cohen's benchmarks. However, it accounts for only 25% of the variance, leaving 75% of the variance as nonoverlapping between the two variables. Remain cognizant of these interpretive difficulties as you peruse the research literature.

Rates, Ratios, Selectivity, and Predictive Power

Mental health and addiction research often refers to a host of rates, ratios, and derivative measures. In this section, we identify the most frequently used indexes within this plethora of percentages and provide examples of interpretation for each index.

Prevalence Rates and Related Ratios

A **prevalence rate** identifies the percentage of a population having a particular characteristic. For example, the prevalence rate for mental retardation is approximately 1% in the general population of the United States. Writers in the clinical literature usually prefer the term *prevalence rate*, but in other contexts the term **base rate** carries the same meaning: the percentage of a population having a certain characteristic.

Separate prevalence rates may apply for persons (1) having the characteristic at any one time or (2) having ever had the characteristic. We can usually define the prevalence rate for a single time by a certain period of time, 1 year providing a common definition (i.e., referred to as the "1-year prevalence rate"). The percentage of the population having ever had the characteristic is the *lifetime prevalence rate*. Distinguishing among these various uses of the term becomes critically important. Consider how the percentages (prevalence rates) would change in answer to these questions: Are you abusing alcohol right now? Have you abused alcohol in the past 12 months? Have you ever abused alcohol?

When examining research literature, keep four important points in mind about prevalence rates. First, as just noted, one must distinguish carefully between the one-time and the lifetime definitions of prevalence rate. They can be, and usually are, quite different.

Second, remain very careful about drawing conclusions about prevalence rates in entire populations when comparing the prevalence rates between two groups. For example, bulimia nervosa may occur ten times more often in women than in men. That sounds dramatic—and it is. But it does not mean that most women will likely suffer that condition. Similarly, boys have five times more likelihood than girls of manifesting ADHD. That does not mean the typical boy has ADHD. We expand on this matter of comparing prevalence rates later.

Third, varying prevalence rates can have a substantial impact on test validity, especially when we use the test for purposes of selection or identification. Suppose we want to use a test to identify persons likely to attempt suicide. The one-time prevalence rate for this characteristic is very low, less than 1%. No matter how good the test, we are likely to maximize correct classifications (attempters vs. nonattempters) by simply classifying everyone as a nonattempter. That is not very helpful in a clinical context. Consider the case where a prevalence rate is very high (e.g., where 90% of college students drink alcohol). Use of a test to distinguish between students who will or will not use alcohol is virtually hopeless. Simply predict that everyone will drink and you will guess correct 90% of the time—hard odds to beat. Test validity, in the sense of usefulness of the test for identification, tends to become maximized when prevalence rates reach a moderate level, the best case being 50%.

Fourth, prevalence rates can vary substantially among subgroups, and this fact has important implications for the potential effectiveness of tests or other indicators. For example, while the prevalence rate for suicide attempters is less than 1%, the prevalence rate for attempters among those who score above a certain point on a measure of depression may jump to 30%. Among that group, a test might prove very helpful in identifying attempters in clinical contexts.

Internet searches for "base rate" or "prevalence rate" AND (name of disorder) will yield much useful information. For a compilation of data on lifetime prevalence rates for mental and addictive disorders, see Karpiak and Norcross (2005) and Kessler et al. (2005).

 The CD contains hyperlinks for prevalence rates for ADHD, suicide, HIV/AIDS, and mental retardation to show how such information is typically reported. Links are also provided for the respective sources.

Odds Ratio and Relative Risk

A variety of techniques exist to assist with comparisons of prevalence rates among groups. We note increasing use of the **odds ratio (OR)**, an abbreviation for the more complete term "ratio of conditional odds" (Kennedy, 1992). Let's apply the technique to a comparison of ADHD in boys and girls in a school system (see Table 5.2). The data are hypothetical, and for simplicity, we disregard the subtypes of ADHD.

If you roll an unbiased die, the probability that you will get a 6 is 1/6, but the odds of getting a 6 are 1:5 (read, one to five). We express odds as (number of favorable outcomes):(number of unfavorable outcomes); in the case of the die, the favorable outcome is a 6 and there are five unfavorable outcomes. In our example, the odds that a boy is ADHD are 16:175. The odds that a girl is ADHD are 5:190. These odds can be written as ratios: 16/175 for boys and 5/190 for girls. We can calculate the OR as the ratio for boys divided by the ratio for girls, resulting in OR = 3.47. In words, in this hypothetical example, boys are about three and one-half times more likely than girls to have ADHD.

When the two groups under comparison have the same prevalence rates, OR = 1.00. As the rate in the first group exceeds the rate in the second group, OR can become infinitely large. As the

Table 5.2. **Hypothetical Data to Illustrate Use of Odds Ratio**

	ADHD	**Non-ADHD**	**Total**
Boys	16	175	191
Girls	5	190	195
Total	21	365	386

rate in the first group (in the numerator) becomes less than the rate in the second group (in the denominator), OR approaches 0.

Switching the position of the groups (i.e., whether the first or second group becomes the denominator) results in the OR moving above or below its central value of 1. However, the one OR will equal the reciprocal of the other. In our ADHD example, using the ratio for boys as the numerator and the ratio for girls as the denominator yields OR = 3.47. Reversing numerator and denominator gives OR = .288 (i.e., girls have less than one-third the likelihood of an ADHD diagnosis). Note that 3.47 and .288 are reciprocals of one another (1/3.47 = .288 and 1/.288 = 3.47).

The OR is asymmetrical around its "equal point" of 1.0. Below 1, the OR can go only to 0, so values in that range just do not appear as very startling. Above 1, OR values can go to infinity, and even values like 15 or 20 do seem startling. Translating ORs back and forth using the reciprocal relationship just described helps to counteract this disparity in viewpoints.

We usually find a specific OR accompanied by a CI, most commonly a 95% CI. The **OR confidence interval** is determined by log transformation and, therefore, will not seem obvious to the nonmathematician. However, we interpret the OR CI in the usual way. It provides a range within which the "true OR" probably falls. Since an OR of 1 means equal odds for the two groups, we must ask the crucial question of whether an OR's CI includes 1.00. If it does, then no important difference may exist between the odds for the two groups. And, like all CIs, the OR's CI will prove heavily dependent on the number of cases in the groups involved in calculating the OR. Small numbers of cases result in wide CIs for the OR; large numbers of cases result in narrow CIs.

Relative risk (RR) is another way to compare prevalence in two groups. Like the OR, RR is also a ratio; but it is a ratio of the actual prevalence rates in the two groups. Consider the data in Table 5.2. The risk of ADHD for boys is 16/191 (number of boys divided by total number of boys) = .084. The risk of ADHD for girls is 5/195 (number of girls divided by total number of girls) = .026. The *relative* risk of ADHD for boys (in comparison with girls) is .084/.026 = 3.23. The *relative* risk of ADHD for girls (in comparison with boys) is .026/.084. = .31. The RR for boys is the reciprocal of the RR for girls.

Four characteristics of RR correspond to characteristics of OR. First, the "balance point," where the rates are equal in two groups, is 1.0. Second, on the high side both can go to infinity, while on the low side they can only go to 0. Third, as for OR, RR in one direction is the reciprocal of RR in the other direction. Fourth, we can construct a CI for RR. It, too, relies on logarithms, and once again, the key question is whether the CI includes 1.0.

Selectivity, Specificity, and Predictive Power

Consider a test designed to identify ADHD patients. More precisely, the test needs to distinguish between ADHD cases and non-ADHD cases. Let's call the ADHD cases the "target group." Contrasts between any condition and absence of the condition, for example, depressed and nondepressed or cocaine user and nonuser, would serve equally well for illustrating the following points.

The concepts of "selectivity" and "specificity" describe the efficiency with which the test functions in distinguishing the target group from the nontarget group. **Selectivity** is the percentage of cases correctly identified as falling within the target group. Some sources use the term **sensitivity** as an equivalent to selectivity. **Specificity** is the percentage of cases correctly identified as falling within the nontarget group.

Application of the concepts of "selectivity" and "specificity" requires the use of a **cut-score** on the test. We tag people above the cut-score as belonging to the target group. We tag people below the cut-score as not belonging to the target group. In this instance, high scores on the test indicate presence of the disorder ADHD. A test using binary scores (e.g., 1, 0 or Yes, No) has a built-in cut-score. Most tests used in clinical practice have a continuous score scale, but it becomes a binary system (above, below) when we apply the cut-score.

Table 5.3 illustrates the application of a cut-score to our test designed to identify ADHD patients. The table shows the cut-score, set here at 16+, applied to distributions of scores for ADHD and non-ADHD cases. We assume that careful evaluation of the patients has resulted in correct placement in their respective groups. This is often a tenuous assumption in actual practice. For example, the non-ADHD group may contain some real ADHD cases which have simply escaped notice. (Refer to Figure 7.1 for a sample decision tree on Jonathon's ADHD diagnosis.) Conversely, the ADHD group may contain some cases that were incorrectly diagnosed. However, we make the assumption of correct classification in order to develop the notions of selectivity and specificity.

In Table 5.3, the test's selectivity, with a cut-score of 16+, is 60% (i.e., 60% of the ADHD cases scored above the cut-score).

Table 5.3. **Distributions of Test Scores to Illustrate Selectivity (Sensitivity) and Specificity**

Test Score		Group	
		ADHD	Non-ADHD
20	Selectivity = 60%	1	
19		2	
18		6	8
17		9	12
16		12	20
15		10	60
14		6	40
13		3	24
12		1	16
11	Specificity = 80%		12
10			8
Total		50	200

The test's specificity is 80% (i.e., 80% of the non-ADHD cases fell below the cut-score and we correctly identified them as non-ADHD). Notice that using a cut-score of 16+ means that we "missed" 40% of the ADHD cases and incorrectly tagged 20% of the non-ADHD cases as ADHD.

Observe what happens if we move the cut-score down to 15+ with the hope of capturing more of the ADHD cases. That move does indeed capture more ADHD cases, improving selectivity from 60% to 80%. However, we have simultaneously decreased specificity from 80% to 50%. As always, we face a trade-off between selectivity and specificity, so we should always present them together. Consider these extreme cases. If we set the cut-score at 12+, we will have a wonderful-looking selectivity of 100% but specificity will plunge to 10%—we have classified 90% of the non-ADHD cases as ADHD. At the other extreme, setting the cut-score at 19+ yields marvelous specificity of 100% but selectivity plummets to 6%—we have missed 94% of the ADHD cases.

Let us convert Table 5.3 to a 2 x 2 table (Table 5.4), classifying cases only as above and below the cut-score of 16+ for the ADHD and non-ADHD groups. With the information in this format, we introduce the notions of "positive" and "negative predictive power." **Positive predictive power** (PPP) is the percentage of actual ADHD cases of all the cases falling above the cut-score. In Table 5.4, this is 30/70 = 43%. **Negative predictive power** (NPP) is the percentage of non-ADHD cases correctly classified as non-ADHD. In Table 5.4, this is 160/180 = 89%. Thus, based on these data, there is approximately a 40% chance that a previously unevaluated child with a score of 16+ is ADHD. There is approximately a 90% chance that a non-ADHD child will be correctly identified as non-ADHD.

Obviously, placement of the cut-score affects PPP and NPP, generally going in opposite directions. The effect of the

Table 5.4. **A 2 x 2 Arrangement for ADHD and non-ADHD Cases Above and Below Cut-Score**

	ADHD	non-ADHD	Total	Predictive Power
Above cut-score	30	40	70	PPP = 30/70 = 43%
Below cut-score	20	160	180	NPP = 160/180 = 89%

prevalence rate for the condition does not appear so obvious. As noted earlier, when a condition has an extremely low prevalence rate, it is very difficult to identify. Thus, both selectivity and PPP will typically prove poor.

For brief, useful applications of the concepts of "selectivity" (or "sensitivity"), "specificity," "PPP," and "NPP," see Rich and Eyberg (2001) and Dumont, Willis, and Stevens (2001).

False Positives and False Negatives

We often use the terms *false positive* and *false negative* in the clinical literature to describe the relationship between test performance and an external criterion. The external criterion might require a thorough evaluation resulting in a diagnosis, such as depressed and nondepressed or successful and not successful. The relationship between standing on the test and standing on the external criterion may appear as shown in Figure 5.9. The figure shows classification of individuals into depressed and nondepressed cases, based on careful evaluation and diagnosis of the individuals and their test performance, specifically in terms of whether they scored above or below a cut-score. In this example, a high score is indicative of depression.

False positive cases fall above the cut-score on the test but, in fact, are not depressed individuals (i.e., the test categorized these people as depressed, but they were not). **False negative** cases fall below the cut-score on the test but come from truly depressed people (i.e., the test categorized these people as not depressed, but they indeed do suffer from depression). **Hits** refer to agreements between the test classification and the external criterion classification. Some sources call the cases in the upper right quadrant

Clinician's Guide to Evidence-Based Practices

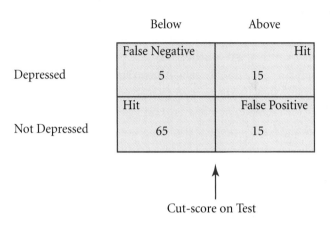

Test Performance

	Below	Above
Depressed	False Negative 5	Hit 15
Not Depressed	Hit 65	False Positive 15

Cut-score on Test

Figure 5.9 False positives, false negatives, and hits in a 2 x 2 table.

"true positives." The test identified them as depressed, and they indeed qualify as depressed, according to the external criterion. Correspondingly, we would call cases in the lower left quadrant "true negatives." The test correctly identified these people as not depressed.

Placement of the cut-score clearly affects all the numbers in the figure. Most importantly, increasing the cut-score (moving it to the right in Fig. 5.9) will decrease the number of false positives but, simultaneously, increase the number of false negatives. Similarly, as a general rule, decreasing the cut-score will decrease the number of false negatives but increase the number of false positives. We can see many similarities between this way of looking at classification decisions and the treatment of selectivity and specificity described earlier.

Outliers

An **outlier** is an aberrant data point, one that lies well outside other data points in a distribution or in a configuration of data points. A **univariate outlier** is a data point that lies noticeably far out in a single distribution. A **bivariate outlier** is a data point noticeably outside the *pattern* formed by the data points in the array, for example, in a scattergram. A bivariate outlier may fall within the normal range of data points on both of its variables but outside the pattern formed by the variables.

Several common definitions of a univariate outlier exist (see Hogan & Evalenko, 2006) and a plethora of less common definitions (see Barnett & Lewis, 1994). Among the common definitions, several rely on the *SD*, defining an outlier as beyond 2 or 3 *SD*s. The most common definition of an outlier (Tukey, 1977) utilizes the **interquartile range (IQR)**, which is the difference between the third quartile (Q_3 or 75th percentile) and the first quartile (Q_1 or 25th percentile). An outlier is then defined as 1.5 x IQR above Q_3 or below Q_1.

These definitions of outliers refer to individual cases in individual research studies. We also have outliers for statistics, including measures of ES, encountered when summarizing results from many studies. A meta-analysis of ESs for cognitive behavior therapy, for example, may identify an aberrant result—one very much higher or lower than the ESs reported in the other studies.

Regardless of their particular definition, outliers can have a pernicious effect on data summaries, particularly when dealing with small samples. What should you look for when interpreting research results? Look for evidence that the authors examined

Clinician's Guide to Evidence-Based Practices

the data for outliers. If they did examine for outliers, you are probably safe in relying on their judgment as to whether they should include the outlying data points in the data analysis or not. If the authors do not address the issue of examining data for outliers, then keep in mind that outliers lurking in the data might have a profound effect on conclusions, especially for small samples.

Checklist for Reading Research

- ♦ When interpreting test scores for individuals, apply the *SEM* to create a CI.
- ♦ When interpreting a statistic, such as a mean, apply the *SE* of the statistic to create a CI.
- ♦ When interpreting tests of statistical significance, for example, between a treatment and a control group, apply the concept of ES to help determine "practical" significance.
- ♦ Apply the benchmarks for measures of ES (*d* and *r*) to aid interpretation.
- ♦ When examining prevalence rates, make sure you know the time frame used for defining the rate (e.g., now, within last year, lifetime).
- ♦ Use the OR or RR ratio to aid in interpreting differences between groups in prevalence rates.
- ♦ Use the concepts of "selectivity" and "specificity," of "false positives" and "false negatives," and of "PPP" and "NPP" to interpret the effectiveness of a test in

separating groups. Recognize the effect of the placement of cut-off scores in creating trade-offs between
these contrasting categories.

♦ Be alert to the possible influence of outliers on summaries of data, especially with small samples.

Key Terms

base rate

bivariate outlier

Cohen's *d*

confidence interval (CI)

cut-score

effect size

effect size benchmarks

error score

false negatives

false positives

hits

interquartile range (IQR)

negative predictive power

obtained score

odds ratio

OR confidence interval

outlier

parameter

positive predictive power

prevalence rate

proportion of variance in common

relative risk

selectivity

sensitivity

specificity

standard error of a statistic

standard error of measurement (*SEM*)

statistic

true score

univariate outlier

Recommended Readings and Web Sites

Cohen, J. (1988). *Statistical power analysis for the behavioral sciences* (2nd ed.).
    Hillsdale, NJ: Erlbaum.

Grissom, R. J., & Kim, J. J. (2005). *Effect sizes for research: A broad practical
    approach*. Mahwah, NJ: Erlbaum.

Karpiak, C. P., & Norcross, J. C. (2005). Lifetime prevalence of mental
    disorders in the general population. In G. P. Koocher, J. C. Norcross, &

S. S. Hill III (Eds.). *Psychologists' desk reference* (2nd ed., pp. 3–6). New York: Oxford University Press.

National Comorbidity Survey Replication. (2005). National comorbidity survey (NCS) and national comorbidity survey replication (NCS-R). www.hcp. med.harvard.edu/ncs/

Tukey, J. W. (1977). *Exploratory data analysis.* Reading, MA: Addison-Wesley.

Wolf, F. M. (1986). *Meta-analysis: Quantitative methods for research synthesis.* Newbury Park, CA: Sage.

▌▌▌▌▌
CHAPTER 6

Appraising Research Reports

The typical practitioner will take, on average, 15–30 min to access electronically the research literature as described in Chapter 3. Now, prepped with the results of the information search and armed with knowledge of research designs and measures, the practitioner is prepared to engage in **critical appraisal**. This process entails assessing and interpreting research evidence by systematically considering its relevance to an individual clinician's work (Parkes et al., 2001).

In this chapter we concentrate on the first part of this process: interpreting research reports. We begin with a description of the individual research report and then consider summaries of reports, especially the techniques of meta-analysis. Then, we examine the problems you should consider for all types of research reports, regardless of their design or statistical analysis.

Individual Reports

Research reports constitute the backbone of evidence-based practice. Such reports appear primarily as articles in professional, peer-reviewed journals but also in papers presented at meetings of professional associations and in technical reports from research institutes.

Principal difficulties with the individual research report include the following:

- Each usually represents only one study or a closely related cluster of similar studies. Such small or unitary studies never "prove" a point. Establishing solid generalizations requires a whole string of studies, preferably involving different investigators and sites, thus forming the basis for generalizability.
- Many reports do not provide sufficient detail about the nature of the participants and the nature of the independent variable (e.g., a treatment) to allow for meaningful interpretation, especially for understanding possible limitations of the study.
- Stated conclusions do not always follow from the data. Because of these second and third points, one should never rely fully on simply reading the abstract. We return to and expand on these points in a few pages.

Summaries: Narrative Reports and Meta-Analysis

The scientific literature typically contains numerous studies on any given topic. For example, thousands of studies have examined the effectiveness of various types of psychotherapy (versus no therapy or versus pharmacotherapy). The results of these studies yield varying data and conclusions. To the unsophisticated, these differences are disconcerting, sometimes suggesting irreconcilable confusion. To those accustomed to conducting research, such differences are a normal part of science, which seldom appears as simple, clean, and uniform as textbooks on research methods might suggest. Results may differ simply due to random sampling effects. Results may also differ because of variations in the operational definitions of variables. In psychotherapy, we apply different therapies for varying lengths of time; we define outcomes in terms of changes in test scores in some studies and by self-reports of improvement in other studies; patient samples vary by age; and so on for other types of differences in detail. Despite the variations from one study to another, we wish to develop generalizations about the topic. What general truisms apply to the effectiveness of psychotherapy?

Narrative Review

The traditional method for developing generalizations from many studies on a single topic is the **narrative review**. In this method, the reviewer assembles the relevant studies and then tries to identify common trends in results. The reviewer may discount results that are clearly aberrant or that come from flawed designs. The reviewer may assign special import to studies with particularly good designs or based on a large number of cases. In the end, the reviewer provides generalizations about the topic, often with qualifications about softer parts of the research base and with suggestions for further research.

Meta-Analysis Defined

Meta-analysis is a statistical technique—more accurately, a family of techniques—that enables researchers to formally combine or summarize results from many studies on a given topic. Meta-analysis takes the actual results from the relevant studies and combines them. This technique has the same purpose as the narrative review: to develop generalizations. Furthermore, both approaches begin the same way (i.e., by assembling relevant studies of the topic). The two approaches differ in the formality of combining results. In recent years, meta-analysis has become the "industry standard" for summarizing results of multiple studies on a topic. Prior to the 1980s, summaries in the published literature consisted entirely of the narrative variety. For descriptions of meta-analytic procedures, see Glass, McGaw, & Smith (1981); Hedges and Olkin (1985); Hunter and Schmidt (2004); and Lipsey and Wilson (2000).

Simple Meta-Analysis

Meta-analyses proceed at varying levels of complexity. Let's begin with two simple examples, then suggest how more complicated methods proceed. Meta-analysis ordinarily summarizes measures of effect size (e.g., Cohen's d or a correlation coefficient, r; see Chapter 5 on effect size). At the simplest level, a meta-analysis averages the d or r values, weighted by their respective sample size (N).

Figure 6.1 shows an example for the correlation coefficient (r). Recall the point made earlier that the key problem with the individual report arises from its status as just one study. The person who encountered study 1 in Figure 6.1 would conclude that a strong correlation exists. The person who encountered study 2

Study	r	N
1	.75	100
2	.25	25
3	.40	40
4	.55	35
5	.50	200

Average $r = .54$

Figure 6.1 Sample meta-analysis for *r*.

would conclude that only a slight correlation exists. The person who came across both studies 1 and 2 would feel left in a quandary. The person who looked at the meta-analysis would conclude that the correlation approximates .54, with fluctuations around this value likely due to sampling error or minor differences in study design.

Figure 6.2 shows an example for *d*. A person who came upon study 2 first would conclude that the independent variable (treatment) had a rather potent effect. A person who came upon study 3 would conclude that the same treatment had no effect or perhaps even a slightly deleterious effect. A person who came upon the meta-analysis would conclude that on average, across several studies, the independent variable had a modestly positive impact.

Advanced Meta-Analytic Techniques
The simple methods presented above comprise a "bare bones" meta-analysis, while we would call more advanced methods

Study	d	N
1	.10	100
2	.65	50
3	-.05	50
4	.02	30
5	.35	100

Average $d = .23$

Figure 6.2 Sample meta-analysis for *d*.

"psychometric meta-analysis" (Hunter & Schmidt, 2004). We hint here at how these work. Recall from elementary statistics that group heterogeneity affects the magnitude of *r* (i.e., the greater the variability in the group, the higher the value of *r*; lesser variability in the group tends to reduce *r*). We sometimes call this phenomenon the **range restriction** problem. Some relatively simple formulas allow for correcting a given *r* for differences in group heterogeneity or range. Recall also that reliability restricts validity. Again, some relatively simple formulas, often called **corrections for attenuation**, allow us to correct a given *r* for imperfect reliability in either or both of the variables involved in a correlation. We might apply either or both of these corrections to the data in Figure 6.1 to provide a more sophisticated analysis.

Still another extension of bare bones meta-analysis involves coding characteristics of the studies themselves and then determining whether these characteristics relate systematically to the measures of effect size in the studies (*r* or *d*). Examples of study

Clinician's Guide to Evidence-Based Practices

characteristics include year of publication, age of patients, and type of dependent variable. One meta-analysis of the effect of psychotherapy for the treatment of depression found that investigator allegiance (i.e., commitment of the investigator to the type of therapy applied) linked to the effectiveness of the therapy (Prochaska & Norcross, 2007).

We conclude this brief exposition with a few notes on procedural matters. The first step in the meta-analytic process involves assembling the studies for analysis. The typical meta-analysis describes this process in considerable detail. The report usually includes a list of the studies. The process is similar to that used for a narrative review. However, the meta-analyst must limit the list to those studies that include the required statistics; in some instances, the analyst may have the ability to compute the required statistics from other information given in a study. For example, we might convert a *d* to an *r* or vice versa using formulas covered in the section on effect size in Chapter 5. The entire process may sound quite mechanical. It is not. See the following checklist for potential biases in meta-analytic reports. The analyst must make judgments about which studies qualify for inclusion. We should not limit inclusion to studies that show significant results; in fact, the significance of results in individual studies should not get them special attention. A report of a meta-analysis often includes a confidence interval (CI) for the average measure of effect size. Most reports use a 95% CI. We can interpret such CIs in the same way as CIs for any type of statistic. Consider these as a range within which the "true" population value for the measure of effect size lies, with a certain degree of probability (see Chapter 5 for a full description of CIs).

Checklist of Potential Methodological Problems
with Meta-Analytic Reports

- ◆ Potential for bias in the process of locating and selecting studies for inclusion in the analysis.
- ◆ Studies with significant results are more likely to get published than studies without significant results, leading to publication bias.
- ◆ Among published studies, those with significant results will more likely win citation by others, thus being more likely to appear repeatedly, leading to citation bias and multiple publication bias.
- ◆ Possible presence of bias in sensitivity analyses (analyses of study features potentially related to outcomes, e.g., sample size).

Some reports of meta-analysis also include a **fail-safe statistic**. This statistic attempts to deal with the "file drawer" problem: the tendency to publish "significant" results and to put "nonsignificant" results in the file drawer. The fail-safe statistic indicates the number of unpublished studies that one would need to uncover and include in the meta-analysis to reduce the reported effect size to 0 or some small value. For example, Walters (2003) reported that one would need to uncover approximately 30 unpublished studies with nonsignificant results in order to negate his conclusions from his meta-analysis of 42 published studies related to institutional recidivism.

Critical Appraisal of How the Study Was Conducted and Reported

Regardless of the type of study design, we need to pay attention to the actual conduct of the study in order to safely draw practice conclusions from it. Furthermore, what we know about the conduct of the study depends on reporting of details. Thus, for many practical purposes, the manner of conducting and reporting the study merges into a single consideration. Note that these concerns apply even to the true experimental design. Five important features of the conduct and reporting of studies require attention: the sample, the independent variable, the dependent variable, the comparison groups, and the relation of conclusions to actual results.

The Sample

First, we need to carefully examine the nature of the patients or cases used in the study. As we already noted, only rarely will a study use a random sample from a meaningful and well-defined population. Even when a randomized clinical trial (RCT) employs random assignment to conditions, the groups in the study do not usually originate as random samples from a population. Rather, they typically consist of ad hoc **convenience samples**: We use whomever we can easily recruit. The practical situation calls for us to stand the textbook problem of inferential statistics on its ear. The textbook problem involves having a random sample from a well-defined population and trying to draw an inference from the sample to the population. The practical situation, applicable to nearly all studies in mental health and addictions, is that we have a convenience sample and we have to figure out to what population we can generalize the results.

Estimating to what population we might generalize the results depends critically on having sufficient information about characteristics of the sample. Unfortunately, many reports provide insufficient information. The prototypical examples are reports that say that the participants studied included "42 depressed students from a midwestern university" or "76 alcohol-abusing clients at a private clinic" without further specification. It is very difficult—essentially impossible—to generalize from such descriptions to any larger groups.

What information should investigators provide? The answer depends greatly on the nature of the problem under study. In many circumstances, we would want to know age, gender, racial/ethnic group, socioeconomic status, and educational or ability level. If specific exclusion criteria applied in the selection of individuals, the report should specify those criteria and describe the effects of applying them (e.g., percentages excluded). The National Institute of Mental Health's Treatment of Adolescent Depression Study (TADS), for example, screened out 85% of the target group of depressed adolescents, while still claiming applicability of the results to the entire target group (Westen, 2006).

In some circumstances, information about physical condition, medical status, job classification, family situation, and personal history might be important. For example, if the 42 depressed students at a midwestern university had all participated in a project on the effects of psychotherapy on their depression, we would certainly want to know about their depression, comorbid diagnoses, current medications, and so on. In contrast, if recruitment of the student participants occurred through a project about the effects of aerobic training, we would want to know about their age and physical condition.

The **simple random sample** is the "benchmark" type of probability sample, but it is only one type. Other probability samples include **stratified samples** and **cluster samples**, and each of these categories has several subcategories. For a given sample size (*N*), a stratified sample yields a smaller standard error than does simple random sampling to the extent that the basis for stratification relates to the characteristic under study, thus making the strata different on the characteristic. If the basis for stratification is unrelated to the characteristic under study, stratified sampling offers no advantage over simple random sampling. For a given *N*, cluster sampling yields a larger standard error than does simple random sampling to the extent that clusters are internally homogeneous in comparison to the entire population for the characteristic under study. One often encounters studies that apply formulas for the standard error based on simple random sampling when the investigator has actually used some other type of sampling (see, e.g., Alf & Lohr, 2007). The most important point to make about sampling in mental health and addictions involves the use convenience samples with limited generalizability in the great majority of studies.

For RCTs, questions about the nature of the sample expand to include not only allocation of cases but also such matters as loss of cases, for a host of reasons, anywhere in the research process. Notice that "allocation" relates directly to the randomization process described in Chapter 4, a crucial requirement for a true experimental design. To help account for such losses, an increasing number of investigators use the CONSORT (Consolidated Standards of Reporting Trials) flowchart (see Fig. 6.3). It begins with "assessment for eligibility" (i.e., in the study, e.g., women self-referred for chronic depression—like Annique). The flowchart then tracks cases through the research process, right up to the point of final data analysis. How well do the final data

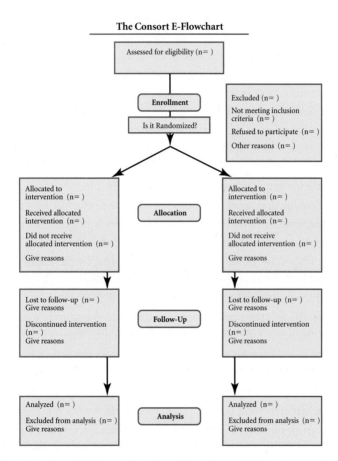

The Consort E-Flowchart

Assessed for eligibility (n=)

Enrollment

Is it Randomized?

Excluded (n=)

Not meeting inclusion criteria (n=)

Refused to participate (n=)

Other reasons (n=)

Allocated to intervention (n=)

Received allocated intervention (n=)

Did not receive allocated intervention (n=)

Give reasons

Allocation

Allocated to intervention (n=)

Received allocated intervention (n=)

Did not receive allocated intervention (n=)

Give reasons

Lost to follow-up (n=)
Give reasons

Discontinued intervention (n=)
Give reasons

Follow-Up

Lost to follow-up (n=)
Give reasons

Discontinued intervention (n=)
Give reasons

Analyzed (n=)

Excluded from analysis (n=)
Give reasons

Analysis

Analyzed (n=)

Excluded from analysis (n=)
Give reasons

Figure 6.3 The CONSORT Flowchart. From Moher, Schulz, , & Altman (2001a). In the public domain at www.consort-statement.org/Downloads/download.htm

represent what you started with in the first box? Even research reports that do not formally use such a flowchart still need to address this question. (Also see Table 7.1 for the 22 CONSORT guidelines for RCTs.)

The Independent Variable

A second problem is *fuzzy definition of the independent variable*. The study certainly has an independent variable as its focus. For example, a study may compare efficacy of cognitive therapy with a control (i.e., no therapy) condition. But if we assume the investigator detects some effect, we always need to ask what really happened. Did the particular cognitive therapy produce the changes? Or did the therapeutic relationship, quite apart from the type of therapy, evoke the change? Or did the fact that any therapy took place, regardless of its type, make the difference? Or did the fact that something, almost anything, happened to the people in the treatment group? Authors of a meta-analysis of 32 randomized trials of psychotherapies noted the difficulty of drawing conclusions because "so many of the studies failed to provide necessary information: for example, on therapists . . . on the interventions . . . and on the location(s)" (Weisz, Jensen-Doss, & Hawley, 2006, p. 686).

Customarily, the research literature refers to *the* independent variable as if it constituted some pure, simple element. In mental health research, that situation rarely exists. Rather, *the* independent variable typically includes a complex mixture of elements, much like a chemical compound. For example, a treatment consists of who applies it, under what circumstances, for what length of time, to what degree of fidelity, and so on. Even each of these elements of the independent variable consists of more refined elements. For example, "who" includes the therapist's gender, ethnicity, theoretical orientation, level of training, and interpersonal skills. Disentangling these elements is no mean feat. Within the context of a single study, it is ordinarily impossible to isolate all elements of the compound, as we might have the ability to do in the chemistry lab. Nevertheless, when referring to *the* independent variable, we must always remember that it constitutes a very complex compound. Thinking of the issue in this way allows us to introduce two useful terms, perhaps confused because of their phonetic similarity: *mediator* and *moderator.*

A **mediator** is a variable or factor that makes up the specific mechanism by which a given result happens. It is the causal agent. In our example about a treatment, the real mediator may be the "who" (the therapist), with all other elements in the compound being unimportant; or it may be the particular therapy method. The mediator may also be the conjunctive force of two of the elements (e.g., length of treatment and therapy method), with either one by itself proving ineffectual and all others proving inert or unimportant. The mediator may also constitute a spinoff from the treatment situation, such as family members' reactions to the fact that treatment of the patient has occurred.

We distinguish a mediator from a moderator. A **moderator** variable differentiates (in a noncausal sense) the influence of an independent variable. For example, chronological age may constitute a moderator for the effectiveness of a treatment. The treatment may be quite effective with recreational cocaine users, somewhat effective for cocaine abusers, and ineffective for chronic cocaine abusers. Detection of moderators is one of the principal targets of factorial designs (see Chapter 4) when one of the independent variables is a patient variable. The distinction between mediators and moderators plays a prominent role in structural equation modeling (see Edwards & Lambert, 2007).

The Dependent Variable

A third issue relates to the *dependent variable*. It may prove off-target or less than satisfactory. A treatment may have an effect but not on whatever we operationally defined as the dependent variable; for example, a patient's score on a depression test may have missed the effect. Sometimes the test may prove roughly on-target but has such low reliability that the "real effect" becomes swamped by measurement error variance (see Chapter 4 on types of error and power). Or perhaps the treatment has an effect on the dependent variable, but we have no real interest in that particular dependent variable. For example, the dependent or outcome variable in a study of the effectiveness of psychotherapy will often involve a client's report of satisfaction, but the client's condition may not have actually improved (Norcross & Lambert, 2006). We can take pleasure in the fact that the client feels satisfied (that is one dependent variable), but we would hope that the condition has diminished (a different dependent variable).

Research reports ordinarily refer to the "reliability" and "validity" of the measures used for dependent variables. Treatment of these topics requires special attention. Everyone in the social/behavioral sciences is familiar with the concepts of "reliability" and "validity" for psychological tests. At a general level, *reliability* deals with the consistency of scores and *validity* deals with what the test actually measures. However, some special considerations with how we use these terms in research reports merit attention. In order to interpret research intelligently, we must use greater precision about these terms than what we would normally require for a general understanding of them.

Suppose you treat Francesco, the 30-year-old man suffering from generalized anxiety disorder (GAD) and alcohol dependence. You search the literature for treatments for his disorder. The "Method" section of a relevant article says "GAD was measured with the Scranton Behavior Rating Scale (SBRS), which has demonstrated adequate reliability and validity (Hogan, 2008 [a sham reference here])." Journal policies say that authors should address the reliability and validity of any measures used in the study. The foregoing sentence seems to satisfy that requirement: It gives a citation for the reliability and validity of the test. But does it? The citation is to the manual for the SBRS, which Hogan has authored. Naturally, the manual for the SBRS will report it as a reliable and valid instrument. But what exactly does the manual say? We need to remain wary of any blanket statements that a test is (simply) reliable and valid. No instrument is perfectly reliable and valid. Some test authors claim reliability based on rather thin evidence and express satisfaction with reliability levels that would make most people blush. The SBRS may have internal consistency reliability of, say, .75, which makes Hogan quite happy but is really rather marginal in acceptability. Furthermore, the internal consistency reliability of .75 does not tell us anything about the temporal stability of the scores. We must establish the validity of a test for use of particular scores for particular purposes. What particular scores and what particular purposes were at the root of the test manual's claim for validity?

Although the tests used in a research study are not ordinarily a major focus of attention, the entire array of analyses and conclusions depends critically on the reliability and validity of the tests used. Low reliability contributes to error variance not only for individual scores but also for group summary statistics. Low reliability leads to low power in the same way that a low number of cases does. Less than satisfactory validity means, in essence, that we have only measured the dependent variable partially or inappropriately. Thus, to make sense out of research reports, we need to pay careful attention to the evidence presented for the reliability and validity of tests used.

The Nature of the Comparison Group

Textbook descriptions of the RCT design typically present a comparison between a treatment and a control group. Usually, the treatment receives considerable attention, but the control group merits little comment, other than the fact that it is not the treatment. However, from a practical perspective, the nature of the control group is crucial. It deserves careful description by researchers and careful scrutiny by research consumers.

Think of the nature of the control group as falling into one of several categories arranged in a hierarchy of clinical realism (Wampold, 2001). At the lowest level, the control group gets literally "nothing at all." At one step up, the control group has some contact with the researcher. At yet another level up, members of the control group receive a **placebo**. By *placebo* we mean some action or substance not expected (by the researcher) to have any real effect. The classic example of a placebo in pharmaceutical studies is a "sugar pill." Thus, members of the control group get a pill that may look like the genuine drug but should not have therapeutic effect. In the best-designed studies, neither the subjects nor the researchers know who gets the "real" pill (i.e., supposedly active ingredient) and who is getting the placebo. We call this a *double-blind* design. While easily implemented with pills, it is difficult to implement with psychotherapy. We can distinguish between a *sham* placebo, a token action of some sort, and a realistic placebo that mimics certain features of the treatment, such as duration and amount of contact.

Another important type of control condition is **treatment-as-usual (TAU)**. Here, we contrast the treatment under investigation—the one whose value we seek to establish—with treatment that cases would ordinarily receive. Treatment-as-usual provides a more realistic contrast than "nothing at all." We might demonstrate that a new treatment works better than "nothing at all," but the real question is whether the new treatment is better than what patients would ordinarily receive. A research report should describe exactly what TAU involves.

At still higher levels in our hierarchy of control conditions are treatments of structural equivalence (duration, intensity, amount of contact, etc.) and, even better, structural equivalence accompanied by researcher allegiance. The latter provides the most rigorous contrast in the investigation of a treatment.

As you read research about the contrast between a treatment and a control group, try to place the control group in the hierarchy just described. The control condition should provide a meaningful contrast with the treatment under investigation. Virtually any treatment can outperform no treatment. The more realistic

Clinician's Guide to Evidence-Based Practices

question is: Which of several alternative, structurally equivalent treatments is most effective?

Conclusions versus Actual Results

The fifth issue involves whether the conclusions drawn in the report really follow from the results presented. Making a judgment here requires careful examination of the results related to the conclusions. We often find at least a partial mismatch between data and conclusions—sometimes even a complete mismatch. Researchers, after all, have a vested interest in confirming their research hypotheses. Thus, one finds "tendencies although not significant" or "qualitative observations" turning into firm conclusions. You must also stay alert to hints of causal connections from designs that do not permit such conclusions.

In many research reports, the five issues just outlined are more important than all the statistical matters that occupy our attention. As a reminder about these five important matters, we provide the following checklist.

Checklist for Appraising Research
The Sample

- ♦ Does the report adequately describe the sample?
- ♦ Does the study use a random sample from a clearly defined population?
- ♦ If the study focused on a convenience sample, to what population might results generalize?
- ♦ Might results of the study prove different for other populations?

The Independent Variable

- Does the report adequately describe the independent variable (e.g., a treatment)?
- Does the report present evidence or a discussion about which features of the independent variable (e.g., treatment components, therapeutic relationship, homework assignments) might prove crucial?
- Do the analyses focus on the independent variable (e.g., a treatment) separately from the person who provided it?

The Dependent Variable

- Does the report adequately describe the dependent variable?
- What evidence does the investigator present about the reliability and validity of the dependent variable?
- What effect might unreliability of the dependent variable have on the power of the statistical analysis?
- Would alternate definitions of the dependent variable yield similar results?
- Did the investigator omit attention to completely different dependent variables of importance?

The Comparison Group(s)

- Does the report adequately describe the control condition (comparison group)?
- Does the comparison condition make meaningful clinical sense, for example, comparable in terms of such factors as length of exposure and therapist allegiance?

Clinician's Guide to Evidence-Based Practices

Relation of Conclusions to Data

- ◆ Do the data clearly support the conclusions drawn?
- ◆ Does the investigator make any attempt to draw causal conclusions from a design other than a true experimental design?
- ◆ Does the report properly qualify groups to which results might generalize?

The first step in critical appraisal involves understanding typical research reports, knowing how to read them, and determining their value. This chapter treated this first step. Then, critical appraisal continues with considering its relevance to a particular case and translating that research into practice. We do so in Chapter 7.

Key Terms

cluster sample	moderator
convenience samples	narrative review
correction for attenuation	placebo
critical appraisal	range restriction
fail-safe statistic	simple random sample
mediator	stratified sample
meta-analysis	treatment-as-usual (TAU)

Recommended Readings and Web Sites

Alderson, P., & Green, S. (2002). Cochrane collaboration opens learning material for reviewers, www.cochrane-net.org/openlearning/

Hunter, J. E., & Schmidt, F. L. (2004). *Methods of meta-analysis: Correcting error and bias in research findings* (2nd ed.). Newbury Park, CA: Sage.

Lipsey, M. W., & Wilson, D. B. (2000). *Practical meta-analysis.* Thousand Oaks, CA: Sage.

Moher, D., Schulz, K. F., & Altman, D. G. (2001). CONSORT E-checklist and flowchart. Available from www.consort-statement.org/Downloads/download.htm

Sudman, S. (1976). *Applied sampling.* New York: Academic Press.

Wampold, B. E. (2001). *The great psychotherapy debate: Models, methods, and findings.* Mahwah, NJ: Erlbaum.

Weisz, J. R., Jensen-Doss, A., & Hawley, K. M. (2006). Evidence-based youth psychotherapies versus usual clinical care. *American Psychologist, 61,* 671–689.

▐ ▐ ▐ ▐ ▐
CHAPTER 7

Translating Research into Practice

Having now critically appraised the research reports, you begin to translate the research into practice. You become a critical consumer and interpreter of the research evidence as it applies to your clinical situation at hand. Beyond browsing the literature, your aim now involves actually using the information in solving patient problems (Guyatt & Rennie, 2002).

In this chapter we will assist you in translating that evidence for direct application to your patients. First, we address the imperative of translational research and the stance of the reflective practitioner. We then help you translate the results of randomized clinical trials (RCTs) into practice by applying the CONSORT standards (as graphically illustrated in Chapter 6) by working through the CONSORT checklist. Next, we help you to consider potential harms that might accrue to your patients in translating the research to them, as individuals. We also discuss the process of identifying which interventions do not work—discredited practices. Finally, we provide a quick lesson in applying clinical decision analysis, using decision trees to explore choices at critical junctures.

Translational Research: Identifying What Works

The mental health and addiction fields have increasingly become aware that the science-to-service or (lab) bench-to-bedside process runs along a two-way street. Basic scientists or clinical investigators provide practitioners with new tools; practitioners often make novel observations about the nature and progression of disorders that stimulate additional investigations. Patient and family member reports of outcomes help close the feedback loop and generate more research ideas.

Perhaps the worst feeling experienced by a practitioner is the sense of helplessness when one lacks sufficient knowledge to alleviate a client's distress. Each year, more than 6 million adults and 3 million children in the United States experience debilitating symptoms at the termination of treatment (National Advisory Mental Health Council on Behavioral Science, 2000). Although advances in science and practice have greatly improved treatment outcomes (Lambert & Ogles, 2004), a pressing need remains to develop more effective interventions for the many patients who do not respond to current treatments (Hannan et al., 2005).

In an effort to promote development of innovative treatments, the National Institute of Mental Health (NIMH) has placed strong emphasis on **translational research**. The NIMH uses the following definition: "Translational research in the behavioral and social sciences addresses how basic behavioral processes inform the diagnosis, prevention, treatment, and delivery of services

Clinician's Guide to Evidence-Based Practices

for mental illness, and, conversely, how knowledge of mental illness increases our understanding of basic behavioral processes" (National Advisory Mental Health Council on Behavioral Science, 2000, p. iii).

You may begin by considering how significant methodological decisions, made by the researchers whose work you read, offer clues about translating their data to your patients. Five methodological foci characterize successful programs of translational research: (1) time span, (2) scope of hypotheses, (3) dose adjustments, (4) determining contraindications, and (5) patient population selections. Early-phase translational research usually begins with short-duration time frames, addresses hypotheses with relatively narrow scope, delivers small doses of treatment, closely monitors any potential for harm (contraindications), and studies relatively healthy patient populations. The defining features of translational research generally become clearly evident in the middle phases, when time and scope of hypotheses broaden and doses of presumed active intervention components increase in trials with low-risk patient populations. In later-phase translational research, larger, full-scale clinical trials begin to test the efficacy and effectiveness of interventions with diverse patient populations (Tashiro & Mortensen, 2006). Research in the middle and later phases can be translated into daily clinical practice.

Becoming a Reflective Practitioner

In critically appraising what you have found in your search of the research literature, we recommend the old German proverb: "To believe everything is too much, to believe nothing is not enough."

Beginners tend to follow one of two error-prone paths. First, some give in to the pervasive temptation to prematurely dismiss or trash the research literature as "not like my patient" or "not compelling research." Rarely, if ever, will any single research study or review perfectly match your patient and context. We must assume that any piece of research suffers from imperfections, especially with respect to any direct translation from the laboratory to the consulting room. But will the data prove good enough to let us draw reasonable guidance? Second, other beginners succumb to the temptation to worship all publishable research and automatically apply it to their particular circumstances. Nonresearchers often find it difficult to appreciate the contextual and subjective limits of science. We must thoughtfully ask, Can the research translate to my patient?

We adopt Peterson's (1995) notion of the reflective practitioner, seeking to integrate research into clinical practice. Frequently, we find a tension between scientific rigor, on the one hand, and clinical relevance, on the other. This tension is frequently characterized as efficacy research versus effectiveness research. We cannot easily control and randomize all important variables, such as empathy, therapeutic relationship, and patient comorbidity. However, practitioners need not "fly off into an intuitive never-neverland." Reflection in action draws on past research and documented theory wherever pertinent research has occurred and well-tested theories exist. "Whenever high ground appears, we need to seize it, hold it, and work from it in the public benefit" (Peterson, 1995, p. 980).

The reflective, sophisticated practitioner will rely on empirical research when available and when relevant to a particular case.

In the words of the APA Task Force on Evidence-Based Practice (2006, p. 285): "The treating psychologist determines the applicability of research conclusions to a particular patient. Individual patients may require decisions and interventions not directly addressed by the available research."

The task confronting the reflective practitioner consists of recognizing boundary conditions when deciding if research (and, if so, which research) applies. At least three key questions flow from this line of reasoning (Semple et al., 2005):

♦ Does the quality of the research pass muster (validity), as detailed in Chapters 4, 5, and 6?
♦ Does the research hold enough relevance to warrant attempting to apply it?
♦ Does the research match my patient and context (**transportability**) closely enough?

In the hierarchy of evidence, the results of RCTs and summaries of multiple RCTs have emerged as the gold standard of research evidence to inform evidence-based practices (EBPs). Thus, we concentrate on extrapolating from clinical trials to individual patients with a focus on RCTs. As noted in Chapter 4, these studies come closest to allowing us to draw causal conclusions from our data.

Evaluating Randomized Clinical Trials

Novices and nonresearchers sometimes have difficulty appreciating the subjectivity of science. An aphorism reminds us: Scientists are scientific about everything but their own science! Decisions about inclusion criteria, outcome measures, research designs, comparison groups, and the like can bias or even preordain the results. Consider the controversial example of the effectiveness of abstinence-only programs, aimed at reducing sexual activity (hence pregnancies and sexually transmitted diseases in the young). Earlier studies, hailed by social conservatives, suggested that abstinence-only programs proved effective in reducing early sexual activity. But later, well-controlled studies repeatedly found that children and adolescents enrolled in abstinence-only intervention programs had no greater likelihood of abstaining than their control group counterparts. We need to just say "no!"—to bad science (Begley, 2007).

Undeniably, RCTs constitute an advance in health care as a means of determining treatment effects when controlling other factors that might affect patient outcomes. At the same time, significant mismatches exist between the evidence provided by RCTs and the needs of practitioners. Because many factors other than the treatment itself profoundly alter a patient's outcome, determining the best treatment (or assessment, prevention, etc.) for any particular patient in any given situation will differ fundamentally from any determination of which treatment proves best on average (Kent & Hayward, 2007). We do not mean to suggest that RCTs cannot inform but, rather, that they cannot alone determine our direction and should never shackle us.

Reporting a single number from an RCT, such as an effect size or an absolute risk reduction, gives the misleading impression that the treatment method alone accounted for the outcome. Such impressions ignore the interaction between the multifaceted method and the complex risk–benefit profile of a particular group of patients (Kent & Hayward, 2007). Even when RCT results yield no differentially beneficial effects, some patients may still benefit substantially from the treatment. Alternatively, a treatment which benefits many on average may prove ineffective for particular others. Some hidden risks and hidden benefits also occur in clinical trials, going undetected because study designs mask individual differences.

Another concern arises from the fact that RCTs have evolved more recently, appear with less frequency, and use less rigorous methodologies in mental health and addictions than in biomedical research. The RCTs reported in behavioral journals tend to reflect more analytic weaknesses than those reported in medical journals, particularly in specifying primary outcomes, analyzing intention-to-treat, randomizing all participants, and accounting for missing data (Spring et al., 2007). Simply put, RCTs in medical journals are generally more sophisticated and complete.

An international group of researchers, known as the CON-SORT (Consolidated Standards of Reporting Trials) group (Moher et al., 2001a, 2001b), created reporting guidelines for RCTs. These guidelines have won wide endorsement in biomedical and behavioral journals and have increased standardization and transparency of reporting results. Many journals now require a CONSORT flowchart (see Figure 6.3 for a sample). The CONSORT guidelines provide a particular boon to those trying to evaluate and synthesize research reports. We summarize the 22 CONSORT items in Table 7.1.

As you can see, compliance with the CONSORT standards enables the reader to develop significant translational implications. For example, readers can quickly gauge eligibility, inclusion, exclusion, and elimination criteria to assist in assessing

Table 7.1. **CONSORT Checklist for a Randomized Clinical Trial**

Paper Section	Item	Description
Title and abstract	1	How participants were allocated to interventions (e.g., "random allocation," "randomized," or "randomly assigned").
Introduction or background	2	Scientific background and explanation of rationale.
Methods, participants	3	Eligibility criteria for participants and the settings/locations where the data were collected.
Interventions	4	Precise details of the interventions intended for each group and how and when they were actually administered.
Objectives	5	Specific objectives and hypotheses.
Outcomes	6	Clearly defined primary and secondary outcome measures and, when applicable, any methods used to enhance the quality of measurements (e.g., multiple observations, training of assessors).
Sample size	7	How sample size was determined and, when applicable, explanation of any interim analyses and stopping rules.
Randomization— sequence generation	8	Method used to generate the random allocation sequence, including details of any restrictions (e.g., blocking, stratification).
Randomization— allocation concealment	9	Method used to implement the random allocation sequence (e.g., numbered containers or central telephone), clarifying whether the sequence was concealed until interventions were assigned.
Randomization— implementation	10	Who generated the allocation sequence, who enrolled participants, and who assigned participants to their groups.

Table 7.1. **(Continued)**

Paper Section	Item	Description
Blinding (masking)	11	Whether or not participants, those administering the interventions, and those assessing the outcomes were blinded to group assignment. If done, how the success of blinding was evaluated.
Statistical methods	12	Statistical methods used to compare groups for primary outcome(s); methods for additional analyses, such as subgroup analyses and adjusted analyses.
Results, participant flow	13	Flow of participants through each stage (a diagram is strongly recommended). Specifically, for each group report the numbers of participants randomly assigned, receiving intended treatment, completing the study protocol, and analyzed for the primary outcome. Describe protocol deviations from study as planned together with reasons.
Recruitment	14	Dates defining the periods of recruitment and follow-up.
Baseline data	15	Baseline demographic and clinical characteristics of each group.
Numbers analyzed	16	Number of participants (denominator) in each group included in each analysis and whether the analysis was by "intention-to-treat." State the results in absolute numbers when feasible (e.g., 10/20, not 50%).
Outcomes and estimation	17	For each primary and secondary outcome, a summary of results for each group and the estimated effect size and its precision (e.g., 95% confidence interval).

Table 7.1. **(Continued)**

Paper Section	Item	Description
Ancillary analyses	18	Address multiplicity by reporting any other analyses performed, including subgroup analyses and adjusted analyses, indicating those prespecified and those exploratory.
Adverse events	19	All important adverse events or side effects in each intervention group.
Discussion, interpretation	20	Interpretation of the results, taking into account study hypotheses, sources of potential bias or imprecision and the dangers associated with multiplicity of analyses and outcomes.
Generalizability	21	Generalizability (external validity) of the trial findings.
Overall evidence	22	General interpretation of the results in the context of current evidence.

how closely the study sample matches particular patients. We can trace the sequence of participants through the study, evaluate the relevance and utility of the outcome measures, and even check for common adverse effects. Finally, the CONSORT standards specifically mandated that investigators address the generalizability of the findings. As we read through the flowchart and focus on the CONSORT criteria, we imagine precisely how any of our particular patients might have wound their way through the study.

In addition to these 22 specific items, we suggest attending to a few other vital considerations when critically appraising RCTs and systematic reviews for mental health and substance abuse outcomes.

- ◆ What determined the salubrious effect reported? Consider the treatment method, therapist characteristics, patient attributes, and the therapeutic relationship. Over and above the effects of the therapeutic relationship itself, does the treatment method appear to receive credit due to the clinician? Do the clinicians receive credit for work done by the patients?

- ◆ With respect to cultural, ethnic, or racial minority groups, can we safely assume that efficacious EBP assessments, treatments, and preventions validated on a homogeneous patient population will work equally well for other groups?

- ◆ Do the inclusion and exclusion criteria seem reasonable, or do they constrain validity by narrowing the study sample too much? In a meta-analysis of published outcome studies on three disorders, investigators estimated the average inclusion rates to be 32% for depression, 36% for panic disorder, and 35% for generalized anxiety disorder (Westen & Morrison, 2001). The typical study excluded the majority of the individuals who sought treatment for one of these disorders.

- ◆ Should we feel concerned about publication bias? For example, does the journal or online resource have a peer review policy or a narrow theoretical perspective that might cause us concern?

- ◆ Can we feel confident about effect sizes: Do we find credible evidence of clinical significance, apart from statistical significance? (See Chapter 5 for explanation of effect size.)

- ◆ Do the outcome measures have relevance for the symptoms or concerns we seek to treat in our clients?
- ◆ Does the RCT use bona fide comparisons? The data show the treatment worked, but compared to what? For example, was a new treatment compared against an existing standard or treatment-as-usual (TAU) or against no treatment, a waiting list, or a sham control group of some sort? It is relatively easy to show that a treatment, any treatment, outperformed no treatment, but it is comparatively difficult to show that a treatment outperformed a bona fide alternative treatment (Wampold, 2001).
- ◆ Do the lead researchers have a particular theoretical allegiance that may reflect a bias in conducting the study or analyses? The researcher's allegiance has been shown to account for more than one-half of all purported outcome differences among different psychotherapies (Luborsky et al., 1999).
- ◆ Can we detect a funding bias? This can prove a particular concern in medication trials funded by drug companies or others with an agenda in mind. For example, in the *Daubert* case described in Chapter 9, a legal team tried to submit research from drug studies run chiefly as potential evidence for the litigation. Some corporate entities fund research with a requirement that they retain the right to block publication of the data, if they so choose. Should we trust such research? Do such studies constitute dispassionate scientific evidence or subtle efforts to selectively market or promote commercial products?

Clinician's Guide to Evidence-Based Practices

- Is the EBP under study the only one or the most effective one of its kind? Have the researchers ignored or overlooked important alternatives?
- What probabilities of relapse exist (see Witkiewitz & Marlatt, 2007)?
- Do the findings apply reasonably well to our particular treatment setting?

By asking yourself these questions as you read an RCT, you can avoid uncritical acceptance of relatively useless information, while focusing on the most generalizable components with the greatest relevance to the particular patient(s) of concern to you.

Potential Harm

Recall the old saw, "The operation was a success, but the patient died." Even with the best of evidence-based care, not everyone gets better. When translating research into practice, pay particular attention to the percentage of patients in RCTs showing no change or deterioration. Heed the Hippocratic Oath: "First, do no harm."

Approximately 5%–10% of patients will deteriorate during the course of mental health and addiction treatment (Lambert & Ogles, 2004; Mohr, 1995). Note that these figures apply *during* the course of treatment, not necessarily *because* of the treatment. Nonetheless, a small portion of patients may actually experience harm as a result of treatment, and we must consider this possibility when translating the research into clinical practice. What is the likelihood that this patient may suffer harm?

What price is the cure? One way to reduce the risk of patient harm or deterioration during the course of treatment involves conducting a **decision analysis**, as we discuss later in this chapter. Simpler processes involve cost–benefit analysis and risk–benefit analysis. The primary difference between these two involves whether one focuses on all risks or only economic hazards.

Economic costs include the total dollar amount paid to a clinician or agency for treatment, whether the patient pays the full fee out of pocket, covers a copayment charge, or is covered by health insurance. Additional fiscal components include incidental costs (such as prescription drugs, transportation, child care) and opportunity costs (such as time lost from work or school). Of course, mental disorders and substance abuse have economic costs of their own (lost productivity, disability payments, and so on). Some treatments will prove more costly than others, and the costs will be borne by different parties.

Annique's health insurance probably covers some of the cost of her psychotherapy and medications. Depending on her coverage, some medications may cost her significantly more than others; some providers may not qualify as reimbursable under her plan; the number of sessions and types of services may fall under managed care restrictions; and her preferred treatment options (or the most effective EBP providers) may not fall under her coverage mandates. On the other hand, Annique's health insurance may favor EBP and providers known to use such approaches. The company may offer her incentives (such as lower copayments) to use such providers or may require providers seeking to serve their clients to certify that they practice EBPs.

Francesco has neither employment nor insurance, so he must rely on state services for the uninsured or take advantage of agencies offering very low fees. In that sense, the rest of society contributes (via taxes or higher fees) to cover the cost of any services he receives. Different EBPs pose different costs and different potential benefits for him, but much relies on his preferences and motivations. For example, outpatient treatment with cognitive-behavior therapy focused on his anxiety and delivered through a community agency might help him, but alcohol abuse may erode those gains. An intensive inpatient program coupling cognitive-behavior therapy with state-of-the-art substance abuse treatment might prove more effective or have a more enduring effect but lie beyond his (and society's) financial means. Whether he will have access to EBPs remains unclear, but the costs of not treating him can rise steeply. If his anxiety leads to continued unemployment or his alcohol abuse leads to liver disease requiring medical attention or results in incarceration as a result of acts committed while intoxicated, very substantial public costs accrue.

From a purely economic perspective, patients and society will, more likely than not, benefit economically from the ready availability of EBPs in the long run because the average patient will improve and become more productive (or cease becoming an economic drain) more quickly. Making such services available, however, may prove more expensive in the short run (providing necessary education and training to providers and assuring patient access to same).

In a risk–benefit analysis, cost becomes but one factor. Other hazards include side effects of biological treatments (such as medication, electroshock, deep brain stimulation) and risks associated with treatment (diagnostic errors, misapplied techniques, therapist negligence). In general, properly applied EBPs tend by their very nature to minimize risk, when used appropriately (see the discussion of professional liability in Chapter 9).

The Dark Side: Identifying What Does *Not* Work

The President's New Freedom Commission on Mental Health in 2003 called attention to both the *underuse* of evidence-based treatments and the *overuse* of treatments for which no favorable empirical evidence exists. Practitioners are encouraged to simultaneously use EBPs to promote what *does* work and avoid discredited practices to eradicate what does *not* work. In other words, translational research can be prescriptive as well as proscriptive.

Specific assessments, treatments, and prevention programs that have not been subjected to systematic empirical testing cannot be assumed to be either effective or ineffective; they are simply untested to date. The absence of evidence, we must recall, is not evidence of absence.

But there exist assessment, treatment, and prevention practices that are probably discredited, even harmful. **Discredited practices** are those unable to consistently generate treatment outcomes (interventions) or valid data (assessments) beyond that obtained by the passage of time alone, expectancy, base rates, or credible placebo. *Discredited* subsumes ineffective and detrimental interventions but forms a broader and more inclusive characterization (Norcross et al., 2006, 2007).

In two recent Delphi polls, we asked respected experts to rate the degree to which various practices in mental health and addictions were discredited (Norcross et al., 2006b; Norcross et al., 2007). Table 7.2 summarizes expert consensus on the most discredited treatments and tests. These are generally to be avoided. As one example, consider the research on critical incident stress debriefing (CISD). The RCTs show CISD heightens risk for posttraumatic stress symptoms in some individuals (Lilienfeld, 2007).

Another potentially harmful set of interventions, described as sexual orientation conversion or reparative therapies, purport to resolve unwanted same sex attraction via verbal psychotherapy laced with significant religious overlay. Some clients uncomfortable with same sex attraction have sought and benefited from psychotherapy, but rigorous empirical studies fail to show that conversion therapies work (Greene et al., 2007; Schneider et al., 2002). We must therefore ask whether offering such treatments comports with the therapist's ethical responsibility and consumer welfare.

Clinical Decision Analysis

Let us walk through a **decision analysis** for a particular patient to illustrate the stepwise progress in translating research into practice. In its most simplified form, traditional decision analysis texts often attempt to teach would-be decision makers about the influence of probabilities and preferences using the hypothetical "stranded on a desert island without food or water" scenario. The instructor tells the students to assume that a bottle washes

Table 7.2. **Expert Consensus on Discredited Practices in Mental Health and Addictions**

Top 10 Discredited Mental Health Treatments

1. Angel therapy for treatment of mental/behavioral disorders
2. Use of pyramids for restoration of energy
3. Orgone therapy (use of orgone energy accumulator) for treatment of mental/behavioral disorders
4. Crystal healing for treatment of mental/behavioral disorders
5. Past life therapy for treatment of mental/behavioral disorders
6. Future lives therapy for treatment of mental/behavioral disorders
7. Treatments of posttraumatic stress disorder caused by alien abduction
8. Rebirthing therapies for treatment of mental/behavioral disorders
9. Color therapy for treatment of mental/behavioral disorders
10. Primal scream therapy for treatment of mental/behavioral disorders

Top 10 Discredited Substance Abuse Treatments

1. Electrical stimulation of the head for alcohol dependence
2. Past life therapy for drug addictions and for alcohol dependence[a]
3. Metronidazole for alcohol dependence
4. Electric shock for alcohol dependence
5. Psychedelic medication for alcohol dependence
6. Ultrarapid opioid detoxification under anesthesia for alcohol dependence
7. Neurolinguistic programming for drug and alcohol dependence
8. Scared Straight for prevention of alcohol dependence and for prevention of drug abuse[a]
9. Stimulant medications for alcohol dependence
10. DARE programs for prevention of substance abuse

Clinician's Guide to Evidence-Based Practices

Table 7.2. **(Continued)**

Top 10 Discredited Psychological Tests

1. Lüscher Color Test for personality assessment

2. Szondi Test for personality assessment

3. Handwriting analysis (graphology) for personality assessment

4. Bender Visual Motor Gestalt Test for assessment of neuropsychological impairment

5. Eneagrams for personality assessment

6. Lowenfeld Mosaic Test for personality assessment

7. Bender Visual Motor Gestalt Test for personality assessment

8. Anatomically detailed dolls or puppets to determine if a child was sexually abused

9. Blacky test for personality assessment

10. Hand Test for personality assessment

[a]These practices rated as discredited for both alcohol and drug abuse in separate items.

From Norcross, Koocher, & Garafalo (2006). Norcross, Koocher, Fala, & Wexler, (2007).

ashore, they uncork it, and in so doing they release a genie who offers a food reward for releasing him but with a catch. The stranded hungry person must play a game of chance with three potential outcomes: a 95% chance of winning a moldy, stale loaf of bread and glass of tepid water; a 50% chance of winning a sandwich and beverage of choice; or a 25% chance of winning a sumptuous seven-course meal imported from a five-star restaurant. Which will you choose? The ultrarational survivalist would pick the nearly certain win of bread and water. But wait:

Perhaps the castaway only just arrived on the island does not feel particularly hungry, has an intense mold aversion, and anticipates rescue in the near future. Perhaps in those circumstances, the other options become more appealing. The intrinsic message: People's preferences, beliefs, and perceptions of probable outcomes exert a powerful influence on their decisions.

When making clinical decisions in the context of mental health treatment, clinicians often behave in similar fashion—relying on internalized preferences and probability estimates. They weigh preferences and perceived probabilities in deciding what course to follow. Sometimes they will decline a highly effective treatment because they perceive the cost as too high or the value as too low. Sometimes the costs involve economic factors (price); other times the decision may flow from perceptions about quality of life or likely outcome.

Let's see how a clinical decision analysis might unfold in Jonathon's treatment. We have devised two decision trees to illustrate the possibilities. Figure 7.1 shows a simplified decision tree for Jonathon's diagnosis. As good clinicians we cannot assume the accuracy of the referring diagnosis and should evaluate Jonathon's status as a precursor to formulating a treatment plan. The referral information from the school psychologist informs us that "Psychological testing, behavioral observations, and record review supported a diagnosis of ADHD (mixed type) and mild to moderate oppositional defiant disorder (ODD) accompanied by family tensions."

Figure 7.1 shows the array of potential diagnoses that could account for Jonathon's problems under the span of the line composed of dashes. Your review of the literature suggests that the

Simplified Decision Tree for Diagnosis of Jonathon

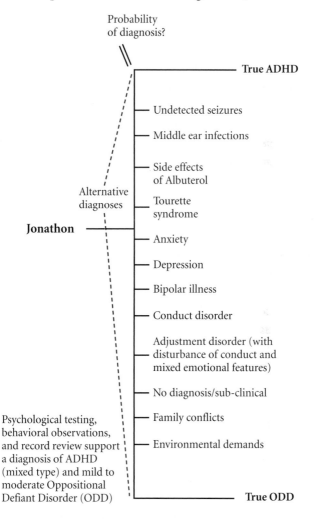

Figure 7.1 Simplified decision tree for diagnosis of Jonathon.

probability of a valid ADHD diagnosis in boys Jonathon's age approximates 4%–8%; thus, we might consider assigning a probability value of 6% at the decision choice point for making an ADHD diagnosis, indicated by the double line. If we simply guess that the ADHD diagnosis applies, we will have a 6% shot at accurate diagnosis by chance alone. Similarly, a valid diagnosis of Tourette syndrome would prove accurate only .03% of the time, based on epidemiological rates alone. We know that his asthma medication, albuterol, can cause nervousness, irritability, restlessness, and sleep problems; but the side effect incidence studies become difficult to interpret because of dosing differences and the small numbers of child participants in drug company studies. Published incidence data range 3%–20% for "moderate-level" symptoms.

In this case, knowledge of **epidemiology** can guide us in asking the right questions; for example, Do Jonathon's difficulties increase on days when he needs to make use of his asthma inhaler? Has his physician tried other asthma medications that might reduce physiological correlates of agitation? Such data can also help us to eliminate low-incidence conditions such as Tourette syndrome, especially if Jonathon's symptoms do not seem fully congruent with them (e.g., no reports of tics or coprolalia). While the incidence-related probabilities offer a degree of guidance, we know (and suspect) that Jonathon's behavior difficulties most likely arise as an interaction of multiple causes.

We know that the reliability of assigning diagnoses, particularly in childhood, suffers from many shortcomings. Research generally finds poor reliability among different diagnostic methods and different diagnosticians. One set of researchers (Lewczy et al., 2003), for example, studied agreement between diagnoses for 240 youths generated through parent and youth interviews with the structured Diagnostic Interview Schedule for Children (DISC) and diagnoses assigned by clinicians in community-based practice settings. The agreement between the two assessment methods proved very weak, with coefficients of agreement (kappa) ranging from -.04 for anxiety disorders to .22 for ADHD. Such discrepancies raise grave concerns about diagnostic reliability and assessment measures among children (Hoagwood, 2002).

We cannot be certain that Jonathon actually suffers from ADHD or ODD, but as clinicians we must make decisions. Researchers can respond to uncertainty with abstraction and curiosity; however, practitioners must resolve uncertainty through action (Greer, 1994). We must make diagnostic and treatment decisions on the basis of the best research at hand.

This necessity takes us to Figure 7.2, representing a simplified decision tree for treating Jonathon. For this tree we assume that we have eliminated all diagnoses other than ADHD and ODD. For each of those two conditions we show branches for both psychosocial and pharmacological treatments. Following the dotted lines, we could assign probabilities of likely beneficial response to each treatment based on published research and our confidence in those results. Note, however, the line of dashes at the points where the psychosocial and pharmacological options branch off. We know that patient characteristics, culture, and preferences all play a critical role in determining the choice of treatment (see Chapter 8).

Simplified Decision Tree for Treatment of Jonathon

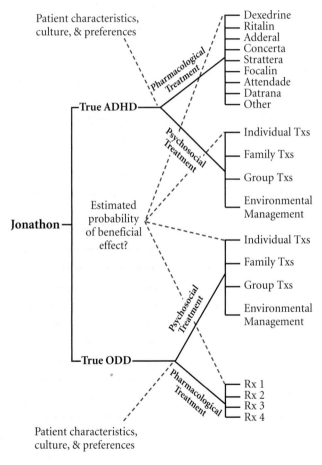

Figure 7.2 Simplified decision tree for diagnosis of Jonathon.

Clinician's Guide to Evidence-Based Practices

We also know that ". . . Jonathon's father firmly resists any psychotropic medication at this time. Both parents are genuinely concerned about Jonathon and willing to participate in a few family meetings, but their demanding work schedules and marital conflicts prevent extensive outpatient treatment." If we could convince Jonathon's father to allow a trial of stimulant medication, the next set of choices would involve a medication consultation to choose among the drugs with a record of documented success in treating ADHD through RCTs. In making the choice we would have to consider the pluses and minuses of specific drug actions, side effects, interactions with Jonathon's other medication, and dosing (short-acting, sustained-release, delivered orally or by transdermal patch).

In one sense, the father's reluctance to try additional medication could help if the ODD diagnosis proved more appropriate than ADHD. Although some prescribers have readily used atypical antipsychotic or other medications to treat ODD, these would all qualify as "off-label" uses under Food and Drug Administration regulations. Treating ODD with medication has practically no research support; thus, the risks far outweigh any benefit.

Given the record of family and school problems, however, any good child-clinician will know that Jonathon will need more intervention than simply medication. We know the parents have demands on their time and a conflictual relationship, so the clinician will probably conclude that any intervention with the family will need a tight focus and prompt reinforcement for the frustrated parents. The clinician may want to use a well-established parent training intervention but knows that she has little chance of getting them to sign on for multiple sessions. She may find herself selecting those components of an EBP that she can adapt quickly in the hope of engaging the parents and helping them get a handle on the difficulties with their son. She will also have to make a clinical decision about whether she will have the best results delivering the parent training to the parents as a couple or as individuals, given the tensions between them. She will have a number of solid EBPs to guide her but will most likely not have the ability to deliver any of them to this family in the way the protocol authors conducted the underlying research.

Interestingly, the clinician faces a very similar pattern of decisions if she determined ODD as the primary diagnosis. The target behaviors that she might focus on would differ—managing temper outbursts for ODD as opposed to increasing planful behaviors with ADHD—but the need to focus on helping the parents and school with behavior management would not change.

This walk through the diagnostic and therapeutic decision trees for Jonathon was intended to demonstrate the process of translating published research into clinical practice. The final step in critical appraisal entails integrating the patient and clinician with the research, which is our goal in the next chapter.

Key Terms

cost–benefit analysis
decision analysis
discredited practices
effectiveness research
efficacy research

epidemiology
risk–benefit analysis
translational research
transportability
validity

Recommended Readings and Web Sites

Calculating risks of harm, www.clinicalevidence.com/ceweb/resources/calculate_risk.jsp and www.cmaj.ca/cgi/content/full/171/4/353

Figueira, J., Greco, S., & Ehrgott, M. (Eds.). (2005). *Multiple criteria decision analysis: State of the art surveys.* New York: Springer.

Gambrill, E. (2005). *Critical thinking in clinical practice: Improving the quality of judgments and decisions* (2nd ed.). Somerset, NJ: Jossey-Bass.

Petitti, D. B. (2000). *Meta-analysis, decision analysis, and cost-effectiveness: Methods for quantitative synthesis in medicine* (2nd ed.). New York: Oxford University Press.

President's New Freedom Commission on Mental Health, www. mentalhealthcommission.gov

Turk, D. C., & Salovey, P. (Eds.). (1988). *Reasoning, inference, and judgment in clinical psychology.* New York: Free Press.

Westen, D., Novotny, C. M., & Thompson-Brenner, H. (2004). The empirical status of empirically supported psychotherapies: Assumptions, findings, and reporting in controlled trials. *Psychological Bulletin, 130,* 631–663.

▌▌▌▌▌
CHAPTER 8

Integrating the Patient and the Clinician with the Research

You have asked a specific clinical question, accessed the research literature, appraised that research, and, as illustrated in the last chapter, begun to translate it into clinical practice. Now, we advance to the task of integrating that research with the two other pillars of evidence-based practice (EBP): clinical expertise and patient characteristics. This chapter demonstrates the core skill of integrating the best available research with the clinician and the patient.

A fundamental premise of EBP holds that research alone will never suffice to make a clinical decision (Guyatt & Rennie, 2002). Indeed, the simple extrapolation of controlled research to practice should *not* be characterized as EBP. Such a linear approach lacks clinical sophistication, sensitivity, and real-world application. Clinicians understandably rail against such naiveté and deride it as untenable "cookbook practice."

In practice, determining the optimal plan for a given patient constitutes a recursive process. After asking "What does the research tell us?" we must always inquire "What does the patient desire? What is available and realistic? What fits this context? What about the cost–benefit ratio?" and a host of related questions. Then, we ask "Given these circumstances and contexts, what does the research tell us now?" And so on, until we secure a seamless blend, a practical integration of best research, clinical expertise, and patient values.

In the words of George Eliot (the pen name of Mary Ann Evans) from the novel *The Mill on the Floss*, "we have no master-key that will fit all cases." We must make clinical decisions, like Eliot's moral decisions, by "exerting patience, discrimination, and impartiality" and an insight earned "from a life vivid and intense enough to have created a wide, fellow feeling with all that is human."

Yet, the integration of the three pillars of EBP remains the least developed (or most neglected) of the EBP skills. Proponents of evidence-based medicine tend to minimize this step; in fact, many simply conjoin it with translating the research. Apart from the literature on clinicians' decision making regarding psychological assessment (e.g., Garb, 1998; Turk & Salovey, 1988), only a handful of empirical studies have examined clinical decision making about treatment (Chambless & Crits-Christoph, 2005). As practitioners, we are left with a dearth of EBPs about decision making in realistic, complex situations. Until we possess better research, we depend upon generalizations from the extant, limited research and clinical expertise.

In a given case, we will need to make dozens of minidecisions, and there will never be empirical research to guide all of them.

There remain many problem constellations and clinical situations for which empirical data are sparse. We cannot possibly expect that every practitioner's action will flow from research data (Chambless & Crits-Christoph, 2005). In such instances, clinicians use their clinical expertise and the best available research evidence to develop coherent, realistic treatment strategies (APA Task Force on Evidence-Based Practice, 2006).

Enlarging the Decision Making

We do know that blending clinical expertise and patient characteristics, culture, and preferences with the research evidence will necessarily broaden our decision making. In biomedicine, the prevalent model of treatment tends toward:

Interventions → operate on patient's disease → to produce effects

The traditional medical model assumes that the curative power rests primarily on the method or intervention; that the relationship is hierarchically structured, with the provider serving as the expert; and that the patient's role is to comply and participate as "prescribed" (Bohart, 2005).

In mental health and addictions, by contrast, the psychosocial model anticipates a more comprehensive and bidirectional process:

Treatment method			
Therapeutic relationship	←→ collaborate	←→ with unique patient in specific context	←→ to reach goals
Individual practitioner			
Active client			

The psychosocial model assumes that the curative power rests not only with the treatment method but also within the therapeutic relationship, the person of the practitioner, and the active client. Further, the treatment relationship works through collaboration, empathy, and empowerment. We filter and focus all decisions through the lens of the patient's characteristics, values, and culture. The client collaborates, remains informed, and works hard to participate and self-heal.

The psychosocial model requires us to abandon a parental stance and passive image of patients and move toward a more collaborative stance and an active image of clients. The psychosocial model, likewise, rejects monocultural, one-size-fits-all treatments for a particular diagnosis in favor of culturally informed, individually tailored treatment plans. This chapter adopts the psychosocial model, championed by mental health and addiction professionals, as its template.

Clinical Expertise

Clinical expertise is used to integrate the best research evidence with clinical data (e.g., information about the patient obtained over the course of treatment) in the context of the **patient's characteristics, culture, and preferences** to deliver services that have a high probability of achieving the goals of treatment (APA Task Force on Evidence-Based Practice, 2006). This description sounds accurate, but it begs the question of what exactly constitutes clinical expertise.

Let us begin by defining what clinical expertise is *not*. Clinical expertise does not refer to extraordinary performance that might characterize an elite group (e.g., the top 2%) of clinicians. As an aside, the concept of rating someone a "top 2% clinician" ignores the obvious fact that no single clinician (regardless of wisdom, skill, and sophistication) will qualify as equally adept with every potential patient. It refers instead to skills expected of all well-trained mental health professionals. Nor should we equate clinical expertise with "clinical experience" (Collins et al., 2007). Although clinical experience is required to develop clinical expertise and ongoing clinical experience can enhance it, clinical expertise is a far more complicated and inclusive construct (as defined shortly). Nor can we simply equate clinical expertise with "theoretical orientation." To be sure, we expect clinical know-how to flow from a (testable) theory of psychopathology and behavior change. However, clinical expertise transcends the shackles of a single theoretical orientation to embrace specific, transtheoretical skills.

As the APA Task Force on Evidence-Based Practices (2006, p. 276) put it, clinical expertise

> *encompasses a number of competencies that promote positive therapeutic outcomes. These competencies include a) conducting assessments and developing diagnostic judgments, systematic case formulations, and treatment plans; b) making clinical decisions, implementing treatments, and monitoring patient progress; c) possessing and using interpersonal expertise, including the formation of therapeutic alliances; d) continuing to self-reflect and acquire professional skills; e) evaluating and using research evidence in both basic and applied psychological science; f) understanding the influence of individual, cultural, and*

contextual differences on treatment; g) seeking available resources (e.g., consultation, adjunctive or alternative services) as needed; and h) having a cogent rationale for clinical strategies. Expertise develops from clinical and scientific training, theoretical understanding, experience, self-reflection, knowledge of current research, and continuing education and training.

Here, we shall punctuate just four of these competencies as they relate specifically to integrating the patient and the clinician with the research. First, clinical expertise includes a *scientific attitude* toward clinical work, characterized by openness to data, clinical hypothesis generation and testing, and a commitment against theoretical preconceptions overriding clinical or research data. Second, clinical expertise also entails the *skillful and flexible* delivery of treatment. Skill and flexibility require proficiency in delivering interventions and the ability to adapt the treatment to the particular case. Flexibility is manifested in tact, timing, pacing, and framing of interventions, maintaining an effective balance between consistency of interventions and responsiveness to patient feedback. Third, clinical expertise does not end with determining an initial treatment plan; it entails the *monitoring of patient progress* (and of changes in the patient's circumstances, such as job loss or major illness) that may suggest the need to adjust services. Should progress prove insufficient, the clinician considers alternative diagnoses and formulations, consultation, supervision, or referral. Fourth, clinical expertise requires an *awareness of the individual, social, and cultural context* of the patient. Such cultural sensitivity allows clinicians to adapt interventions and to construct a therapeutic milieu that respects the patient's worldview, values, and preferences.

Patient Characteristics, Culture, and Preferences

Mental health and substance abuse services prove most effective when responsive to the patient's specific problems, strengths, personality, sociocultural context, and preferences. In fact, many patient characteristics, such as functional status, readiness to change, and level of social support, have a documented relationship to therapeutic outcomes (see Norcross, 2002b, for reviews).

The APA Task Force on Evidence-Based Practice (2006) presented several important patient characteristics to consider in forming a treatment relationship and in implementing specific interventions. These include the following:

- ♦ variations in presenting problems or disorders, etiology, and comorbid syndromes
- ♦ chronological age, developmental status, developmental history, and life stage
- ♦ sociocultural factors, including gender, gender identity, ethnicity, race, social class, religion, disability status, and sexual orientation
- ♦ environmental context (e.g., institutional racism, health-care disparities) and stressors (e.g., unemployment, major life events)
- ♦ personal preferences and values related to treatment (e.g., goals, beliefs, worldviews, and treatment expectations)

The explicit enumeration and delicate balancing of these multiple patient considerations bring the underlying value judgments into bold relief (Guyatt & Rennie, 2002). Whose values—researchers, practitioners, patients, insurers—do we see reflected in treatment decisions? And do we find those values (and their sources) explicitly articulated?

Many treatment guidelines, in particular, possess implicit values derived from the authors. For example, the outcomes of interest focus almost exclusively on symptom reduction (as opposed to, for example, increases in joy or insight), and the independent variables are typically treatment methods that can be controlled and randomized (as opposed to, say, a strong therapeutic relationship). In addition, most investigators study the performance of graduate students or licensed health-care professionals (as opposed to indigenous healers or spiritual counselors). The investigators implicitly assume that the disorders should always be treated (e.g., as opposed to accepting diversity in functioning) and that treatments should continue until achieving maximum benefit (as opposed to good enough or cost considerations). We rarely hear patient/consumer voices in the writing of treatment guidelines or compiling of research reviews.

We cannot anticipate the hundreds of patient considerations that potentially enter the decision-making mix, but we have repeatedly noted several reality constraints intruding.

♦ *Readiness to change.* Only a minority of mental health and substance abuse patients enter treatment highly motivated and ready to immediately change their behavior (Prochaska, Norcross, & DiClemente, 2005). Instead, most enter treatment minimizing their problem, ambivalent about change, or contemplating taking action.

♦ *Acceptability.* Not all patients (or patient groups) will find the research-recommended intervention acceptable. Preference relates to what the patient desires; acceptability relates to what the patient finds minimally suitable.

♦ *Availability.* Access to the service (e.g., assessment, prevention, treatment) exists locally and is affordable and available to the patient. Those individuals who are most in need of mental health and addiction treatment are frequently those who experience the most barriers to it. State-of-the-art, expensive services remain unavailable to many impoverished and rural patients. Even if available and affordable, patients without reliable, private transportation cannot easily access some services.

♦ *Probability of payer approval.* Even if available, the chance that the insurance carrier or other third-party payer will approve the optimal treatment plan remains an open question. Anyone who has struggled to convince a health-maintenance organization (HMO) to approve an extended hospital or residential treatment knows of what we speak.

♦ *Caregiver approval.* The research and the practitioner may agree on an optimal treatment plan, but the parents or caregiver may not. For children and youth, the referring caregivers, rather than the identified patient, will likely choose the therapist and make other treatment decisions. However, children naturally have their own preferences and agendas.

♦ *Incongruous recommendations.* At the national level, different mental health disciplines offer disparate, even competing, treatment guidelines. At the local level, professionals from different disciplines may offer disparate treatment plans. For example, a cocaine addict who recently consulted us was offered, in the course of several weeks, four different "evidence-based" treatments. A psychologist recommended intensive outpatient psychotherapy (without medication), a psychiatrist recommended outpatient medication (without psychotherapy), an addictions counselor recommended inpatient detoxification and 14-day rehabilitation, and a pastoral counselor recommended Cocaine Anonymous and spiritual counseling.

◆ *Prior treatment failures.* Many patients present with chronic histories—both of their long-term suffering and of many unsuccessful treatment episodes, including with EBPs. "Been there, done that" is a familiar refrain among staff in community clinics when faced with such patients.

◆ *Intolerable side effects.* Some patients cannot tolerate the side effects of the finest EBP treatments, be they psychotropic medications or intense psychotherapies.

Take the case of Francesco. He has no insurance coverage and little money. Even if he could obtain a few free or low-cost sessions of outpatient therapy for his generalized anxiety disorder from his case manager, he would probably not receive a cutting-edge, state-of-the-art EBP treatment. In all likelihood, Francesco would receive a prescription for an antianxiety medication from his personal care physician. His enrolling in an extensive alcohol rehabilitation program seems improbable given his lack of health insurance and inability to pay privately. Even if offered, Francesco's low readiness to change would probably lead him to decline at this time. Moreover, Francesco's chronic history of alcohol dependence, two previous inpatient rehabilitations, and current minimization of his substance abuse all conspire to lower his odds of a good prognosis without extensive treatment. Any EBP that does not consider the patient's unique characteristics, culture, and preferences is ripe for failure.

Clinicians can commit the error of underestimating the uniqueness of patients, on the one hand, or overstating the uniqueness of patients, on the other. Having now emphasized the former, let us remind ourselves of the folly of the latter. If we place undue, exaggerated emphasis on patient uniqueness, then we may undercut the potential influence of clinical research findings. We may then fall prey to the heuristic (Chapter 7) of justifying what we are accustomed to doing regardless of the research evidence (Wilson, 1995). The task ahead is to thoughtfully and impartially integrate all three components.

Integrating the Three Components

The EBP trinity—best research, clinical expertise, and patient characteristics, culture, and preferences—is not an equal partnership. Research stands as the first and primary source of evidence. According to our (and other's) definition, practitioners integrate research with clinical expertise in the context of patient characteristics, culture, and preferences.

EBP decisions occur at the intersection of these three components, as graphically illustrated in Figure 8.1 (based on Walker et al., 2006). Figure 8.1 portrays in Venn diagram format an ideal situation in which the research literature, clinical expertise,

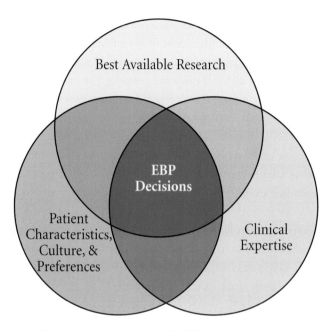

Figure 8.1 The three evidence-based practice (EBP) components demonstrating major convergence.

and patient characteristics largely converge. A substantial overlap exists; all three evidentiary sources are largely in agreement on how to proceed in practice—whether in assessment, prevention, or treatment. If only all treatment decisions proved so consensual and easy!

Consider the assessment and treatment of Annique's recurrent major depression. Research tells us that several psychometrically sound and clinically useful measures can assess her depression and monitor her symptom improvement (or deterioration) throughout the course of treatment. As a bright and informed

Clinician's Guide to Evidence-Based Practices

patient, Annique concurs that periodic assessment of her depression would serve her well. Such assessment fits congruently with her preferences and values. Her private practice psychologist knows the research on the assessment of depression and routinely employs self-report depression measures every third or fifth session. Similarly, the research evidence, the clinician's expertise, and Annique's preferences all align with interpersonal psychotherapy (IPT), an evidence-based psychotherapy for treatment of acute depression and prevention of its recurrence. The research, clinical expertise, and patient all converge—an optimal, Figure 8.1 situation.

Figure 8.2 displays a clinical case in which the patient and research fit together harmoniously but the practitioner's expertise remains out of synch with both. Two of the circles show considerable overlap with each other but not with the third. Here, the clinical decision is decidedly more complex and challenging.

To follow with our example, Annique and the research both support IPT (or another research-supported treatment, say, cognitive behavioral therapy, short-term psychodynamic therapy, or emotion-focused therapy). However, the practitioner favors a Therapy X, which Annique does not prefer and for which no controlled outcome research exists (for acute or maintenance treatment of depression). The practitioner has skill in rendering diagnoses, conceptualizing cases, forming facilitative relationships, and in other critical areas but lacks both training in IPT and the inclination to obtain it (or, for the sake of illustration, the other research-supported therapies for major depression).

How to proceed toward a clinical decision? In the face of evidence that IPT works for this disorder, it is not sufficient for the

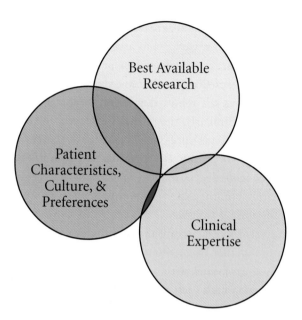

Figure 8.2 The three EBP components demonstrating major convergence between available research and patient preferences but minimal overlap with clinical expertise.

practitioner who prefers Therapy X to rest upon the fact that no one has proven it ineffective. The research-supported treatment remains the EBP and probably the most ethical choice in the majority of cases.

Nonetheless, in some cases, other factors will mitigate that decision. Three such mitigating factors are:

- ◆ The success of Therapy X has been recently documented in controlled research.
- ◆ In the process of obtaining informed consent, the clinician describes the alternatives and the evidence

for each, permitting the client to make an educated decision for Therapy X. (However, recognize that a depressed and dependent patient such as Annique might well uncritically accede to a clinician's theoretical inclinations, if strongly expressed.)

♦ Annique has undergone treatment on two occasions with the research-supported psychotherapy but has not improved, and now the clinician persuades her that they should opt for an alternative treatment.

The ethics codes of mental health professions argue in favor of offering research-supported treatments, absent such mitigating circumstances. The clinician need not have proficiency in all treatments and may thus refer Annique elsewhere if not trained in the EBP. We believe that most clinicians would, in fact, refer Annique to a colleague offering the indicated treatment should she maintain her strong treatment preference for the EBP.

Of course, the converse frequently occurs as well: the practitioner's expertise and the best research converge, but they diverge from the patient's preferences and culture. Figure 8.3 depicts this clinical situation.

In Annique's case, this scenario would occur when the best available research and clinical expertise converge in recommending the EBPs of IPT and antidepressant medication to treat her recurrent depression, but Annique rejects these. She might

♦ elect to discontinue antidepressant medications due to intolerable side effects or a philosophical objection to "chemical solutions"

♦ prefer a psychotherapy specifically developed for and evaluated on African American women

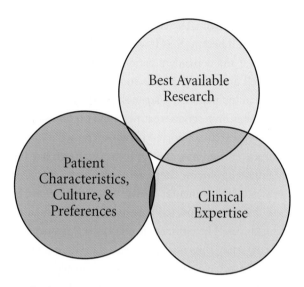

Figure 8.3 The three EBP components demonstrating major convergence between available research and clinical expertise but minimal overlap with patient preferences and culture.

- ◆ opt for a discredited treatment, say, sitting an hour a day in an Orgone energy accumulator to absorb (nonexistent) orgone energy (Norcross et al. 2006)
- ◆ decide that her primary goal in this course of psychotherapy lies in developing insight into the intrapsychic and family origins of her depression, as opposed to focusing on symptom reduction. In such a case, an EBP primarily devoted to, and validated in research on, symptom reduction might not be the treatment of choice. More than 90% of outcome measures in published mental health RCTs concern symptoms (Farnsworth et al., 2001).

Jonathon's case provides an exemplar of the clinical situation portrayed in Figure 8.3. The research supports the efficacy of parent management training, stimulant medication, and classroom management for Jonathon's ADHD. And the clinical expertise of the practitioner supports all three treatments. Yet, Jonathon's father firmly resists any psychotropic medication, thus taking that EBP off the table, at least in the short run. Both parents express a willingness to participate in a few family meetings, but their demanding work schedules and marital conflicts prevent extensive outpatient treatment. Can parent management training deliver its benefits in a few sessions with discordant parents? Perhaps a classroom behavior management program runs in Jonathon's elementary school, but the teacher already feels overwhelmed by the needs of the other 29 children in her classroom and insists on the parents medicating Jonathon. The teacher advocates for special services for Jonathon in the classroom; if not, then she argues for placement in a substantially separate classroom for the emotionally disturbed.

Figure 8.4 illustrates a different decision-making scenario: the patient's values and the clinician's expertise align well, but the best research stands apart. Annique, to continue with our example, presents to psychotherapy with definite cultural-driven preferences for an African American female therapist who will actively engage Annique's larger community, including her church group and pastor, in her psychological treatment. Meta-analyses show that ethnic minority clients definitely tend to prefer ethnically similar therapists over European American therapists (Coleman et al., 1995) but that ethnic minority therapists achieve no better or worse treatment outcomes (Sue & Lam, 2002). Hundreds of

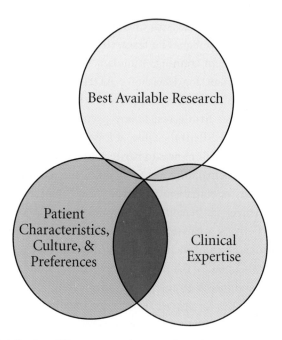

Figure 8.4 The three EBP components demonstrating major convergence between clinical expertise and patient preferences and culture but minimal overlap with available research.

controlled research studies have investigated the efficacy of family and community interventions, but none, based on our knowledge and literature search, specifically involved church groups in the treatment of depression. Annique's preferences enjoy no support in the research literature, but neither do we find data in the research literature to contradict them. Annique's preferred therapist, an African American woman, possesses training and competence in working with larger systems, views therapy as a collaborative endeavor, and responds effectively to the patient's

Clinician's Guide to Evidence-Based Practices

values and preferences. She works with Annique's inclinations, to their mutual satisfaction. Although this particular treatment approach would not appear on a list of "evidence-based" treatments or in a practice guideline, their treatment plan certainly qualifies as "evidence-based" in the best sense of that term.

Another example of patient characteristics and clinical expertise trumping the research-supported treatment is when the values of the patient contrast with those embodied within the EBP. Annique might decide that restructuring her relationships in IPT or her cognitions in cognitive behavior therapy does not coincide with her worldview. She elects a spiritual or existential psychotherapy whose philosophy feels more congruent with her personal values. Clinical expertise would lead most professionals to determine these therapies probably hold the greatest probability of benefit given the strength of Annique's values and the possible iatrogenic effect of imposing a treatment over those values. One goal of EBP is to maximize patient choice among effective alternative interventions (APA Task Force on Evidence-Based Practice, 2006).

In the interest of completeness, we should acknowledge one final, logical relationship among the three EBP components: all three spheres barely overlapping with each other. We have found this to occur very rarely in ordinary practice. Almost always, at least two of the components overlap considerably.

Complex Cases

What works in mental health and addictions? The definitive answer, the only evidence-based answer, is "It depends." Successful intervention necessarily considers the individuality of the patient, the singularity of the context, the nature of the patient's problems, the availability of resources, the likely prognosis, and expected benefits. Frequently, knowing the person who has the disorder proves far more important than knowing the disorder the person has. Most of our cases are, in a word, complex.

In fact, practitioners' concerns about the value of EBPs for complex patients, who may differ in significant ways from the samples in clinical trials, contribute to underutilization of EBP (Ruscio & Holohan, 2006). Patient complexity can be defined in many ways, as summarized in Table 8.1. All features of patient complexity tend to decrease a favorable prognosis, and all complicate the integration of best research with clinical expertise and patient contributions.

Table 8.1. **Common Features of Complex Cases**

Symptom presentations

Severe symptoms

Chronic course

Comorbid disorders

Severe functional impairment in multiple domains

Symptoms maintained by factors that are difficult to change

Presenting problem generally considered difficult to treat

No EBPs available for presenting disorders

Legal entanglements

Court-mandated treatment

Secondary gain to preserve impairment, e.g., disability evaluations

Table 8.1. **(Continued)**

Strong motivation to present or fake "good," e.g., child custody evaluations

Repeated charges or formal complaints against health-care professionals

Suicidal and safety concerns

Suicidal and self-destructive behaviors

Parasuicidal or self-injurious behaviors

Past suicide attempts

Homicidal impulses or tendencies

Frequent hospitalizations

Ongoing physical danger

Physical/medical complications

Chronic pain

Multiple, diffuse somatic symptoms

Medical condition causes psychological symptoms

Physical disability maintains psychological condition

Physical factors limits treatment

Intellectual limitations

Limited intellectual ability

Low education level

Cognitive impairment

Interpersonal impediments

Personality disorders that undermine the therapeutic alliance

Severe personality traits, e.g., hostility, suspiciousness, dependence

Pervasive tendency to externalize problems

Low psychological mindedness

Low self-esteem or self-efficacy

Table 8.1. **(Continued)**

Psychosocial factors

History of chronic or repeated trauma

Multiple, significant stressors

Severe financial instability

Social isolation

Unstable or insecure social environment

Family and social system undermines treatment

Motivational factors

Severe hopelessness and demoralization

Precontemplation stage (denial of problems)

High level of reactance/resistance

Low expectancy for improvement

Strong belief in problematic beliefs or behaviors

External contingencies reinforce the sick role

Poor commitment to therapy

Treatment noncompliance

Treatment history

Repeated prior treatment failures

History of premature termination and dropout

Unsuccessful prior treatment with EBPs

Adapted from Ruscio & Holohan (2006).

It would be impossible to discuss all the features of complex cases listed in Table 8.1 in a brief, how-to manual on EBPs. Nonetheless, we can profitably work a couple of examples to demonstrate the process of arriving at an EBP decision.

Clinician's Guide to Evidence-Based Practices

Comorbid disorders confound any simple or linear determination of a treatment plan from the research literature. Consider the frequent co-occurrence of major depression and generalized anxiety disorder. In a prospective longitudinal **cohort** study, a birth cohort of 1,037 people was followed to age 32 years (with an impressive 96% retention). Cumulatively, 72% of lifetime anxiety cases from this group demonstrated a history of depression, and 48% of lifetime depression cases also had anxiety. In this comorbid group, depression onset occurred first in one-third of the participants, anxiety onset occurred first in one-third of the participants, and depression and anxiety onset began concurrently in one-third of the cases (Moffitt et al., 2007).

Presenting with major depression, Annique has almost a 50% chance of experiencing clinical levels of anxiety as well. Presenting with generalized anxiety disorder, Francesco has a 72% chance of experiencing clinical depression at some point. As every seasoned psychotherapist knows, anxiety and depression rarely present as discrete disorders.

The cultural context challenges us to think in terms of idiographic cases as contrasted to the normative probabilities of group research. Does the applicability of research results depend, for example, on the nation and time period? Case in point: Does the applicability of the research results from the prospective longitudinal study mentioned above change in your mind as you learn that the particular study took place in Dunedin, New Zealand, starting in 1972–1973? To what extent do we base the probability of comorbid diagnoses for Annique and Francesco on such findings?

Then, we have that subset of patients who present with high levels of reactance or resistance, meaning that they become easily provoked and respond oppositionally to external demands. Research finds that high client resistance consistently associates with poorer therapy outcomes in 82% of studies. Fortunately, research has determined that matching therapist directiveness to client level of resistance improves therapy outcome in 80% (16 of 20) of studies (Beutler et al., 2002). Specifically, clients presenting with high resistance benefit more from self-control methods, minimal therapist directiveness, and **paradoxical interventions**. By contrast, clients with low resistance benefit more from therapist directiveness and explicit guidance.

In order to sensitively integrate the research with the patient and the clinician, we increasingly need to know not simply which treatments work for which disorder but which treatments work for which person. Different folks demand different strokes.

Here, it seems to us, lays the central difference between EBPs in medicine and EBPs in mental health: the relentless complexity of people. We do not minimize the complexity of the physical body or disease states. Rather, mental health and addiction professionals address all of that pathology complexity on top of the immense complexity of human behavior.

Adopt, Adapt, or Abandon

After evaluating the confluence of the three components of EBP and considering the complexity of patient characteristics, we must make a clinical decision and act accordingly. Practitioners have three basic options for a particular patient with regard to a research-supported intervention: **adopt it, adapt it, or abandon it**. Given the paucity of research on choosing among the options and the seemingly infinite number of competing considerations, the practitioner confronts a difficult decision.

We *adopt* the research-supported EBP when we believe it is a "good enough" fit for this particular patient and context. Providing the EBP in its original form affords several benefits (Ruscio & Holohan, 2006):

- The treatment has been tested and shown to be efficacious for alleviating the target problem, thus maximizing the probability of client success.
- The clinician will probably feel more confident in using an EBP and communicate that confidence to the patient.
- The client, as a part of informed consent, will learn that she is receiving a demonstrably effective, scientifically supported treatment with low attrition.

In our experience, the majority of mental health and addiction patients make a good enough match with at least one EBP for one or more of their presenting problems.

We *adapt* an EBP when we believe it has utility but does not quite seem adequate for this particular patient, problem, and context. Adaptations can entail modifying, supplementing, or sequencing the treatment, in ways not studied in the research trials, to accommodate the needs of the patient. The obvious advantages include our hope the treatment aligns better with the patient's needs and that the proven efficacy of the EBP will generalize to this case. The disadvantages include the unknown impact of the adaptation on the efficacy of treatment and the possibility that the modified EBP loses its curative ingredients. Indeed, early research suggests that adapting EBPs to tailor treatment to an individual patient seldom improves treatment outcome (Ruscio & Holohan, 2006). However, adapting EBPs may mean the difference between some treatment gains by engaging the patient versus no treatment gains at all by imposing a treatment deemed "unacceptable" by the patient.

Dynamic tension occurs in resolving the conflict between **fidelity** and fit, both essential elements of EBP. We seek fidelity of implementation in the delivery of the manualized intervention as found effective in controlled research. At the same time, we seek fit in adapting the service to accommodate the needs of the specific patient (Castro et al., 2004).

Consider two examples of **cultural adaptations** of research-supported interventions—one in substance abuse prevention and the other in parent management training. An innovative substance abuse prevention program in the Southwest built in adaptation to enhance program fit while maintaining fidelity of implementation. The cultural adaptation involved modifying some program content and the form of program delivery. The latter included characteristics of the clinicians (lay health workers rather than health educators), the channel of services (on the Internet rather than formal presentations), and the location of services (a community hall rather than school classroom) (Castro et al., 2004).

Parent management training has a long and well-established evidence base (Kazdin, 2005) but has shown some racial/ethnic disparities in outcomes (Lau, 2006). The wide variation in parenting practices and family values across ethnic groups has led several researchers to adapt the treatment. Some changes lie at the surface, such as including community-relevant examples, modifying pictures to depict ethnically similar families, and respecting cultural values. Other changes have a more structural nature, for example, recruiting in community networks, matching the ethnicity of the clinician to the clientele, conducting the treatment groups in churches, and addressing basic living needs. The outcomes of the adapted parent training typically equate to the standard versions; however, the cultural adaptation frequently results in marked improvements in client recruitment, satisfaction, and retention (Lau, 2006).

Of course, research evidence must systematically guide adaptation of EBPs to cultural contexts and other patient characteristics. Data can selectively identify target problems and communities that would most benefit from an adaptation and then direct the design of the treatment adaptation (Lau, 2006). We also need to factor in the bottom-line question of whether the outcomes justify the additional costs of cultural adaptation. The consensus in the field points to selective and conservative adaptations—balancing fidelity with fit.

We *abandon* a research-supported intervention either before treatment commences because we believe it does not apply to the particular patient and context or during treatment when it does not produce the desired results. Before treatment, clinicians may decide that the research-supported intervention lacks applicability and generalizability (for one or more of the reasons reviewed in Chapter 7 and in this chapter). During treatment, clinicians may decide to abandon the research-supported option because the patient shows signs of deteriorating, is not making any progress with it, refuses to continue it, threatens to drop out, or insists on an alternative.

When treatment with a research-supported intervention is failing, the clinician can proceed in many ways. Possible strategies entail:

- determining, in a nonblaming style with the patient, the reasons the current treatment plan is not working
- revisiting the therapeutic contract and asking if the treatment had a sufficient chance, or "dose," to work
- adapting the research-supported treatment in some manner
- delaying or resequencing the particular treatment
- returning to the research literature to discover other research-supported interventions for the particular patient and context
- reconsidering the patient's diagnoses and treatment goals
- evaluating the patient's readiness to change or motivational level
- evaluating the therapeutic relationship, particularly for ruptures in the therapeutic alliance
- obtaining peer consultation or supervision on the case
- transferring the patient to another clinician

The Reflective, Evidence-Based Practitioner

Decision trees (see Figures 7.1 and 7.2), overlapping circles (Figures 8.1–8.4), and case examples can only begin to capture the enormous complexity of integrating the best available research with clinical expertise and patient characteristics, culture, and preferences. Risk–benefit analyses, likelihood ratios, and decisional balances are simply paths through the tangled thicket of complex and conflicting considerations. Sensitive application and thoughtful integration of the research can be taxing. At times, we secretly crave the older, discarded practice of mindlessly providing all patients with the identical treatment!

But clinical experience and controlled research convincingly demonstrate the error of that old way. Michels (1984, p. xiii) has written:

> *The easiest way to practice is to view all patients and problems as basically the same, and to apply one standard therapy for their treatment. Although some may still employ this model, everything we have learned in recent decades tells us that it is wrong—wrong for our patients in that it deprives them of the most effective treatment, and wrong for everyone else in that it wastes scarce resources.*

His words underscore the overarching purposes of EBPs, which, as you will recall from Chapter 1, are to improve the care of the individual patient and to enhance the health of the entire population.

In the end, the practitioner performs the integration with skill, flexibility, scientific attitude, and cultural sensitivity while monitoring patient progress and adjusting treatment as necessary. We rely on research but soberly acknowledge that not all research applies and that individual patients may require decisions and interventions not directly addressed by the available research. Effective practice requires delicate balancing, recursive decision making, and collaborative relationships to ensure that patients understand the probable costs, risks, and benefits of different choices.

Key Terms

adopt it, adapt it, or abandon it
clinical expertise
cohort
comorbid disorders
cultural adaptation

fidelity
paradoxical interventions
patient characteristics, culture, and
    preferences

Recommended Readings and Web Sites

Bohart, A. C., & Tallman, K. (1999). *How clients make therapy work: The process of active self-healing.* Washington, DC: American Psychological Association.

Centre for Evidence-Based Medicine. Applying Evidence to Patients, www. cebm.utoronto.ca/practise/apply/

DiClemente, C. C. (2003). *Addiction and change: How addictions develop and addicted people recover.* New York: Guilford.

Garb, H. N. (1998). *Studying the clinician: Judgment research and psychological assessment.* Washington, DC: American Psychological Association.

Hunink, M. G. M., Glasziou, P. P., Siegel, J. E., Weeks, J. C., Pliskin, J. S., Elstein, A. S., et al. (2001). *Decision making in health and medicine: Integrating evidence and values.* Cambridge, UK: Cambridge University Press.

Lambert, M. J. (Ed.). (2004). *Bergin and Garfield's handbook of psychotherapy and behavior change* (4th ed.). New York: Wiley.

Lau, A. S. (2006). Making the case for selective and directed cultural adaptations of evidence-based treatments: Examples from parent training. *Clinical Psychology: Science and Practice, 13,* 295–310.

▌▌▌▌▌
CHAPTER 9

Incorporating Evaluation and Ethics

The final core step in evidence-based practice (EBP) involves evaluating the effectiveness of the entire process. In the literature, we see this skill typically referred to as monitoring, measuring, or auditing clinical performance. We study clinical performance using three different levels of evaluation: the individual practitioner, the program or administrative unit, and the profession as a whole.

Interestingly, we can track the evaluation process using the stages of change model often used to describe behavior change and psychotherapy progress (Prochaska et al., 1992 1994). Individual practitioners will move through five stages— precontemplation, contemplation, preparation, action, and maintenance—as they adapt their work and implement EBP. By taking seriously this book you have demonstrated movement past precontemplation and probably even past contemplation. You have gone beyond the "Who cares about EBP?" attitude of the precontemplator and probably past the "Do I really want to do this?" of the contemplator. You have plunged deep into the book and should hopefully feel prepared to take action. This will likely require altering your practice in significant ways and may necessitate some continuing education to acquire familiarity with new assessment, prevention, or treatment approaches. Success will also require follow-through and follow-up (i.e., implementing the EBPs and evaluating the outcome of your work). Table 9.1 enumerates the stages of change as applied to EBP in mental health and addictions.

This chapter begins with an evaluation of EBPs at three levels: the individual practitioner, the program or administrative unit, and the profession as a whole. Next, we focus on risk management, liability standards, and ethical issues—matters typically and tragically too often ignored when considering EBPs.

Three Levels of Evaluation

Evaluating One's Own Performance

A good evaluation of an individual practitioner's performance involves both self-evaluation and evaluation by others. One might think that well-intentioned, highly educated, clinically skilled practitioners trained in EBP would know about their own competence or skill level based on introspective self-awareness. However, quoting from the lyrics of George Gershwin in *Porgy and Bess*, "It ain't necessarily so." Difficulties in recognizing one's own incompetence can easily lead people to hold overly favorable views of their abilities in many contexts (Kruger & Dunning, 1999). Personal biases and the intense wish for one's patients

Table 9.1. **Stages of Change in EBP Adoption**

Stage of Change Relative to EBP	Characteristic Questioning	Suggestions for Promoting Movement
Precontemplation	Who cares about EBP? The status quo is fine with me.	Encourage reevaluation and self-exploration; recognize risks of doing nothing.
Contemplation	Do I really want to do this? What are the benefits and risks?	Consider the pros and cons of adopting EBPs, as well as potential positive outcomes.
Preparation	Okay, I bought the book and am intrigued. Now what?	Identify any obstacles, acquire necessary skills, and begin taking small steps.
Action	I want to do it, but can I? Let's see how this goes.	Practice the core EBP skills, improve self-efficacy, and focus on long-term benefits.
Maintenance	Can I sustain this? How did I ever do without it?	Follow-up and document patients' successes, prevent relapse, self-reinforcement.

to improve further complicate objective outcome assessment in mental health and the addictions.

Humans absorb and process massive amounts of sensory data and attempt to make sense of it all using various organizing strategies or cognitive anchors, often without specific awareness. We typically seek to optimize our understanding of the world using interpolative and probabilistic cognitive processes, as opposed to extrapolative and nonprobabilistic thinking. We typically attempt to insert new data into our preexisting worldviews, as opposed to expanding our thinking outward based on the new data or observations. Some refer to these human organizing strategies as **heuristics**—"mental rules of thumb" that we use to perform abstract reasoning in cognitively economical ways. These strategies generally operate below our threshold of awareness and save us time and effort, but they often fail when confronted by data at variance with or outside of our domains of expertise.

Such failures often tend to pass without notice. For one thing, the cognitive processes responsible for judging the quality of our thinking fall prey to these biases as well. In addition, such biases apply so broadly and seem so natural that few people notice them. Finally, decisions made based on heuristics often simply feel good or correct. Such ways of conceptualizing our world leave us intuitively satisfied regardless of their correctness. Illustrative examples of heuristic biases appear in Table 9.2.

What does the research evidence tell us about countering such heuristics? The strategy of simply informing people about a particular bias and warning them to avoid falling under its influence turns out to be nearly worthless. But five strategies to de-bias judgment have research support:

- *Consider alternative outcomes.* Actively considering alternatives, whether diagnoses or treatments, reduces unwarranted overconfidence and increases our humility.
- *Increase attention to usually ignored data.* Chief among such data are research findings, which help us to think realistically about probabilities and perhaps to even calculate likelihoods for our patients.
- *Minimize the role of memory.* Fallibility of recall should lead us to try to decrease our reliance on memory.

Clinician's Guide to Evidence-Based Practices

Table 9.2 **Examples of Heuristic Biases**

Name	Description
Anchoring effect	Failure to adjust sufficiently from initial anchor points, even when the points are arbitrary.
Base rate neglect	Overlooking background frequencies in favor of salient anecdotal evidence (e.g., "All my clients are liberal Democrats, so…").
Confirmation bias	Seeking out opinions and facts that support our own beliefs and hypotheses (e.g., "I'm sure I'm right, I just need to find the proof").
False consensus bias	Inclination to assume your beliefs are more widely held than they actually are (e.g., "Family therapists pretty much agree on this").
Fortune teller effect (or Barnum effect)	Tendency of people to accept general descriptions as uniquely relevant to them (e.g., "You think about sex from time to time").
Framing effect	Disparities in estimates when identical problems or data are arrayed in different configurations or sequences.
Gambler's fallacy	Pervasive false beliefs about the nature of random sequences (e.g., "I'm due for a win any time now").
Groupthink	Pressure to irrationally agree with others in strong team-based cultures (e.g., "I better keep my odd ideas to myself because the rest of the team thinks the sky is green").
Homogeneity bias	Exaggerated conclusions about large populations based on small samples (e.g., "My three clients typify the universe").
Lake Wobegon effect	Coined by Garrison Keillor, the tendency of people to assume they are "above average."

Table 9.2. **(Continued)**

Name	Description
Not my fault bias	If the patient does not improve, it could not have been me (e.g., "They must have not followed my advice or screwed up some other way").
Truthiness	Coined by Comedy Central's Stephen Colbert, referring to the human propensity for determining truth by what we feel in our gut, independent and frequently in opposition to objective reality or scientific research.
Wow effect	Salient memories override normative reasoning

+ *Use a disconfirmation strategy.* Instead of immediately searching for clinical information to support our initial hunch, search for information that would disconfirm it.
+ *Rely on* **actuarial judgment** *when available.* Hundreds of studies demonstrate the robust superiority of actuarial over clinical judgment in making health-care decisions.

Mental health practitioners have historically proved lousy at gauging their clients' success and experiences of empathy, although therapists frequently believe they do so with great accuracy (Hannan et al., 2005). One meta-analysis found that client and therapist ratings of the quality of their therapeutic relationship only correlated .33 on average (Tryon et al., 2006). Therapists also do not judge very accurately who is doing well in therapy; they tend to overestimate client gains and satisfaction.

How might these play out in the clinical context? The effects of *confirmation bias* may lead the clinician to see success where expected and to overlook evidence of failure. When clinicians tap their memories for a treatment method that worked with similar clients in the past, they risk making decisions biased on the *wow effect* or *homogeneity bias.* Thinking of examples about an intervention's particularly memorable success or failure will influence estimations of the likelihood that the treatment will help in the present case. One or two successful cases may prove sufficient to override memory of cases for which the same approach did not work. The *not my fault bias* comes into play when clinicians' self-assessments lead them to ascribe the reason for treatment failures to clients' behaviors or characteristics, while attributing successes in treatment to themselves and their skills.

We can begin to evaluate ourselves by asking questions that force us to bypass heuristic biases, as suggested by Straus and colleagues (2005):

- Have I asked myself any clinical questions lately?
- If so, have I asked well-formulated questions about both "foreground" and "background" questions (see Chapter 2)?
- Have I attempted to identify my own knowledge gaps and to frame questions focused on those domains?
- Do I routinely note questions that occur to me in daily practice so that I can follow up with research later?
- Are there better treatments than the one that I successfully employ now?

Once we get into the habit of routinely questioning ourselves about our clinical work, the next step involves actively seeking answers. So ask yourself the following:

- Have I done any searching of the research literature?
- Do I know the best sources of current evidence for my professional discipline and patient population of interest?

- Do I have easy access to resources for finding the best available evidence suited to my needs?
- Have I had success finding the research evidence I need?
- Have I become more efficient in my searches?
- Have I begun to critically appraise the evidence I discover?
- How do my searches and critical appraisals compare with those of respected colleagues who share my interest in seeking out and adopting the best EBPs?
- Have I become more critically sophisticated and accurate in applying in clinical practice what I have learned from the research?

If you ask yourself these questions, breaking free of heuristic biases whenever possible, you have essentially begun to **audit** your work. An audit represents the next step in self-evaluation by focusing on your performance in terms of outcomes. We will discuss application of audit principles to a clinic or program.

As an individual practitioner, you can (1) track patient outcomes, (2) check your work against evidence-based **practice guidelines**, and (3) compare patient outcomes to established **benchmarks**. For example, one could measure treatment completion or dropout rates and use outcome measures (e.g., symptom changes in depression and anxiety with self-report instruments or observable behavioral indices such as days of sobriety or days missed from school/work). You might check yourself against the work of other practitioners at the same institution or as reported in the literature. You can also determine how your patient's progress compares to national benchmarks (see Hunsley & Lee, 2007, for practical examples).

Tracking Patient Outcomes

In the words of the APA Task Force on Evidence-Based Practice (2006, p. 285): "The application of research evidence to a given patient always involves probabilistic inferences. Therefore, ongoing monitoring of patient progress and adjustment of treatment as needed are essential" to EBPs. We recommend that mental health practitioners employ a four-pronged approach to outcome data: patient self-report, ratings by other observers, quantifiable observable behaviors, and, when available, physiological data. Selection of the actual instruments can link directly to the individual circumstances of the client, using well-validated tools targeted to the patient's specific needs (see Chapter 3 on accessing tests and measures). Consider how this might apply to our three index patients.

In Jonathon's case, we would typically track his ADHD and ODD symptoms by asking him and his parents to complete self-report checklists and other diagnostic instruments to assess their experience of his dysfunction. We might also ask for teacher reports and take care to address discrepancies among informants' ratings (De Los Reyes & Kazdin, 2004). If Jonathon were to undertake a course of neurofeedback (or electroencephalographic/EEG feedback) for his ADHD, then we would also seek to monitor the changes in the proportion of his brain waves. We could look for congruence of opinion and critically evaluate noncomporting data. For example, following multimodal intervention, it may turn out that parent and teacher reports reflect improvement. At the same time, Jonathon's acting out behaviors decrease and activity level moderates. If all of these changes occur with no concomitant brain wave changes, perhaps we should discard brain wave measurement as a meaningful outcome variable.

In Francesco's case, we might ask for self-report measures of life stresses, anxiety, and substance abuse. We might engage his primary care physician to report on correlated physiological factors, for example, heart rate, blood pressure, or signs of hepatic disease. If available, we might, with Francesco's consent, also seek input from his family members or fellow workers regarding his alcohol consumption, emotional status, or days missed from work. And we might desire some concurrent monitoring of Francesco's blood alcohol levels with breathalyzer or urine sample. Of course, we must take care to ascertain that the instruments we use are linguistically and culturally appropriate for Francesco, particularly if we wish to use comparative norms to track his progress.

In Annique's case, we can certainly rely on well-validated depression measures; but with her consent, we can also seek data from her spouse and psychiatrist for their views of her progress using standardized measures. We can also consider her absences from work and performance evaluations, use of alcohol or tobacco, sleeping, appetite, reports of somatic symptoms, and so on.

Because our three index patients, like the rest of the world, manifest differences in age, sex, ethnicity, culture, socioeconomic class, and other characteristics, we must choose our assessment and outcome measures carefully, avoiding **arbitrary metrics**. Many psychological tests have arbitrary metrics but remain appropriate for testing theories (Blanton & Jaccard, 2006). For example, suppose we measure depression by asking someone "How depressed do you feel on a scale of 1 to 7, where 1 equals not at all depressed and 7 equals totally depressed?" Such a scale might help us to track changes in that person's depression level over time, but a score of 5 on the scale has no absolute meaning apart from any arbitrary criteria or cut-points that we set. The same factors or symptoms that contribute to one person's rating of 5 might lead a different person to offer a rating of 4 or 6.

Mental health and addiction research has traditionally relied heavily on such metrics, and investigators may find themselves unable to determine whether patients receiving EBPs have improved daily lives or have changed in significant ways, apart from the arbitrary metrics. What if Jonathon's parents rate him as improved on instrument norms but his teacher finds him unmanageable in class? Suppose Francesco reports less anxiety than the test manual specifies for the average Latino male but he took the test while intoxicated. Perhaps Annique will report improved quality of life according to the test manual, despite the fact that her spouse witnesses continued chronic tearfulness and sleep disturbance. In translating EBP case by case, we must better connect arbitrary measures to real-world referents (Kazdin, 2006).

As all practitioners know, assessing patient outcome and treatment success usually proves far more complicated than conveyed in a single, global category of "improved" or "not improved."

In reviewing research, we would categorize this as a **criterion problem**: What criteria are most appropriate for determining effective treatment and who should decide?

We embrace the tripartite view of mental health outcomes (Strupp & Hadley, 1977): the individual patient's perspective, family and societal perspective, and the treating clinician's perspective. The same individual may qualify simultaneously as cured, improved, or deteriorating depending upon the criteria used. The same treatment may simultaneously qualify as successful evidence-based, unsuccessful evidence-based, or non-evidence-based depending upon the person setting the criteria.

We have thus far discussed the evaluation of patient outcomes largely in terms of symptom improvement at the end of a course of treatment. However, experienced clinicians know that we must consider evaluating the ongoing process that includes the treatment relationship. We recommend assessing patient satisfaction with treatment, monitoring patient progress, and making midcourse treatment corrections or adjustments as needed.

Research has underscored the effectiveness of systematically seeking patients' feedback as a way to materially improve the success of therapy. One meta-analysis (Lambert, 2005) demonstrated that collecting feedback from patients periodically throughout treatment reduced deterioration rates by 15%–21%. We can improve outcomes by detecting deteriorations early and altering the course of treatment.

The EBP moral: Regularly and proactively request real-time feedback from clients on their response to the therapy relationship. Focus on emphasizing the merits of the *client's* experience of the treatment relationship and success, not the therapist's perspective. The benefits of doing so include empowering clients, promoting explicit collaboration, allowing for midtherapy adjustments as needed, and enhancing the success of treatment (Miller et al., 2005).

The data—both empirical and clinical—on continuously collected feedback from patients appear compelling. Many clinicians will tell us "Of course, I do this stuff with my patients." However, the research indicates that they do *not* do such assessment regularly. Even when clinicians solicit such information, they often do not do it *explicitly* (instead, they intuit or infer). They often prove inaccurate when guessing or inferring. Some find it awkward to broach a discussion of the relationship with the client and may attribute blame to the patient for any disappointments or ruptures. EBP demands that we follow the evidence on how to collect feedback, conceptualize patient dissatisfaction as a mutual problem, and hold paramount the patient's experience of treatment.

Checking Your Work Against Evidence-Based Practice Guidelines

Individuals can compare their performance against the guidelines introduced in Chapters 1 and 3. The most exhaustive listings of health-care guidelines probably appear at the National Guideline Clearinghouse (www.guideline.gov) and the National Institute for Health and Clinical Excellence (www.nice.org.uk).

Comparing Patient Outcomes to Established Benchmarks (When Available)

Using Jonathon as an example, we have already noted how a practitioner could track patient outcomes using self-rating, parent rating, and teacher rating. We can also compare our ability to retain the family in treatment against dropout rates reported in the literature, against retention rates for colleagues at our institution, or against rates for other similar patients in our practice. Then, we can compare our treatment of Jonathon against established professional guidelines.

If we were Jonathon's pediatrician, for example, we could check our management of his asthma against standards for inhaled medication (see, e.g., guidance.nice.org.uk/TA38/?c=91527) and for the comprehensiveness of his ADHD treatment plan (see, e.g., aappolicy.aappublications.org/cgi/content/full/pediatrics;108/4/1033). Regarding the ADHD, the American Academy of Pediatrics would recommend that Jonathon's primary care physician attend to five foci: (1) establishing a treatment program that recognizes ADHD as a chronic condition; (2) making sure that the treating clinician works in collaboration with parents, child, and school personnel, while specifying target outcomes; (3) recommending stimulant medication and/or behavior therapy to improve target outcomes; (4) if the selected management program does not meet target outcomes, re-evaluating the original diagnosis, using all appropriate treatments, considering adherence to the treatment plan, and considering the presence of coexisting problems; (5) providing periodically a systematic follow-up for the child directed at the target outcomes with information gathered from parents, teachers, and the child.

Obviously, a mental health practitioner could follow a similar plan in close concert with the primary care physician. This model tracks well with the diagnostic and decision trees illustrated in Figures 7.1 and 7.2.

Clinician's Guide to Evidence-Based Practices

Evaluating a Program

In addition to evaluating your own use of EBPs, it becomes important to examine the group, program, or organization within which you practice. Organizational structures may create barriers to change that prove as difficult or more difficult to alter than individual practitioner's behavior.

One strategy involves implementing a plan–do–check–act cycle (Straus et al., 2005). Typical barriers encountered in group practice or institutional settings include personnel at disparate levels of acceptance (different stages of change) and people with varying levels of education and training. Professionals responsible for different activities—say, for example, intake, screening, evaluation, assignment, record keeping, and in-service training—can inhibit change.

Some types of EBPs will prove easier to implement than others. Establishing in-service training programs, continuing professional education opportunities, focused case conferences, and journal clubs can all contribute to upgrading practitioner competence. After initial planning and targeting the barriers to implementation, the next phase of the audit will involve the "doing." We can conceptualize this as undertaking a pilot period of testing the ability to change. Ideally, this will involve solid efforts to measure change by establishing initial or historical base rates and then reviewing comparison data after attempting the new model. Follow this period with a "checking" activity aimed at answering these questions: Did the expected changes occur? Do patient outcome data seem congruent with administrative systems data? What worked? What did not work? Why?

In the final step of the organizational practice audit, we look at how to systematize and extend the gains documented in a review of the pilot data, or we revisit our plan in an effort to fix the parts that did not work as anticipated. Very often, this will involve adapting to the human element of the equation. For example, we may find that some practitioners have resisted or otherwise failed to adapt their ways of working. Introduction of benchmark comparisons, particularly from external sources, or practice guidelines can help overcome resistance and motivate change.

Alternatively, we may find that the idealized EBP model does not fit our population well. Jonathon's parents, for example, may have significant difficulty in following the clinician's suggestions consistently, thus nullifying the effect of our best efforts at parent management training. Francesco's lack of health insurance and the agency's inability to offer reduced-fee or pro bono services may result in his dropping out of treatment. Annique may become acutely suicidal and require hospitalization before her treatment with cognitive behavior therapy and new medication get under way.

Successful application of the audit will require careful, objective analysis of any failures and modification of planning to address root issues in a revised series of steps. Optimal success occurs when this pattern of planning, doing, checking, and acting becomes routine.

Evaluating the Profession

Health-care professionals must actively engage in defining and implementing EBPs in a manner that best serves their clientele

and professional values. Otherwise, we will find ourselves grop-
ing in the wake created by the other health professions' inexo-
rable movement in that direction. We must consider whether
our educational and training programs tend to create unin-
volved professionals or colleagues actively engaged in continuous quality improvement. Early debate and dialogue on EBP
among mental health professionals seemed to revolve around
fears of criticism and narcissistic injury—"Your criticisms about
the way I practice just aren't fair, because. . . ." Books on the
topic tended toward the descriptive and interpretive, aimed at
informing practitioners and defusing tensions (Norcross et al.,
2006a). We recognize, however, that passive dissemination of
EBP materials will prove insufficient to bring about real change
(see Chapter 10).

This book represents movement from the preparation stage to
the action stage of EBPs by providing practical how-to applications. We hope to trigger change in individual behavior that will
ultimately evoke broader professional change in mental health
and addictions practice. Medicine has seen this occur as insurers
and government agencies begin to designate preferred providers. For example, some hospitals with better surgical outcomes
for specific procedures have won preferred provider designations
by some payers. Of course, debate will center on the appropriateness of outcome variables. Most of us would prefer reduced
symptoms, absence of side effects, and improved quality of life
as outcomes but fear that some payers in the health-care industry will value cost of services more highly than patient-centered
variables. Health-care costs decrease when surgical outcomes
go well and no additional hospitalizations or expensive tests

are required. Subsequent health-care costs also drop when the patient dies in surgery.

Managed care organizations and other third-party payers have begun to deploy their own outcome measures for subscribers utilizing medical, mental health, and substance abuse services. Some refer to this as a "quality assurance plan," but others describe it as a **pay-for-performance (P4P)** plan intended to improve the quality of health care. The P4P programs yield valuable outcome data but also pose significant implementation concerns (Bachman, 2006) and ethical challenges (e.g., collection of large databases filled with confidential information that patients may prefer not to disclose to their insurance company). In addition, outcome measures designed by and for third-party payers will likely raise the same questions highlighted in our opening chapter: What data will best validate the preferred outcome for which patients?

Risk Management and Evidence-Based Practices

Risk management uses retrospective evaluation for the prospective assessment of practice hazards. Risk management may involve addressing ethical violations, carelessness, simple errors, or even unfortunate outcomes without any actual negligence. The key to basic risk management requires understanding standards of care.

From a legal perspective, the clinician must possess and use the knowledge, skill, and care ordinarily possessed by members of the profession in good standing. From an ethical perspective, **standard of care** means the prevailing professional judgment of peers engaged in similar activities in similar circumstances, given the knowledge the clinician had or should have had at the time. From a risk management perspective, EBP, when properly implemented, tends to lower one's risk of adverse incident.

Since we must adapt EBP to fit individual patients, how much risk does adaptation or innovation with established protocols incur? Conservative decision making often proves safest and most faithful to the established practice, but one can quite reasonably take prudent risks when they offer good probability of improving treatment outcomes without substantially increasing risk of harm. Prudent risk taking implies collegial consultation and good documentation. Such steps enable the clinician to demonstrate that good care was provided; that the clinician behaved as a competent, prudent professional; and that he or she engaged in ethically sound conduct, consistent with law and the standard of care.

As an example of prudent risk taking, let us consider Annique's return to psychotherapy. As in treating any depressed patient, the usual standard of care would include inquiring about suicidal ideation. Suppose that Annique's therapist asks and she reports that she has "thought about it from time to time." This response would trigger additional questions from the prudent practitioner. Let us assume that further inquiry reveals the following: Annique has no history of suicide attempts, has not formulated a plan, has articulated the importance of and delight she takes in interacting with her young grandchild, and has forged a positive alliance. In this context, one could reasonably rate her risk of self-harm as low and put aside any thoughts of seeking inpatient treatment.

Another example focused on Francesco might involve the clinician making a collateral referral to a community agency providing blue-collar job placement. Some clinicians might wonder "Will I offend him by suggesting he ought to be looking for work? Will he feel uncomfortable about returning to therapy if he does not follow the suggestion? Will his anxiety increase if the program rejects him?" All of these questions do raise potential risks, but they are worth taking. By making such a referral, the clinician conveys an interest in addressing Francesco's sources of anxiety and demonstrates a concern that reaches beyond the traditional domain of the therapeutic relationship.

Keep in mind that the greatest risk may be to stop taking any risks—with the end result that EBPs may stifle creative, innovative, and nimble practice. Clinicians must remain responsive and innovative. The challenge involves blending innovation with empiricism. Either extreme—too much risk or too little restraint, on the one hand, or too rule- and research-bound, on the other—probably harms patients.

Mistakes versus Negligence

People cannot avoid making mistakes, but a mistake does not equal negligence. Practitioners can and will make "judgment call" errors. We need not attain perfection but must strive to be at least a "good enough clinician" (Bennett et al., 2007). The two terms that signify the most risk are **departure from standard of care** and **gross negligence**. A practice representing *departure from standard of care* means that many practitioners would not do it, while *gross negligence* represents an extreme departure from usual professional conduct. In this sense, implementing EBP as a result of cogent reasoning and thoughtful consultation will tend to insulate the practitioner from risks associated with lawsuits and licensing board complaints alleging negligence.

For a lawsuit to succeed, a plaintiff's attorney must generally prove the **four Ds of legal liability**: *d*ereliction of *d*uty leading *d*irectly to *d*amages (Bennett et al., 2007).

- A duty applies when the clinician agrees to provide services to the patient and they begin to work together in a professional relationship.
- Dereliction implies a breach of duty and, by extension, negligence. Dereliction or negligence may include acts of commission (e.g., as Jonathon attempts to leap from the therapist's desk, he breaks a prized clock; the angry clinician attempts to restrain the child and, grabbing his arm, causes Jonathan to fall, sustaining a fracture in the process) or acts of omission (e.g., failure to inquire about whether Annique has any thoughts of suicide during three sessions, only to learn that she subsequently killed herself).
- Attorneys usually attempt to demonstrate direct causation using a doctrine of proximal cause. In so doing they will seek to prove that the clinician's negligence led directly (or proximally contributed) to the harm suffered by the patient.
- In order to document damages, the plaintiff's attorney will use actual invoices (e.g., hospital bills or fees paid to subsequent therapists) or experts (e.g., a forensic economist to testify about the lifetime earnings lost

by Annique's death or the toll on her spouse for loss of consortium).

You can take charge of your practice and reduce the likelihood of a lawsuit by (Bennett et al., 2007):

♦ maintaining a working knowledge of ethics codes and legal standards governing practice
♦ conservatively evaluating your competence to perform
♦ maintaining intellectual, technical, and emotional competence
♦ documenting your actions and consultation with peers
♦ keeping your knowledge up to date

At times you may have to consider termination of a client whose behavior becomes risky or prevents you from delivering optimal care. For example, if Jonathon failed to improve after rigorous efforts with an EBP for externalizing behaviors and his parents still declined to consider medication, you should consider the ethical obligation to terminate or refer a client who has not benefited from your efforts. A similar situation might occur if Annique ceased taking her medication and experienced a worsening depression, despite your best therapeutic efforts.

Liability and Innovation

If we only conduct EBP, how will innovation occur? What standards apply when attempting to assess liability and innovation in patient care? One clear standard involves what courts regard as scientifically acceptable evidence.

The ruling in *Daubert v. Merrell Dow Pharmaceuticals, Inc.* (1993) provides some valuable guidance. Prior to that case the standard for introducing scientific evidence in court was *general acceptance*, sometimes known as the Frye standard, dating from 1923. The *Daubert* case focused on the admissibility of novel scientific evidence in federal courts and firmly established the judge as gatekeeper to ensure that any evidence considered in court has both relevance and reliability.

In the *Daubert* case the families of two boys born with birth defects sued Merrell Dow Pharmaceuticals, claiming that the drug doxylamine succinate (Bendectin), used to treat morning sickness, caused the defects. Merrell Dow's expert witness planned to testify that no published scientific studies demonstrated a link between Bendectin and birth defects. Plaintiffs' counsel submitted expert evidence of its own suggesting that Bendectin could potentially cause human birth defects. However, that evidence came from laboratory studies using cell cultures and laboratory animals, reanalysis of other published studies, and methodologies that had not yet gained acceptance within the general scientific community. Furthermore, the court seemed skeptical because the plaintiffs' evidence appeared to have been generated solely for the purpose of the litigation. Without their questionable evidence, the court doubted that the plaintiffs could prove at a trial that the Bendectin had, in fact, caused the birth defects. In essence, the court doubted the methodological validity and generalizability of the evidence used to prove the drug caused the problem. (Parenthetically, this case also provides a good example of a scientific question for which we could not conduct a true randomized clinical trial [RCT]. After all, we could not ethically use random assignment of nauseous pregnant women to a

Bendectin treatment condition if we had any reason to suspect birth defects might result.)

The *Daubert* standard had three key provisions:

1. Expert testimony must have a scientific basis.
2. The scientific knowledge must assist the trier of fact (the judge or jury) in understanding or determining a fact at issue in the case.
3. The judge makes the determination regarding whether the scientific knowledge would indeed assist by ruling whether the reasoning or methodology underlying the testimony stands as scientifically valid and whether that reasoning or methodology properly can be applied to the facts at issue.

The judge's preliminary assessment can focus on whether something has undergone testing, whether an idea has passed scientific peer review or achieved publication in scientific journals, falsifiability and error rates involved in the technique, and even general acceptance, in certain circumstances. The judicial decision focuses on methodology and principles, not the ultimate conclusions generated. Federal courts have strictly applied the standards in *Daubert*, and they have succeeded in excluding "junk science" or "pseudoscience," as well as techniques that qualify as merely experimental.

These standards can assist clinicians facing criticism of their approach or forced to defend an innovation or EBP adaptation in practice by suggesting criteria to guide their efforts. By demonstrating that one's approach has a grounding in valid and reliable science, passes peer review, or has won general acceptance by peer practitioners, the treatment method, prevention program, or assessment measure in question has passed a legal acceptance threshold (at least as evidence).

 Hyperlink to *Daubert* decision.

Ethical Considerations

In a subsequent "junk science" case (*Kumho Tire Co., Ltd. v. Carmichael*, 1999), the courts ultimately excluded a technician's testimony that an exploding tire must have caused an accident because he could find no other reason for the tire's failure. In other words, the technician asserted a causal relationship based on an absence of data. The message for potential mental health innovators: Predicate new approaches on proven foundations, collect pilot data on interventions suspected of being effective, and consider sources of error when attempting to generalize from population to population or setting to setting. Once again, the key to acceptance of science in the courtroom is reliable and valid scientific knowledge.

Suppose Francesco establishes a solid therapeutic alliance with a new clinician who has effectively used EBPs to help bring his anxiety and substance abuse under control. Francesco's referral to the job training program has won him steady employment with health insurance at a new automobile assembly plant across the state. Francesco wants to continue in treatment to consolidate his gains but says he only trusts you. After all, you've helped turn his life around. He wants to continue treatment with you by telephone after he relocates. We may not have an RCT to demonstrate the efficacy of continuity of treatment by telephone, nor will we likely ever have it. Even if we could set up a scientific study of this practice, Francesco would never agree to randomization, and neither would other patients who have solid alliances with their clinicians. One could easily advance ethical arguments against such a study. We do know, however, that Francesco has a therapeutic relationship of proven effectiveness and apparently strong motivation to persist along the same lines. We can certainly make a reasonable argument in favor of attempting the innovative follow up treatment.

Ethics and Evidence-Based Practices

The key ethical considerations in EBP revolve chiefly around matters of competence, consent, and public statements. The American Psychological Association's ethics code (APA, 2002) covers these issues very well. We shall use the APA as an exemplar for the various codes of mental health and addictions professions, and we provide hyperlinks to the ethics codes in the accompanying CD. The central EBP elements of all professional ethics codes focus on basic questions of practitioner competence, patients' sense of autonomy or self-determination as afforded via consent, and the accuracy of public statements about our services.

 Ethics codes of mental health and addiction associations.

Competence

As a starting point, we must remain mindful that the ethics codes of all the mental health professions demand that clinicians have both the scientific and professional skills needed to serve their patients. Our knowledge of the evidence for our chosen treatment method versus other potential methods must have a scientific foundation. The APA code states (section 2.03) "Psychologists undertake ongoing efforts to develop and maintain their competence" and later (2.04) "Psychologists' work is based upon established scientific and professional knowledge of the discipline."

Clinicians have an obligation to work only within the boundaries of their competence, based on education, training, supervised experience, consultation, study, or professional experience. This requires us to remain cautious when evaluating our own expertise. In conducting a new EBP, a professional would need to acquire competence, not merely passing familiarity with it. Reading a treatment manual would probably not constitute sufficient preparation to establish competence. In addition to the strategies and tactics associated with particular approaches, the clinician needs a thorough understanding of psychopathology, diagnostic assessment, and individual differences in order to properly assess and treat the patient. True competence requires a degree of self-awareness that helps us to feel confident of what we know, while recognizing what we do not know.

In some situations, requirements for additional knowledge and integration skills might apply. Each of our index cases, for example, displays somatic features that require the clinician to have, or acquire through consultation, some medical knowledge.

Jonathon may experience an exacerbation of agitation, manifesting hyperactivity as a side effect of albuterol, his asthma medication. Francesco may suffer from medical symptoms related to his history of alcohol abuse. Hormonal changes associated with Annique's menopausal condition may contribute to her mood disorder.

Another subset of competence involves the ability to tailor EBP to the needs of individuals (see also Chapter 8). Where our scientific or professional knowledge establishes that factors associated with age, gender, race, ethnicity, culture, religion, sexual orientation, disability, language, or socioeconomic status in a patient differ from the background of patients described in the research on the EBP in question, we must stand prepared to adapt specific EBPs to reflect the needs, values, and preferences of the particular patient at hand. This may require clinicians to obtain the training, experience, consultation, or supervision necessary to ensure the competence of their services or to make an appropriate referral.

At the same time, we must recognize that no professional will know everything and that the patient's ideal match may not sit waiting for a call. Suppose that Francesco's first language was Spanish, Annique's was Creole, and Jonathon's was Serbo-Croatian. Suppose they are immigrants, perhaps even undocumented; or they may be witnesses to or victims of violence. Now suppose that they present in your office with a moderate level of English proficiency seeking help, and no other mental health or substance abuse professional lives within a reasonable commuting distance. You have a solid knowledge of EBPs that apply to their problem but have never treated anyone exactly like them before. If you stand prepared to listen and learn from your patients and their families (or to consult with others who have special knowledge you lack), you may well have the ability to apply EBPs in ways likely to generalize to and benefit the clients. Doing so remains ethically appropriate with the client's consent, after acknowledging any limitations or constraints.

Consent

When practitioners conduct any professional service, they must obtain the consent of the patient(s). Note from the outset that we have not inserted the adjective "informed" in front of the noun "consent." Doing so actually creates a tautology or redundancy since consent must, by definition, constitute a knowing and voluntary act. The accepted standard holds that, before they can give consent, people must have all of the information that might reasonably influence their willingness to participate in the task at hand. The information must be in a form (language, format, and reading level) that enables them to reasonably grasp it. In addition, the recipient of the information must have the legal authority and personal competence (not comatose or severely cognitively impaired) to make and give voice to the decision.

One can only give consent for oneself, so when a parent or legal guardian authorizes treatment for their child or ward, they have given permission (sometimes called "proxy consent" by ethicists). When the patient lacks the legal competence to give consent because of age or mental impairment, practitioners must nevertheless provide an appropriate explanation, seek the patient's assent, and consider the patient's preferences and best interests.

Competent patients have a right to refuse treatment in most circumstances. Exceptions apply to some patients who pose an urgent threat to themselves or to others or who are incarcerated. Suppose that we recommend a trial of stimulant medication for Jonathon, disulfiram (Antabuse) for Francesco, and lithium for Annique. Now suppose that the adult patients and Jonathon's parents, concerned about potential side effects, say "No, thank you." Some patients may raise religious objections to some interventions. For example, members of the Jehovah's Witness (objections to blood products), Seventh-Day Adventist (objections to hypnosis), and Christian Science (preference for spiritual intervention) faiths may object to specific medical and/or behavioral interventions. Conversely, Jonathon may object to some aspects of a treatment program such as "time-outs" or medication, but his parents have the right to trump his preferences.

Consent with respect to EBP involves active efforts to inform participants of the nature of treatment, potential side effects (if any), and alternative treatments. Enthusiastic proponents of particular EBPs may feel so positively about their interventions that they do not take adequate time to fully discuss the treatment plan with the patient. In almost every case, taking the time to discuss the treatment will actively engage the client in the treatment process, while allowing opportunities for any reservations to emerge. Viewing the consent process as part of forging a therapeutic relationship, rather than an "ethical chore," will prove highly effective.

Advertising and Other Public Statements

A final important ethical consideration entails avoiding false or deceptive public statements about our work, including touting the merits of particular EBPs or criticizing other practitioners. In this context, public statements include paid or unpaid advertising, product endorsements, licensing applications, brochures, printed matter, directory listings, personal resumes, media comments, statements in legal proceedings, oral presentations, and published materials.

Clinicians should not knowingly make public statements that directly or indirectly convey false, deceptive, or fraudulent content. Examples include the following:

- ◆ "Scientific research demonstrates that my treatment is the most effective for anxiety disorders" (an assertion highly unlikely to be accurate without numerous qualifying statements).
- ◆ "Those EBP cognitive behavioral therapies do not produce any lasting changes, and almost always result in relapse or symptom substitution" (yet research demonstrates that many EBPs frequently can and do yield lasting beneficial changes).
- ◆ One of our personal favorites involved a clinician, we'll call him "Jones," who tacked a letter on to the front of a well-known EBP acronym and touted "JCBT—a breakthrough therapy for depression!" It seems that "JCBT" stood for "Jones cognitive behavior therapy," meaning cognitive behavior therapy as performed by him. Unless you asked, you might never learn what the "J" stood for or that he had no data whatever to support his claim.

The key to good ethical practice in EBP (as a subset of mental health and substance abuse practice) centers on clinician competence, full consent, and accurate public statements supportable by hard data.

Key Terms

actuarial judgment
arbitrary metrics
audit
benchmarks
criterion problem
departure from standard
   of care

four Ds of legal liability
gross negligence
heuristics
pay-for-performance (P4P)
practice guidelines
risk management
standard of care

Recommended Readings and Web Sites

Beutler, L. E., & Harwood, T. M. (2000). *Prescriptive psychotherapy: A practical guide to systematic treatment selection.* New York: Oxford University Press.

Cone, J. D. (2000). *Evaluating outcomes: Empirical tools for effective practice.* Washington, DC: American Psychological Association.

Gilovich, T., Griffin, D., & Kahneman, D. (Eds.). (2002). *Heuristics and biases: The psychology of intuitive judgment.* New York: Cambridge University Press.

Hunsley, J., & Lee, C. M. (2007). Research-informed benchmarks for psychological treatments: Efficacy studies, effectiveness studies, and beyond. *Professional Psychology: Research and Practice, 38,* 21–33.

Kahneman, D., & Tversky, A. (Eds.). (2000). *Choices, values, and frames.* New York: Cambridge University Press.

Koocher, G. P., & Keith-Spiegel, P. (2008). *Ethical principles in psychology and the mental health professions: Standards and cases.* New York: Oxford University Press.

National Guideline Clearinghouse, www.guideline.gov

National Institute for Health and Clinical Excellence, www.nice.org.uk

▌▌▐▐▐
CHAPTER 10

Disseminating, Teaching, and Implementing Evidence-Based Practices

The international juggernaut of evidence-based practices (EBPs) has now affected every health-care profession and has increasingly found its way into education and training programs. One can scarcely review announcements for new books or forthcoming journal articles without encountering the tag of *evidence-based*. Accompanying this progress we find a cornucopia of online materials and tools for teaching EBPs (and EBM); simply try any search engine and you will instantly locate hundreds. One can now complete an entire course, secure a certificate, and even obtain a graduate degree in EBPs.

Ironically, despite jumping onto the EBP bandwagon, many of the training tutorials and courses offer no research evidence for their own effectiveness in teaching or implementing EBPs! Having learned from their experience, we begin this chapter with synopses of the empirical research on predicting adoption of EBPs and the research-based principles of effective education. We then turn our attention to specific methods for disseminating, teaching, and implementing EBPs.

Who Is Drawn Toward EBPs?

A small but growing stream of empirical studies has examined the predictors of practitioners' propensity to use EBP and EBM (e.g., Aarons, 2006; Bridges, 2003; Gotham, 2004; Jette et al., 2003; Nelson & Steele, 2007; Pagoto et al., 2007; Sheehan et al., 2007). The studies uniformly find that practitioners continue to rely on the traditional (i.e., non-EBP) information sources of clinical experience, peer opinions, and textbooks. Far fewer practitioners look first to practice guidelines, Cochrane Collaboration Reviews, and related EBP sources.

Across studies, the significant predictors of adopting EBPs and/or expressing positive attitudes toward them include the practitioner's

- ◆ desire to learn and openness to new practices
- ◆ training in EBP, such as taking an EBP class
- ◆ favorable opinion of treatment research
- ◆ perceived receptivity of the workplace toward EBPs
- ◆ supervisors' modeling of, and reinforcement for using, EBPs
- ◆ perception that EBP can be used in daily practice without detracting from clinical productivity (practicality)
- ◆ employment in (or planning a career in) research

- younger age (the only demographic variable that predicts)
- more formal eduction and attainment of a higher degree

While practitioner variables are influential, so too are organizational and economic factors; but these generally prove more difficult to detect in survey studies. Organizations that facilitate learning EBPs by providing release time and in-house training, for example, are more likely to sustain EBPs than organizations primarily concerned with short-term cost containment. Practice settings with high burnout rates, for another example, are unlikely to be conducive to learning EBPs, which often require stepping outside one's comfort zone and acquiring new skills with the support and consultation of colleagues (Addis, 2002).

Negative predictors of EBP use include practitioner age, amount of time spent in direct patient care, negative opinions about treatment research, lack of access to EBP resources at work, and absence of explicit training in EBP. Indeed, the principal barrier appears not to be skepticism but rather a lack of knowledge of EBP and its core skills.

Evidence-Based Practice in Teaching

Several sets of researchers have painstakingly reviewed the thousands of empirical studies on effective teaching in higher education. They converge on several conclusions. Good EBP in higher education (Chickering & Gamson, 1987)

- encourages contacts between students and faculty
- develops reciprocity and cooperation among students

- uses active learning techniques
- gives prompt feedback
- emphasizes time on task
- communicates high expectations
- respects diverse talents and ways of learning

Please note the conspicuous *absence* of several time-honored traditions in education: the extended lecture, the moral exhortation (without skill building), the single bullet or method, and the busy work (without impact or practicality).

As we transition in this chapter into presenting specific methods of training in EBPs, keep these broad evidence-based principles in mind and avoid resorting to discredited educational practices. In other words, let us become evidence-based about teaching evidence-based practices.

Three Training Steps

Getting clinicians to use EBPs in daily practice consists of three distinct but overlapping training steps. The first step involves **dissemination**, which entails raising awareness of EBP resources and their availability, particularly the supporting research evidence. Clinicians need to know about the availability, accessibility, and utility of resources. The second step entails teaching the requisite core EBP skills to competence. Clinicians need to know how to do EBP. And the third step requires **implementation**, which involves getting evidence routinely used in practice. Clinicians need to implement EBP in their daily work. Different strategies and different stakeholders are invoked at each step.

Disseminating Evidence-Based Practices

Reviews of the empirical research on dissemination of EBPs uniformly conclude that passive dissemination of EBP materials by itself exerts no significant effect on practitioner behavior (e.g., National Implementation Research Network, 2005; NHS Centre for Reviews and Dissemination, 1999). In a systematic review of 102 trials on methods to improve health-care practice, for example, the authors (Oxman et al., 1995) concluded that dissemination-only activities result in little or no behavior change.

The findings have directed EBP training efforts in crucial ways. For one, dissemination of information alone does *not* result in positive implementation outcomes (changes in practitioner behavior) or treatment outcomes (benefits to consumers). Only the naive will believe that when research information becomes available, busy clinicians will access, appraise, and then routinely apply it. Dissemination-alone strategies are largely discredited and should be abandoned. For another, practitioner training proves more effective than information dissemination alone (National Implementation Research Network, 2005). Thus, we should focus on actively teaching the EBP skills—to which we now turn—and then on systems implementation—to which we turn in a few moments.

Teaching Evidence-Based Practices

To insure competence in EBPs requires explicit teaching and evaluation of the requisite skills. Consider the task of teaching complex psychotherapy skills to mental health and addiction professionals. Let's use the example of motivational interviewing (Miller & Rollnick, 2002), an evidence-based treatment for patients such as Francesco who deny or minimize their substance abuse. The developers of motivational interviewing have systematically evaluated their teaching methods. The least effective teaching method involved doing nothing: a wait-list control group. Self-guided training proved more effective than nothing. Attending a clinical workshop was superior to self-guided training, but participating in a workshop plus practice was better still. The most effective teaching method involved participating in a workshop plus practice and coaching (Miller et al., 2004).

Learning EBPs will prove more challenging than learning motivational interviewing because it consists of multiple skill sets. Indeed, EBP is both a conceptual framework and a skill set for clinical decision making. In what follows, we offer teaching tips for explaining the EBP conceptual framework and imparting the EBP core skills.

Conceptual Framework
The conceptual framework is the professional expectation and individual commitment to incorporate the best available research into clinical practice. We fondly characterize our 15-minute talk on the central points as "Science is a candle in the dark" (Sagan, 1997). More than 15 minutes tends to generate student sighs, yawns, and eye rolling. A compressed outline and sprinkling of examples of our talk includes these points:

♦ Health care historically relied on nonresearch sources of information. In early days, practitioners followed theoretical doctrine, charismatic pioneers, subjective preferences, and clinical judgments. In modern days, practitioners increasingly look to empirical research to counter inevitable biases, clinical heuristics, and nonprobabilistic thinking.

♦ Controlled research is incomplete and imperfect, of course, but remains superior to the alternatives. It represents our best, self-correcting method for making judicious and accurate decisions. The human mind tends to draw causality from coincidences; controlled research reliably tells us what works. (We then integrate recent examples from the mass media, for example, the controversies concerning hormone replacement therapy and the alleged curative value of magnets, for which randomized clinical trial [RCT] results resolved ambiguity.)

♦ Much of what we now practice derives from empirical research, largely but not exclusively RCTs. Compelling examples from mental health and the addictions include the superiority of actuarial judgment over clinical judgment in reaching diagnoses (Meehl, 1954); the comparability of outcomes obtained with psychoanalysis and briefer psychoanalytic psychotherapy (Wallerstein, 1986); the efficacy of teaching relapse prevention to addicted populations (Marlatt & Gordon, 1985); the inadvisability of using anatomically detailed dolls or puppets to determine whether or not a child experienced sexual abuse (Koocher et al., 1995); the centrality of the therapeutic relationship in predicting and causally contributing to successful psychotherapy outcomes (Norcross, 2002a, 2002b); and the ineffectiveness of various forms of confrontation in treating substance abuse (Miller et al., 2003).

♦ All of these robust research findings initially elicited claims of "impossible!" Computers and statistical formulas will never outpredict the experienced human clinician—never! Psychoanalysis obviously outperforms briefer therapies; the latter will obviously lead to symptom substitution and only fleeting improvement. Relapse prevention will only "encourage relapse" rather than actually reduce the number of relapses. Many of today's standard clinical practices were initially branded as dubious, impossible, or heretical in the past.

◆ Follow the guideposts of research when incorporating them into clinical practice. Research informs us that collaborating with patients and reaching goal consensus lead to improved outcomes (Tryon & Winograd, 2002). Tailoring treatment to the individual patient, his or her preferences, and his or her characteristics also improves outcomes (Norcross, 2002a). Research also guides us in blending our clinical expertise and patient preferences. In fact, research has been conducted to alert us to those situations when clinical expertise might preempt the best available research. The EBP mantra of best available research, clinical expertise, and patient values hails directly and powerfully from the evidence!

◆ We should never consider EBP an academic exercise. On the contrary, it immediately helps you and your patients. EBP improves outcomes for your individual patients as well as the health of the population. Effect sizes and probability values, we must remember, translate into vital human statistics: happier and healthier people.

Core Skills

As featured throughout the preceding chapters, the core skills consist of formulating a specific, answerable clinical question

(Chapter 2); accessing the best available research (Chapter 3); appraising critically that research evidence (Chapters 4–6); translating that research into practice with a particular patient (Chapter 7); integrating the clinician's expertise and patient's characteristics with the research (Chapter 8); and evaluating the effectiveness of the entire process (Chapter 9). Each of these core skills requires mastery by means of practice, coaching, and then implementation to insure they continue.

The research evidence indicates that we can best teach each EBP skill by (National Implementation Research Network, 2005; NHS Centre for Reviews and Dissemination, 1999)

- emphasizing practice of new skills
- using feedback on practice to teach the finer points
- helping trainees integrate thinking and doing during practice sessions (didactic training tends to be linear, while practice tends to be multidimensional and dynamic)
- providing guidance with respect to the boundaries of using a particular treatment, describing when it may be useful and when it may not be useful
- encouraging flexible use of the method (within fidelity)

In addition, clinical teachers of EBP (and EBM) have shared their favorite principles and strategies for helping students acquire the core skills (e.g., Wyer et al., 2004; Straus et al., 2005; Spring & Walker, 2007). Here's a sampling of their—and our—favorites.

- Dispute common myths about EBPs early so that students do not bring their contagious, learning-interfering resistances with them; Table 10.1 provides 12 myths about EBPs in mental health and addictions.

Table 10.1. **Twelve Myths about EBPs in Mental Health and Addictions**

EBPs result in clinical work drained of individuality and creativity; they offer nothing but mindless cookbooks.

EBPs will stifle empathic, warm relationships; they ignore the patient–therapist relationship.

EBPs pertain only to cognitive-behavioral treatments in mental health; insight-oriented and relationship-based therapies are not and can never become EBPs.

EBPs comprise financial rules to deprive practitioners of reimbursement and patients of services.

EBPs apply to doctoral-level, research-producing professionals, not direct-care practitioners.

EBPs ignore clinical expertise and patient preferences.

EBPs focus solely on knowledge gained from randomized clinical trials.

EBPs have arrived on the scene prematurely; we simply do not have sufficient research to guide us yet.

EBPs rarely, if ever, generalize to real-world patients; "my patients are different" from all those used in research studies.

EBPs cannot be taught and will not catch on with senior clinicians; practitioners do not alter their clinical behavior.

EBPs dismiss self-help groups, such as Alcoholics Anonymous and other 12-step groups.

EBPs apply only to psychotherapy, not to assessment, prevention, diagnosis, and other critical decisions.

From Norcross, Beutler, & Levant (2006a); Pagoto et al., 2007; Collins, Leffingwell, & Belar (2007).

Clinician's Guide to Evidence-Based Practices

- Make EBPs practical, relevant, and immediate by using students' real-time cases; historical examples and the teacher's cases hold less relevance and fewer rewards for the learner.
- Capitalize on students' natural curiosity and enthusiasm for helping: Once students realize that we do not expect them to calculate statistics or perform research, they will more likely become highly engaged.
- Role model EBPs in your own work; for example, when you encounter a difficult case, ask aloud about the underlying causes of the disorder, locate and appraise the research evidence, and discuss how the research does and does not apply to the specific patient.
- Teach to the learners' needs: Just as different patients require different strokes, your students will begin at different places, with disparate needs, motivations, and preferences.
- Work as an EBP team: Divide up the learning tasks and ask everyone to be responsible for a task.
- Use online tutorials to supplement instruction; two sample tutorials for mental health and addictions are Evidence-Based Practice for the Helping Professions at www.evidence.brookscole.com and the Centre for Evidence-Based Mental Health at www.cebmh.com/.
- Orient clinic conferences, morning reports, and daily patient discussions around EBPs; to be sure, retain the typical sharing of clinical expertise with similar patients but also strive to infuse the best available

research via literature searches, Cochrane Reviews, practice guidelines, and so on.

♦ Develop journal clubs around EBPs: Learn about advances that should change our practice and/or how to handle vexing patient problems by using the best evidence.

♦ Teach with an eye toward lifelong learning: The goal should focus beyond practicing EBP a few times during training to inculcate a lifetime commitment.

This commitment to transfer of training, from initial training to daily practice, characterizes the most successful teaching of EBP. We seek both **maintenance**—consolidation and continuation of behavior change across time, usually after the training ends—and **generalization**—continuation of behavior change across practice settings, other than those included in training.

Fortunately, from educational and treatment research, we know a fair bit about how to accomplish maintenance and generalization (Kazdin, 2001). The following methods should be built into training programs from the beginning:

♦ Employ incentives that the natural environment already provides for conducting EBP.

♦ Involve the entire system of clinical and administrative staff; a single practitioner should not be a lone EBP wolf.

♦ Gradually, not abruptly, fade or discontinue the training program.

♦ Make the training situation as similar to the practice environment as possible.

- Begin with continuous and rich incentives for using EBPs, but then thin and delay them.
- Use peers and staff to facilitate continued use of EBPs.
- Assess and attend to slips back into previous non-EBP behavior.
- Extend the length of training; brief training typically produces less maintenance and generalization.
- Add reminders and occasional booster training.

In all these ways, we can maintain the core EBP skills over time and generalize them to other practice settings.

Mnemonics

Teachers and supervisors have developed mnemonics to provide easy and memorable ways for students to remember the EBP core skills. Some students (and teachers) appreciate the convenient tool to recall the EBP steps, particularly in the early phase of training. Others find it too cute or simplistic.

In EBM, these are popularly known as the **five As**: *a*sk (a clinical question), *a*ccess (the research literature), *a*ppraise (the research), *a*pply (the research to a particular case), and *a*ssess (the effectiveness of the entire EBP process). In case conferences, clinical supervision, or staff meetings, the professionals are asked to "work" the five As.

In mental health and addictions, the appraisal skill demands more detailed deliberations and more complicated decisions. For this reason, we have divided the skill among three chapters (6, 7, 8) and have concomitantly expanded the mnemonic. In our teaching and supervision, we use **AAA TIE** (or **triple A TIE**): *a*sk a specific clinical question, *a*ccess the research literature, *a*ppraise the research literature for its value, *t*ranslate the research into practice, *i*ntegrate the patient and the clinician with the research, and *e*valuate the entire process (including ethics).

Implementing Evidence-Based Practices

Training practitoners is effective in initial acquisition of EBP skills but will not guarantee incorporation into daily practice. Nor does training individual practitioners automatically yield EBP implementation throughout a unit or system of health care. But longer-term, multilevel implementation can maximize practitioners' behavior change and thus enhance health-care outcomes.

Here's what the research evidence—now totaling hundreds of individual studies—indicates will facilitate longer-term, multilevel implementation of EBPs (Greenhalgh et al., 2004; NIRN, 2005; NHS Centre for Reviews and Dissemination, 1999):

- ◆ Begin by conducting a readiness analysis of the system to identify factors likely to influence the proposed change.
- ◆ Secure the participation of local opinion leaders in the system or surrounding community.
- ◆ Collaborate with all the key stakeholders, including clinicians, consumers, family members, supervisors, insurance organizations, and mental health authorities.
- ◆ Avoid single-bullet and time-limited interventions.
- ◆ Offer training to the entire staff (as described in the previous section).

- Offer training for trainers (and staff leaders) to maximize learning.
- Create peer support to build a culture of acceptance and support.
- Provide administrative and financial resources to sustain the changes.
- Build the PICO framework into record sheets, intake forms, and written documentation.
- Use patient-specific reminders at the point of care for prompting EBPs.
- Assess and track staff **fidelity** in using the EBPs.
- Monitor and evaluate the implementation.
- Reinforce and provide incentives for behavior changes toward EBPs.
- Insist that the new EBPs are conducted with fidelity before adapting to fit local needs; "first do it right, then do it differently."

A case in point is the successful large-scale implementation of evidence-based treatments for children in the state of Hawaii (Chorpita et al., 2002). A multidisciplinary, academic-practice panel reviewed the vast literature on psychosocial treatments for childhood anxiety disorders, depression, ADHD, conduct disorders, and autistic disorder. The panel established a mental health system–university–parent partnership in working toward the design of practice guidelines. Subsequently, the state mental health system authorized a series of training workshops to provide practitioners with the skills to conduct the identified treatments and then revised a number of policies to support the continuing use of EBPs with children. All told, multiple stakeholders and multiple levels were involved in disseminating, teaching, and then implementing EBPs.

Consider as well the multiple structures and supports provided at three implementation levels (external, organizational, and individual) in Ohio. That state, like practically all states, is implementing several mental health and substance abuse EBPs. Ohio worked at each level of influence to facilitate implementation of integrated dual disorders treatment by state-contracted agencies and the state hospital system (Gotham, 2006). Externally, the state provided 2-year grants to nine treatment settings to insure implementation and support. Organizationally, the state provided consultation to the sites in the form of readiness assessments, implementation plans, site visits, fidelity self-studies, and outcomes monitoring. Individually, practitioners received a wide array of training, including statewide conferences, intensive on-site training, monthly follow-ups, and clinical supervision. That's precisely the type of longer-term, multilevel implementation that maximizes practitioners' behavior change and thus enhances health-care outcomes.

Implementation of EBP within health-care systems occurs in predictable stages: exploration, adoption, program installation, initial implementation, full operation, innovation, and then sustainability (NIRN, 2005). Think of systems implementation as a gradual process of behavior change, akin to a patient moving through the stages of change: precontemplation, contemplation, preparation, action, and maintenance (Prochaska, Norcross, & DiClemente, 1995, 2005). Each stage represents a period of time as well as a set of tasks needed for movement to the next stage. We need to consider the organization's readiness to change because each stage and each system will require something a little different. Thus, like EBPs themselves, we must sensitively integrate the best research evidence, clinical expertise, and staff characteristics and preferences into deciding what works for EBP implementation in each unique health-care system.

Key Terms

AAA TIE (or triple A TIE)
dissemination
fidelity
five As

generalization
implementation
maintenance

Recommended Readings and Web Sites

Addiction Technology Transfer Center, www.nattc.org/index.html

Gibbs, L., Armstrong, E. C., Raleigh, D., & Jones, J. (2003). *Evidence-based practice for the helping professions*, www.evidence.brookscole.com

Gotham, H. J. (2004). Diffusion of mental health and substance abuse treatments: Development, dissemination, and implementation. *Clinical Psychology: Science and Practice, 11,* 160–176.

Institute for Behavioral Research. Organizational Readiness for Change, www.ibr.tcu.edu/evidence/evi-orc.html

National Implementation Research Network. (2005). *Implementation research: A synthesis of the literature*, nirn.fmhi.usf.edu

NHS Centre for Reviews and Dissemination. (1999). *Getting evidence into practice*, www.york.ac.uk/inst/crd/ehc51.pdf

Spring, B., & Walker, B. B. (Eds.). (2007). Evidence-based practice in clinical psychology: Education and training issues. *Journal of Clinical Psychology, 63*(7).

Toolkits for Evidence-Based Practices. Shaping mental health services toward recovery, mentalhealth.samhsa.gov/cmhs/communitysupport/toolkits/about.asp

Wyer, P. C., Keitz, S., Hatala, R., Hayward, R., Barratt, A., Montori, V., et al. (2004). Tips for learning and teaching evidence-based medicine: Introduction to the series. *Canadian Medical Journal Association, 171,* 77–81.

▌▌ GLOSSARY ▌▌

***AAA TIE* (or *triple A TIE*)** In EBPs for mental health and addictions, a mnemonic for the core skills: *a*sk a specific clinical question; *a*ccess the research literature; *a*ppraise the research literature; *t*ranslate the research into practice; *i*ntegrate the patient and the clinician with the research; and *e*valuate the entire process, including ethics.

actuarial judgment Using numerical probabilities, as opposed to practitioner judgment, as a basis for clinical decisions; relies on empirically established statistical relationships between patient data and outcome.

adopt it, adapt it, or abandon it The three basic options for practitioners deciding how to proceed with a research-supported intervention in a particular case.

alpha level (α) A probability level (e.g., .05 or .01) used as a definition of a sufficiently low probability in a significance test that, if the obtained result falls below this level, the result is declared "significant."

analysis of covariance (ANCOVA) A type of analysis of variance which makes adjustments in the dependent variable used for comparing groups based on prior information about differences among the groups on some other variable.

analysis of variance (ANOVA) The technique(s) used to test the significance of main effects and interactions in a variety of research designs.

arbitrary metrics The problem of rating psychological constructs with arbitrary numbers. For example, patients can rate their self-esteem as 5 out of 7 on a 7-point scale and track relative shifts over time, but those scores tell us very little about the person in an absolute sense.

audit Examines the performance of practitioners or service units, usually in terms of patient outcome in comparison to clinical standards, which might be general benchmarks, other practitioners, or EBP guidelines. The goal of an audit is to create an ongoing feedback loop to refine and improve the EBP evaluation process.

background questions Broad clinical questions regarding general knowledge about disorders, tests, treatments, and other health-care matters; they typically specify a question root (with a verb) followed by a disorder, treatment, or other health-care issue. Contrast with **foreground questions.**

base rate The percentage of a population having a particular characteristic; in the clinical literature, often called the "prevalence rate."

benchmarks Use of comparative values that indicate desirable or "best practice" standards for assessing the effects of a service. In health care, benchmarking can address such matters as costs, staffing, waiting times, patient retention, and treatment outcomes.

best available research Clinically relevant research, often from basic health science, that will most likely yield accurate, unbiased, and relevant answers to the practice question posed for a particular patient or patient group. One of the three pillars of EBP.

bivariate outlier An aberrant or unusual data point falling well outside the relational pattern of other data points in a bivariate distribution.

Bonferroni correction A common method used to adjust the alpha level when more than one significance test is conducted within a single study. The correction involves dividing the nominal alpha level by the number of tests to be conducted.

Boolean operators Search commands used to logically connect search terms. The most common Boolean operators are AND, OR, and NOT.

Buros A common abbreviation for the *Mental Measurements Yearbook*, after its original editor, Oscar K. Buros. See also ***Mental Measurements Yearbook.***

case study method A research design that concentrates on just one or a very small number of cases, usually providing very detailed description.

clinical expertise Clinician skills that promote positive outcomes, including conducting assessments, developing diagnostic judgments, making clinical decisions, implementing treatments, monitoring patient progress, using interpersonal expertise, understanding cultural differences, and seeking available resources as needed. One of the three pillars of EBP.

cluster sample A sample drawn from a population that consists of predefined clusters or groups; then clusters are drawn from the population, each cluster including all of its constituent cases.

Cochrane Shorthand for the *Cochrane Database of Systematic Reviews*, a filtered database comprised of systematic reviews which identify and synthesize available randomized clinical trials on a given health-care topic.

Cohen's d A measure of effect size determined as the difference between two means divided by the pooled standard deviation for the two groups.

cohort A specified set of people with common characteristics followed over a specified period of time to determine the prevalence, etiology, complications, and/or prognosis of a disorder.

comorbid disorders Two or more disorders occurring simultaneously.

confidence interval (CI) An interval around a statistic (e.g., mean or correlation coefficient) within which the parameter estimated by the statistic should fall with a certain degree of probability, or an interval around an obtained test score within which the true score should fall with a certain degree of probability.

confound A variable associated with or varying with an independent variable so that the effect of the independent variable cannot be separated from possible effects of the confound.

convenience sample A sample obtained by including cases simply because the cases are conveniently available; contrasted with a probability sample.

core EBP skills In sequence, these practitioner competencies are: asking a specific clinical question, accessing the best available research, appraising critically the research evidence, translating that research into practice with a particular patient, integrating the clinician's expertise and patient's characteristics with the research, and evaluating the effectiveness of the entire process. See also **AAA TIE.**

correction for attenuation A statistical correction applied to a correlation coefficient to account for imperfect reliability in one or both variables entering the correlation.

criterion problem The difficulty of determining what constitutes appropriate criteria for determining effective treatment and who should decide on these.

critical appraisal The process of assessing and interpreting research evidence by systematically considering its relevance to an individual's work.

cultural adaptation Modification of clinical services and programs in ways that are culturally sensitive and that are tailored to a cultural group's worldviews.

cut-score The score on a test which divides groups into discrete categories.

ΔR^2 The change or difference in the multiple correlation squared when variables are added to or subtracted from the multiple regression equation. See also **multiple correlation.**

decision analysis An approach for making decisions under conditions of uncertainty by modeling the sequences or pathways of possible strategies (e.g., diagnosis and treatment for a particular clinical problem). Its utility relies on estimates of the probabilities that particular events and outcomes will occur. Decision trees are often used to represent alternative path ways graphically (see Figures 7.1 and 7.2 for examples).

departure from standard of care A treatment course or behavior that many practitioners would not take. It raises a mild degree of liability risk, should harm the result, but may prove reasonable to a percentage of practitioners if it possesses some documented effectiveness.

dependent variable In experimental design, the variable measured to determine if the independent variable had some effect. In correlational design, the variable predicted from the independent variable.

discredited practices Those interventions unable to consistently generate treatment outcomes (interventions) or valid data (assessments) beyond that obtained by the passage of time alone, expectancy, base rates, or credible placebo. *Discredited* subsumes ineffective and detrimental interventions but forms a broader and more inclusive characterization.

dissemination The process of spreading and dispersing evidence-based materials to professionals and the public. See also **implementation**.

epidemiology The study of how often and why diseases occur among different groups of people.

effect size (ES) A measure of difference between means or a correlation coefficient indicating the relative strength; it is calculated independently of measures of significance or random sampling fluctuations.

effect size benchmarks Selected levels to indicate small, medium, and large effect sizes. Often referenced as "Cohen's benchmarks."

error score In classical test theory, the difference between a person's true score and obtained score; error is the result of unreliable variance.

ETS Test Collection An electronic, Web-accessible (sydneyplus. ets.org) database providing basic, descriptive information for approximately 20,000 tests and measures.

evidence-based medicine (EBM) The integration of best research evidence with clinical expertise and patient values. Closely related to, but not identical with, **evidence-based practice**.

evidence-based practice (EBP) The integration of the best available research with clinical expertise in the context of patient characteristics, culture, and preferences.

exact p value The probability of obtaining a result (e.g., a correlation coefficient or difference between means) by chance, i.e., due to random sampling variability, under the assumption that the null hypothesis is true.

factor analysis A family of statistical techniques designed to identify dimensions (factors) accounting for the covariation in a multiplicity of variables.

factorial design A research design involving more than one independent variable operating simultaneously.

fail-safe statistic A statistic indicating the number of unpublished studies that would need to be uncovered and included in a meta-analysis to reduce the reported effect size to zero or some small value.

false negatives In a 2×2 table showing the relationship between performance on a test and on an external criterion, cases that exceed the cut-score on the criterion but not the cut-score on the test.

false positives In a 2×2 table showing the relationship between performance on a test and on an external criterion, cases that exceed the cut-score on the test but not the cut-score on the criterion.

fidelity The degree to which an implemented practice adheres to the original EBP; typically entails fidelity checks to determine compliance with the EBP protocol and staff competence in conducting it.

five As A mnemonic in evidence-based medicine for the five core skills: *a*sk a clinical question, *a*ccess the research literature, *a*ppraise the research, *a*pply the research to a particular case, and *a*ssess the effectiveness.

foreground questions Specific clinical questions typically formatted in searchable PICO terms that include the patient, intervention, comparison, and outcome. Contrast with **background questions**.

four Ds of legal liability These remind us of what a plaintiff must prove in a professional liability (malpractice) lawsuit: *d*ereliction of *d*uty that leads *d*irectly to *d*amages.

F test The *F* ratio, a ratio between two variances, used mainly to test the significance of differences among sample means, as applied in analysis of variance but also having many other applications in statistics.

generalization A continuation of behavior change across real-life settings, other than those included in treatment.

gross negligence A treatment course or behavior that most practitioners would not take. When such behaviors lead to harm, significant liability accrues.

heuristics Mental operating procedures or "rules of thumb" that we usually apply unconsciously to help perform abstract reasoning in cognitively economical ways. These strategies save us time and effort but typically fail when the actual data deviate from or fall outside our usual realms of expertise.

hierarchical regression A common method for entering variables into a multiple regression equation in which the researcher specifies the order of entry, sometimes with entire blocks of variables, according to some theoretical preference.

hits In a 2 × 2 table showing the relationship between performance on a test and on an external criterion, agreements between the test classification and the external criterion classification.

implementation The practical process of having practitioners actually use EBPs and thereby altering their clinical performance. See also **dissemination.**

independent variable In experimental design, the variable being manipulated. In correlational design, the variable used to predict status on another variable.

interaction In a factorial design, the joint effect of two or more independent variables; a differential effect resulting from combinations of different levels of the independent variables. See also **factorial design.**

interquartile range (IQR) The difference between the third quartile (Q_3 or 75th percentile) and the first quartile (Q_1 or 25th percentile).

loading A measure of the relationship between an item or test and the underlying dimensions (factors) in a **factor analysis.**

logistic regression A set of techniques, similar to multiple regression, for expressing the degree of relationship between a dichotomous criterion variable and a composite of predictor variables, some of which may be discrete rather than continuous. See also **multiple regression.**

main effect In a factorial design, the direct effect of one of the independent variables on a dependent variable. See also **factorial design.**

maintenance The consolidation and continuation of behavior change across time, usually after the treatment ends.

margin of error The standard error of a percentage, often reported in survey research.

mediator The specific causal agent within a compound of elements that leads to changes in a dependent variable.

Medical Subject Headings The National Library of Medicine's subject heading system or controlled vocabulary that helps searchers generate targeted searches.

Mental Measurements Yearbook (MMY) A collection of professional reviews of tests; new editions appear approximately every 3 years; reviews are also available electronically.

meta-analysis A family of techniques to formally combine or summarize results from many studies of a given topic using the statistical results from the studies.

moderator A variable that interacts with an independent variable to influence outcomes on the dependent variable.

multiple correlation The correlation, designated by R, between the criterion and the composite of predictor variables obtained in a multiple regression.

multiple regression A set of techniques to express the relationship between one variable (the criterion) and a composite of other variables, with the composite being constructed to apply optimal weights to each entry in the composite.

multiple regression equation The equation giving the prediction of the criterion variable (Y') from the composite of predictor variables, showing the weights assigned to each predictor variable; may be in either raw score or standardized form.

multivariate analysis of variance (MANOVA) A type of analysis of variance designed for use when more than one dependent variable enters the analysis. See also **analysis of variance (ANOVA).**

narrative review A summary of research studies on a single topic that depends on the review author's comprehension of the group of studies. Contrast with **meta-analysis.**

natural group contrasts A research design in which existing groups are compared; cases are not randomly assigned to the groups.

negative predictive power The percentage of cases which actually do not belong to a target group of all the cases falling below the cut-score on a test. See also **cut-score.**

null hypothesis The hypothesis that there is no difference between group means or no correlation between variables. Also sometimes called the "statistical hypothesis." Contrast with **research hypothesis.**

null hypothesis significance test (NHST) The statistical mechanisms (e.g., t test or F test) for determining whether to accept or reject the null hypothesis. See also **null hypothesis.**

observational study A research design that concentrates on obtaining an accurate description of behavior, either holistically or for a specific behavior.

obtained score In classical test theory, the score actually obtained by one individual on one occasion; also known as the "observed score."

odds ratio (OR) The ratio of odds for a particular characteristic applied to rates in two groups, when rates are expressed as odds rather than base rates.

*OR **confidence interval*** The confidence interval for an odds ratio; this confidence interval is asymmetrical around its OR. See also **confidence interval.**

outlier An aberrant or unusual data point, one that falls well outside the distribution of data points or the pattern(s) of relationship among variables.

paradoxical intervention Therapeutic technique in which the clinician gives a patient (or family) an assignment that will probably be resisted, but in so doing, the patient actually changes in a desirable direction.

parameter A descriptive measure (e.g., mean or standard deviation) on a population; often estimated by its corresponding statistic.

partial correlation A procedure for expressing the degree of relationship between two variables (*A* and *B*) with a third variable (*C*) "held constant" or "partialled out."

path analysis One type of causal modeling that draws the paths of imputed causal directions among interrelated variables; the outcome is usually presented as a path diagram.

patient characteristics, culture, and preferences The patient's personality, strengths, sociocultural context, unique concerns, and preferences brought to a clinical encounter that must be integrated into clinical decisions to best serve the patient. One of the three pillars of EBP.

pay-for-performance (P4P) A system of linking practitioner compensation to patient outcomes. Proposed models tend to recognize and reward clinicians whose aggregate outcome results show success relative to some agreed-upon measure (e.g., pre-/postassessment, external benchmark, or criterion).

PICO An acronym for *p*atient, *i*ntervention, *c*omparison, and *o*utcome. Used in formulating searchable clinical questions; also known as "PICOT" when *t*ype of question is added.

placebo An action or substance administered to a group with the expectation that it will not have any meaningful effect; often administered to a control group contrasted with a treatment group.

positive predictive power The percentage of cases which actually belong to a target group of all the cases falling above the cut-score on a test. See also **cut-score.**

power In the context of statistical significance tests, power is the probability of *avoiding* a Type II error, that is, rejecting the null hypothesis when it should be rejected because it is false. Power is defined as $1 - \beta$. See also **Type II error.**

practice guidelines Systematically developed statements to assist practitioner and patient decisions in specific clinical circumstances.

prevalence rate The percentage of a population having a particular characteristic; alternate name for **base rate.**

proportion of variance in common The degree of overlap or covariation between variables, especially as presented graphically in the form of overlapping geometric shapes or as a squared correlation (e.g., r^2, R^2).

quasi-experimental design A research design in which groups are compared but cases are not randomly assigned to the groups.

random Equal probability of being selected or assigned to a group or sample.

random sampling A method of selecting cases from a population such that each case has an equal probability of being selected.

randomized clinical trial The term used in clinical contexts to designate a true experimental design; also known as randomized controlled trial. See also **true experimental design.**

range restriction Restriction in the range or variance of scores, especially as such restriction affects the degree of correlation among variables.

relative risk The ratio of rates for a particular characteristic applied to base (prevalence) rates in two groups.

research hypothesis The hypothesis the researcher wishes to demonstrate or support. Also called the "scientific hypothesis." Contrast with **null hypothesis.**

risk management Retrospective evaluation for the prospective assessment of practice hazards. Risk management may involve addressing ethical violations, carelessness, simple errors, or even unfortunate outcomes without any actual negligence.

sampling frame The specific list of individual elements in a population; used for drawing samples from the population, especially in a survey design.

selectivity The percentage of cases correctly identified by a test as being in the target group; also known as **sensitivity.**

sensitivity The percentage of cases correctly identified as being in the target group; also known as **selectivity.**

significance level Usually means the same as **alpha level.**

significance test The statistical test, usually of a null hypothesis and usually involving F, t, or χ^2, to determine if the null hypothesis should be rejected. See also **null hypothesis.**

simple random sample A sample drawn from a population in such a way that each element of the population has an equal chance of being drawn into the sample.

specificity The percentage of cases correctly identified by a test as being in the non-target group.

standard error of a statistic The standard deviation of a distribution of sample statistics around its parent population parameter. Used for statistical **significance tests** and **confidence intervals.**

standard error of measurement (SEM) The standard deviation of the distribution of many hypothetical obtained scores around the true score; an index of imprecision in the obtained score resulting from unreliable variance.

standard of care The prevailing professional judgment of peers engaged in similar activities in similar circumstances, given the knowledge the practitioner had or should have had at the time.

statistic A descriptive measure (e.g., mean or standard deviation) of a sample; often used to estimate a STET **parameter.**

statistical hypothesis See **null hypothesis.**

stepwise method A common approach to entering variables into a multiple regression equation in which each variable is entered in turn with the variable's contribution examined and with new entries ceasing when a predetermined criterion is met.

stratified sample A sample drawn from a population which is first divided into strata or categories and then elements are drawn, usually proportionately, from the various strata.

structural equation modeling A family of techniques for analyzing the relationships among variables with an attempt to impute causal direction among those variables.

survey design A research design using some type of sampling technique usually to determine status variables such as presence of conditions or respondents' attitudes.

Test Critiques A collection of test reviews, with new volumes appearing periodically.

time series A type of quasi-experimental design in which a treatment group (and possibly a control group) is followed over time as an independent variable (such as a treatment) is turned on and off repeatedly. See also **quasi-experimental design.**

translational research The mutual influence of basic research and health care services; also known as "science-to-service" and "(lab) bench-to-bedside."

transportability The likelihood that an intervention found effective in one setting can be transported to a different setting with equal effectiveness.

treatment-as-usual (TAU) Treatment that patients would ordinarily receive in naturalistic health-care settings, especially in contrast to a treatment under investigation.

true experimental design A research design involving random assignment to groups, manipulation of an independent variable, and then measurement of a dependent variable comparing the groups. All variables other than the independent variable are controlled or allowed to vary at random among the groups.

true score In classical test theory, the score a person would receive on a perfectly reliable test; also conceptualized as the person's average score obtained after an infinite number of tests, varying forms, scorers, and occasions.

truncation A search tool that broadens a search by adding variations to the end of search terms, which can be helpful when searching for the plural of search terms.

t test A statistical significance test used for testing differences between sample means or for testing the significance of correlation coefficients.

Type I error The probability of rejecting the null hypothesis when, in fact, it is true and should not be rejected. The probability of committing a Type I error is alpha. See also **alpha level.**

Type II error The probability of failing to reject the null hypothesis when, in fact, it is false and should be rejected. The probability of committing a Type II error is defined as beta.

univariate outlier An aberrant or unusual data point, one that falls well outside the distribution of data points on a single variable.

wildcards Search tools that broaden searches by automatically searching for variations of search terms. Sometimes notated as *, ?, $, and !, wildcards can be applied to any part of search terms signaling the search system to identify alternate letters for searching.

χ^2 ***(chi-square)*** A test of significance used for data on nominal scales.

▌▌ REFERENCES ▌▌

Aarons, G. A. (2006). Transformational and transactional leadership: Association with attitudes toward evidence-based practice. *Psychiatric Services, 57,* 1162–1169.

Addiction Technology Transfer Center, www.nattc.org/index.html

Addis, M. E. (2002). Methods for disseminating research products and increasing evidence-based practice: Promises, obstacles, and future directions. *Clinical Psychology: Science and Practice, 9,* 367–378.

Alderson, P., & Green, S. (2002). Cochrane collaboration opens learning material for reviewers, www.cochrane-net.org/openlearning/

Alf, C., & Lohr, S. (2007). Sampling assumptions in introductory statistics classes. *American Statistician, 6,* 71–77.

American Psychological Association (2002). *Ethical principles of psychologists and code of conduct.* Washington, DC: American Psychological Association.

APA Task Force on Evidence-Based Practice. (2006). Evidence-based practice in psychology. *American Psychologist, 61,* 271–285.

Bachman, J. (2006). Pay for performance in primary and specialty behavioral health care: Two "concept" proposals. *Professional Psychology: Research and Practice, 37*(4), 384–388.

Barnett, V., & Lewis, T. (1994). *Outliers in statistical data.* New York: Wiley.

Begley, S. (2007, May 7). Just say no—to bad science. *Newsweek,* 57.

Bennett, B. E., Bricklin, P. M., Harris, E. A., Knapp, S., VandeCreek, L., & Youngreen, J. N. (2007). *Assessing and managing risk in psychological practice: An individualized approach.* Rockville, MD: American Psychological Association Insurance Trust.

Beutler, L. E., & Harwood, T. M. (2000). *Prescriptive psychotherapy: A practical guide to systematic treatment selection.* New York: Oxford University Press.

Beutler, L. E., Moleiro, C. M., & Talebi, H. (2002). Resistance. In J. C. Norcross (Ed.), *Psychotherapy relationships that work* (pp. 129–143). New York: Oxford University Press.

Bjorstad, G., & Montgomery, P. (2005). Family therapy for attention-deficit disorder or attention-deficit/hyperactivity disorder in children and adolescents. Cochrane Database of Systematic Reviews, www.cochrane.org/reviews/en/ab005042.html

Blanton, H., & Jaccard, J. (2006). Arbitrary metrics in psychology. *American Psychologist, 61*(1), 27–41.

BMC Medical Informatics and Decision Making, www.biomedcentral.com/bmcmedinformdecismak

Bohart, A. C. (2005). The active client. In J. C. Norcross, L. E. Beutler, & R. F. Levant (Eds.), *Evidence-based practices in mental health: Debate and dialogue on the fundamental questions.* Washington, DC: American Psychological Association.

Bohart, A., & Tallman, K. (1999). *How clients make therapy work: The process of active self-healing.* Washington DC: American Psychological Association.

Boston University. Introduction to evidence based medicine [interactive tutorial], medlib.bu.edu/tutorials/ebm/intro/index.cfm

Brennan, R. L. (2001). *Generalizability theory.* New York: Springer.

Bridges, P. H. (2003). *Factors affecting the propensity to adopt evidence-based practice in physical therapy* (Doctoral dissertation, 2003). Available from www.ebhc.org/2005/presentations/4-11/1%20Bridges%20Patricia.pps

Brunton, L. L. (Ed.). (2006). *Goodman & Gilman's: The pharmacological basis of therapeutics* (11th ed.). New York: McGraw-Hill.

Calculating risks of harm, www.clinicalevidence.com/ceweb/resources/calculate_risk.jsp

Campbell, D. T., & Stanley, J. C. (1963). *Experimental and quasi-experimental designs for research.* Chicago: Rand-McNally.

Castonguay, L. G., & Beutler, L. E. (Eds.). (2006). *Principles of therapeutic change that work.* New York: Oxford University Press.

Castro, F. G., Barrera, M., & Martinez, C. R. (2004). The cultural adaptation of prevention interventions: Resolving tensions between fit and fidelity. *Prevention Science, 5*, 41–45.

Center for Bioinformatics and Molecular Biostatistics, University of California–San Francisco (2006). Power and sample size programs [computer software], www.biostat.ucsf.edu/sampsize.html

Centre for Evidence-Based Medicine, www.cebm.net

Centre for Evidence-Based Medicine. Applying evidence to patients, www.cebm.utoronto.ca/practise/apply/

Centre for Evidence-Based Mental Health, www.cebmh.com

Centre for Health Evidence, www.cche.net

Chambless, D. L., & Crits-Christoph, P. (2005). The treatment method. In J. C. Norcross, L. E. Beutler, & R. F. Levant (Eds.), *Evidence-based practices in mental health: Debate and dialogue on the fundamental questions.* Washington, DC: American Psychological Association.

Chickering, A. W., & Gamson, Z. F. (1987, March). Seven principles for good practice in undergraduate education. *AAHE Bulletin*, 1987, 3–7.

Chorpita, B. F., Yim, L. M., Donkervoet, J. C., Arensdorf, A., Amundsen, M. J., McGee, C., et al. (2002). Toward large-scale implementation of empirically supported treatments for children: A review and observations by the Hawaii Empirical Basis to Services Task Force. *Clinical Psychology: Science and Practice, 9*, 165–190.

Cohen, J. (1988). *Statistical power analysis for the behavioral sciences* (2nd ed.). Hillsdale, NJ: Erlbaum.

Coleman, H.L.K., Wampold, B. E., & Casali, S. L. (1995). Ethnic minorities' ratings of ethnically similar and European American counselors: A meta-analysis. *Journal of Counseling Psychology, 42*, 55–64.

Collins, F. L., Leffingwell, T. R., & Belar, C. D. (2007). Teaching evidence-based practice: Implications for psychology. *Journal of Clinical Psychology, 63*, 657–670.

Cone, J. D. (2000). *Evaluating outcomes: Empirical tools for effective practice.* Washington, DC: American Psychological Association.

Daubert v. Merrell Dow Pharmaceuticals, Inc., 509 U.S. 579, 113 S. Ct. 2786 (1993).

De Los Reyes, A., & Kazdin, A. E. (2004). Measuring informant discrepancies in clinical child research. *Psychological Assessment, 16*, 330–334.

DiClemente, C. C. (2003). *Addiction and change: How addictions develop and addicted people recover.* New York: Guilford.

Dumont, R. P., Willis, J., & Stevens, C. (2001). Sensitivity, specificity, and positive and negative predictive power for continuous performance tests, alpha.fdu.edu/psychology/sensitivity_specificity.htm

Edwards, J. R., & Lambert, L. S. (2007). Methods for integrating moderation and mediation: A general analytical framework using moderated path analysis. *Psychological Methods, 12*, 1–22.

ETS Test Collection, sydneyplus.ets.org

Evidence-Based Behavioral Practice, www.ebbp.org

Evidence-Based Practice for the Helping Professions, www.evidence.brookscole.com

Evidence-Based Resources for the PDA (Dartmouth Medical School), www.dartmouth.edu/~biomed/resources.htmld/guides/ebm_pda.shtml

Farnsworth, J., Hess, J., & Lambert, M. J. (2001, April). *A review of outcome measurement practices in the* Journal of Consulting and Clinical Psychology. Paper presented at the annual meeting of the Rocky Mountain Psychological Association, Reno, NV.

Figueira, J., Greco, S. & Ehrgott, M. (Eds.). (2005). *Multiple criteria decision analysis: State of the art surveys.* New York: Springer.

Forming a Clinical Question, medlib.bu.edu/tutorials/ebm/pico/index.cfm

Gambrill, E. (2005). *Critical thinking in clinical practice: Improving the accuracy of judgments and decisions about clients* (2nd ed.). New York: Wiley.

Garb, H. N. (1998). Clinical judgment. In H. N. Garb (Ed.), *Studying the clinician: Judgment research and psychological assessment* (pp. 173–206). Washington, DC: American Psychological Association.

Geisinger, K. F., Spies, R. A., Carlson, J. F., & Plake, B. S. (2007). *The seventeenth mental measurements yearbook.* Lincoln: University of Nebraska Press.

Gibbs, L., Armstrong, E. C., Raleigh, D., & Jones, J. (2003). *Evidence-based practice for the helping professions,* www.evidence.brookscole.com

Gilovich, T., Griffin, D., & Kahneman, D. (Eds.). (2002). *Heuristics and biases: The psychology of intuitive judgment.* New York: Cambridge University Press.

Giustini, D., & Barsky, E. (2005). A look at Google Scholar, PubMed, and Scirus: Comparisons and recommendations. *Journal of the Canadian Health Libraries Association, 26*(3), 85.

Glass, G. V., & Hopkins, K. D. (1996). *Statistical methods in education and psychology* (3rd ed). Needham Heights, MA: Allyn & Bacon.

Glass, G. V., McGaw, B., & Smith, M. L. (1981). *Meta-analysis in social research.* Beverly Hills, CA: Sage.

Gotham, H. J. (2004). Diffusion of mental health and substance abuse treatments: Development, dissemination, and implementation. *Clinical Psychology: Science and Practice, 11,* 160–176.

Gotham, H. J. (2006). Advancing the implementation of evidence-based practices into clinical practice: How do we get there from here? *Professional Psychology: Research and Practice, 37,* 606–613.

Greene, B., Bieschke, K. J., Perez, R. M., & DeBord, K. A. (2007). Delivering ethical psychological services to lesbian, gay, and bisexual clients. In *Handbook of counseling and psychotherapy with lesbian, gay, bisexual, and transgender clients* (2nd ed., pp. 181–199). Washington, DC: American Psychological Association.

Greenhalgh, T., Robert, G. Macfarlane, F., Bate, P., & Kyriakidou, O. (2004). Diffusion of innovations in service organizations: Systematic review and recommendations. *Milbank Qurterly, 82*, 581–629.

Greer, A. (1994). Scientific knowledge and social consensus. *Controlled Clinical Trials, 15*, 431–436.

Grimm, L. G., & Yarnold, P. R. (Eds.). (1996). *Reading and understanding multivariate statistics.* Washington, DC: American Psychological Association.

Grissom, R. J., & Kim, J. J. (2005). *Effect sizes for research: A broad practical approach.* Mahwah, NJ: Erlbaum.

Guyatt, G., & Rennie, D. (Eds.). (2002). *Users' guides to the medical literature: Essentials of evidence-based clinical practice.* Chicago: American Medical Association.

Hannan, C., Lambert, M. J., Harmon, C., Nielsen, S. L., Smart, D. W., Shimokawa, K., & Sutton, S. W. (2005). A lab test and algorithms for identifying clients at risk for treatment failure. *Journal of Clinical Psychology: In Session, 61*, 155–163.

Hedges, L. V., & Olkin, I. (1985). *Statistical method for meta-analysis.* San Diego: Academic Press.

Hoagwood, K. (2002). Making the translation from research to its application: The *je ne sais pas* of evidence-based practices. *Clinical Psychology: Science and Practice, 9*, 210–213.

Hogan, T. P. (2005). Sources of information about psychological tests. In G. P. Koocher, J. C. Norcross, & S. S. Hill (Eds.), *Psychologist's desk reference* (2nd ed., pp. 105–107). New York: Oxford University Press.

Hogan, T. P., & Evalenko, K. (2006). The elusive definition of outliers in introductory statistics textbooks. *Teaching of Psychology, 33*, 252–256.

Holahan, C. J., Moos, R. H., Holahan, C. K., Brennan, P. L., & Schutte, K. K. (2005). Stress generation, avoidance coping, and depressive symptoms: A 10-year model. *Journal of Consulting and Clinical Psychology, 73*, 658–666.

Huang, X., Lin, J., & Demmer-Fushman, D. (2006, November). *PICO as knowledge representation for clinical questions.* Paper presented at the annual symposium of the American Medical Informatics Association, Washington, DC. Available from www.umiacs.umd.edu/~jimmylin/publications/Huang-etal-AMIA2006.pdf

Hunink, M. G. M., Glasziou, P. P., Siegel, J. E., Weeks, J. C., Pliskin, J. S., Elstein, A. S., et al. (2001). *Decision making in health and medicine: Integrating evidence and values.* Cambridge, UK: Cambridge University Press.

Hunsley, J., & Lee, C. M. (2007). Research-informed benchmarks for psychological treatments: Efficacy studies, effectiveness studies, and beyond. *Professional Psychology: Research and Practice, 38,* 21–33.

Hunsley, J. J., Crabb, R., & Mash, E. J. (2004). Evidence-based clinical assessment. *The Clinical Psychologist, 57*(3), 25–32.

Hunter, J. E., & Schmidt, F. L. (2004). *Methods of meta-analysis: Correcting error and bias in research findings* (2nd ed.). Newbury Park, CA: Sage.

Institute for Behavioral Research. Organizational readiness for change, www.ibr.tcu.edu/evidence/evi-orc.html

Institute of Medicine (2001). *Crossing the quality chasm: A new health system for the 21st century.* Washington, DC: National Academy Press.

Jette, D. U., Bacon, K., Batty, C., Carlson, M., et al. (2003). Evidence-based practice: Beliefs, attitudes, knowledge, and behaviors of physical therapists. *Physical Therapy, 93,* 78–96.

Kahneman, D., & Tversky, A. (Eds.). (2000). *Choices, values, and frames.* New York: Cambridge University Press.

Karpiak, C. P., & Norcross, J. C. (2005). Lifetime prevalence of mental disorders in the general population. In G. P. Koocher, J. C. Norcross, & S. S. Hill III (Eds.), *Psychologists' desk reference* (2nd ed., pp. 3–6). New York: Oxford University Press.

Kazdin, A. (2001). *Behavior modification in applied settings* (6th ed.). Belmont, CA: Thomson Wadsworth.

Kazdin, A. E. (2005). *Parent management training.* New York: Oxford University Press.

Kazdin, A. E. (2006). Arbitrary metrics: Implications for identifying evidence-based treatments. *American Psychologist, 61*(1), 42–49.

Kennedy, J. J. (1992). *Analyzing qualitative data: Log-linear analysis for behavioral research* (2nd ed.). New York: Praeger.

Kent, D., & Hayward, R. (2007). When averages hide individual differences in clinical trials. *American Scientist, 95,* 60–72.

Kessler, R. C., Chiu, W. T., Demler, O., & Walters, E. E. (2005). Prevalence, severity, and comorbidity of 12-month DSM-IV disorders in the National Comorbidity Survey Replication. *Archives of General Psychiatry, 62,* 617–627.

Keyser, D. J. (2004). *Test critiques* (Vol. XI). Austin, TX: Pro-Ed.

Kirk, R. E. (1995). *Experimental design: Procedures for the behavioral sciences* (3rd ed.). Pacific Grove, CA: Brooks/Cole.

Kirk, R. E. (1996). Practical significance: A concept whose time has come. *Educational and Psychological Measurement, 56,* 746–759.

Klem, L. (1995). Path analysis. In L. G. Grimm & P. R. Yarnold (Eds.), *Reading and understanding multivariate statistics* (pp. 65–97). Washington, DC: American Psychological Association.

Kline, R. B. (1998). *Principles and practice of structural equation modeling.* New York: Guilford.

Koocher, G. P., Goodman, G. S., White, S., Friedrich, W. N., Sivan, A. B., & Reynolds, C. R. (1995). Psychological science and the use of anatomically detailed dolls in child sexual abuse assessments. *Psychological Bulletin, 118,* 199–222.

Koocher, G. P., & Keith-Spiegel, P. (2008). *Ethical principles in psychology and the mental health professions: Standards and cases.* New York: Oxford University Press.

Kruger, J., & Dunning, D. (1999). Unskilled and unaware of it: How difficulties in recognizing one's own incompetence lead to inflated self-assessments. *Journal of Personality Assessment and Social Psychology, 77,* 1121–1134.

Kumho Tire Co., Ltd. v. Carmichael, 119 S. Ct. 1167 (1999).

Lambert, M.J. (Ed.). (2004). *Bergin and Garfield's handbook of psychotherapy and behavior change* (4th ed). New York: Wiley.

Lambert, M. J. (Ed.). (2005). Enhancing psychotherapy outcome through feedback. *Journal of Clinical Psychology: In Session, 61,* 141–217.

Lambert, M. J., & Ogles, B. M. (2004). The efficacy and effectiveness of psychotherapy. In M. J. Lambert (Ed.), *Bergin and Garfield's handbook of psychotherapy and behavior change* (4th ed., pp. 139–193). New York: Wiley.

Lau, A. S. (2006). Making the case for selective and directed cultural adaptations of evidence-based treatments: Examples from parent training. *Clinical Psychology: Science and Practice, 13,* 295–310.

Lenth, R. V. (2006). Java Applets for Power and Sample Size [computer software], www.stat.uiowa.edu/~rlenth/Power

Lewczy, C. M., Garland, A. F., Hurlburt, M. S., Gerrity, J., & Hough, R. L. (2003). Comparing DISC-IV and clinician diagnoses among youths receiving mental health services. *Journal of the American Academy of Child and Adolescent Psychiatry, 42*, 349–356.

Lilienfeld, S. O. (2007). Psychological treatments that cause harm. *Perspectives on Psychological Science, 2*, 53–70.

Lipsey, M. W., & Wilson, D. B. (2000). *Practical meta-analysis*. Thousand Oaks, CA: Sage.

Luborsky, L., Diguer, L., Seligman, D. A., Rosenthal, R., Krause, E. D., Johnson, S., et al. (1999). The researcher's own therapy allegiances: A "wild card" in comparisons of treatment efficacy. *Clinical Psychology: Science and Practice, 6*, 95–106.

Maddox, T. (2003). *Tests: A comprehensive reference for assessments in psychology, education, and business* (5th ed.). Austin, TX: Pro-Ed.

Marlatt, G. A., & Gordon, J. R. (Eds.). (1985). *Relapse prevention: Maintenance strategies in addictive behavior change*. New York: Guilford.

Meehl, P. E. (1954). *Clinical vs. statistical prediction*. Minneapolis: University of Minnesota Press.

Messer, S. B. (2004). Evidence-based practice: Beyond empirically supported treatments. *Professional Psychology: Research and Practice, 36*, 580–588.

Michels, R. (1984). Preface. In *Differential therapeutics in psychiatry*. New York: Brunner/Mazel.

Miller, P. M., & Kavanagh, D. J. (Eds.). (2007). *Translation of addictions science into practice*. London: Elsevier.

Miller, S. D., Duncan, B. L., Sorrell, R., & Brown, G. S. (2005). The partners for change outcome management system. *Journal of Clinical Psychology: In Session, 61*, 199–208.

Miller, W. R., & Rollnick, S. (2002). *Motivational interviewing: Preparing people for change*. New York: Guilford.

Miller, W. R., Wilbourne, P. L., & Hettema, J. E. (2003). What works? A summary of alcohol treatment outcome research. In R. K. Hester & W. R. Miller (Eds.), *Handbook of alcoholism treatment approaches* (3rd ed., pp. 13–63). Boston: Allyn & Bacon.

Miller, W. R., Yahne, C. E., Moyers, T. B., Martinez, & Pirritano, M. (2004). A randomized trial of methods to help clinicians learn motivational interviewing. *Journal of Consulting and Clinical Psychology, 72*, 1050–1062.

Moffitt, T. E., Harrington, H. L., et al. (2007). Depression and generalized anxiety disorder: Cumulative and sequential comorbidity in a birth cohort followed prospectively to age 32 years. *Archives of General Psychiatry, 64,* 651–660.

Moher, D., Schulz, K. F., & Altman, D. G. (2001a). CONSORT E-checklist and flowchart. Available from www.consort-statement.org/Downloads/download.htm

Moher, D., Schulz, K.F., & Altman, D.G. (2001b). The CONSORT statement: Revised recommendations for improving the quality of reports of parallel-group randomized trials. *Annals of Internal Medicine, 134,* 657–662.

Mohr, D. C. (1995). Negative outcome in psychotherapy: A critical review. *Clinical Psychology: Science and Practice, 2,* 12–19.

Murphy, L. L., Spies, R. A., & Plake, B. S. (2006). *Tests in print* (Vol. 7). Lincoln: University of Nebraska Press.

National Advisory Mental Health Council on Behavioral Science (2000). Translating behavioral science into action: Report of the National Advisory Mental Health Council's Behavioral Science Workgroup (No. 00-4699). Bethseda, MD: National Institute of Mental Health.

National Comorbidity Survey Replication (2005). www.hcp.med.harvard.edu/ncs/

National Guideline Clearinghouse, www.guideline.gov

National Implementation Research Network (2005). *Implementation research: A synthesis of the literature,* nirn.fmhi.usf.edu

National Institute for Health and Clinical Excellence, www.nice.org.uk

National Registry of Evidence-Based Programs and Practices, www.nrepp.samhsa.gov

Nelson, T. D., & Steele, R. G. (2007). Predictors of practitioner self-reported use of evidence-based practices: Practitioner training, clinical setting, and attitudes toward research. *Administration and Policy in Mental Health, 34*(4), 319–330.

NHS Centre for Reviews and Dissemination (1999). *Getting evidence into practice,* www.york.ac.uk/inst/crd/ehc51.pdf

Norcross, J. C. (2002a). Empirically supported therapy relationships. In J. C. Norcross (Ed.), *Psychotherapy relationships that work: Therapist contributions and responsiveness to patients* (pp. 3–16). New York: Oxford University Press.

Norcross, J. C. (Ed.). (2002b). *Psychotherapy relationships that work: Therapist contributions and responsiveness to patient needs.* New York: Oxford University Press.

Norcross, J. C., Beutler, L. E., & Levant, R. F. (Eds.). (2006a). *Evidence-based practices in mental health: Debate and dialogue on the fundamental questions.* Washington, DC: American Psychological Association.

Norcross, J. C., Koocher, G. P., Fala, N. C., & Wexler, H. K. (2007). *What doesn't work: Discredited treatments in the addictions.* Manuscript in preparation.

Norcross, J. C., Koocher, G. P., & Garofalo, A. (2006). Discredited psychological treatments and tests: A Delphi poll. *Professional Psychology: Research & Practice, 37,* 515–522.

Norcross, J. C., & Lambert, M. J. (2006). The therapy relationship. In J. C. Norcross, L. E. Beutler, & R. F. Levant (Eds.), *Evidence-based practices in mental health: Debate and dialogue on the fundamental questions* (pp. 208–218). Washington, DC: American Psychological Association.

Oxman, A. D., Thomson, M. A., Davis, D. A., et al. (1995). No magic bullets: A systematic review of 102 trials of interventions to improve professional practice. *Canadian Medical Association Journal, 153,* 1423–1431.

Pagoto, S. L., Spring, B., Coups, E. J., Mulvaney, S., Coutu, M., & Ozakinci, G. (2007). Barriers and facilitators of evidence-based practice perceived by behavioral science health professionals. *Journal of Clinical Psychology, 63,* 695–705.

Parkes, J., Hyde, C., Deeks, J., & Milne, R. (2001). Teaching critical appraisal skills in health care setting. *Cochrane Reviews,* articleCD001270.

Pedhazur, E. J. (1997). Multiple regression in behavioral research: Explanation and prediction (3rd ed.). Fort Worth, TX: Harcourt Brace.

Perkins, E. (2001) Johns Hopkins tragedy: Could librarians have prevented a death? Retrieved from newsbreaks.infotoday.com/nbreader.asp?ArticleID=17534

Peterson, D. R. (1995). The reflective educator. *American Psychologist, 50,* 975–983.

Petitti, D. B. (2000). *Meta-analysis, decision analysis, and cost-effectiveness: Methods for quantitative synthesis in medicine* (2nd ed.). New York: Oxford University Press.

PICO Maker, www.library.ualberta.ca/pdazone/pico/

PICO Tutorials, healthlinks.washington.edu/ebp/pico.html

President's New Freedom Commission on Mental Health, www.mentalhealthcommission.gov

Prochaska, J. O., DiClemente, C. C., & Norcross, J. C. (1992). In search of how people change: Applications to addictive behaviors. *American Psychologist, 47,* 1102–1114.

Prochaska, J. O., & Norcross, J. C. (2007). *Systems of psychotherapy: A transtheoretical analysis* (6th ed.). Belmont, CA: Thomson Brooks/Cole.

Prochaska, J. O., Norcross, J. C., & DiClemente, C. C. (1995). *Changing for good.* New York: Avon.

Prochaska, J. O., Norcross, J. C., & DiClemente, C. C. (2005). Stages of change: Prescriptive guidelines. In G. P. Koocher, J. C. Norcross, & S. S. Hill (Eds.), *Psychologists' desk reference* (2nd ed.). New York: Oxford University Press.

Prochaska, J. O., Velicer, W. F., Rossi, J. S., Goldstein, M. G., Marcus, B. H., Rakowski, W., et al. (1994). Stages of change and decisional balance for 12 problem behaviors. *Health Psychology, 13,* 39–46.

Rich, B. A., & Eyberg, S. M. (2001). Accuracy of assessment: The discriminative and predictive power of the Eyberg Child Behavior Inventory. *Ambulatory Child Health, 7,* 249–257.

Ruscio, A. M., & Holohan, D. R. (2006). Applying empirically supported treatments to complex cases: Ethical, empirical, and practical considerations. *Clinical Psychology: Science and Practice, 13,* 146–162.

Sackett, D. L., Richardson, W. S., Rosenberg, W. M. C., & Haynes, R. B. (1997). *Evidence-based medicine: How to practice and teach EBM.* Edinburgh, UK: Churchill Livingstone.

Sackett, D. L., Straus, S. E., Richardson, W. S., Rosenberg, W., & Haynes, R. B. (2000). *Evidence-based medicine: How to practice and teach EBM* (2nd ed.). London: Churchill Livingstone.

Sagan, C. (1997). *The demon-haunted world: Science as a candle in the dark.* New York: Random House.

Schardt, C., Adams, M. B., Owens, T., Keitz, J. A., & Fontelo, P. (2007). Utilization of the PICO framework to improve searching PubMed for clinical questions. *BMC Informatics and Decision Making, 7,* article 16.

Schilling, M. F., Watkins, A. E., & Watkins, W. (2002). Is human height bimodal? *The American Statistician, 56,* 223–229.

Schneider, M. S., Brown, L. S., & Glassgold, J. M. (2002). Implementing the resolution on appropriate therapeutic responses to sexual orientation: A guide for the perplexed. *Professional Psychology, 33,* 265–276.

Semple, D., Smyth, R., Burns, J., Darjee, R., & McIntosh, A. (Eds.). (2005). *Oxford handbook of psychiatry.* New York: Oxford University Press.

Sheehan, A. K., Walrath, C. M., & Holden, E. W. (2007). Evidence-based practice use, training and implementation in the community-based service setting: A survey of children's mental health service providers. *Journal of Child and Family Studies*, *16*, 169–183.

Spring, B., Pagoto, S., Knatterud, G., Kozak, A., & Hedeker, D. (2007). Examination of the analytic quality of behavioral health randomized clinical trails. *Journal of Clinical Psychology*, *63*, 53–71.

Spring, B., & Walker, B. B. (Eds.). (2007). Evidence-based practice in clinical psychology: Education and training issues. *Journal of Clinical Psychology*, *63*(7).

Straus, S. E., Richardson, W. S., Glasziou, P., & Haynes, R .B. (2005). *Evidence-based medicine: How to practice and teach EBM* (3rd ed.). London: Elsevier.

Strupp, H. H., & Hadley, S. W. (1977). A tripartite model of mental health and therapeutic outcomes. *American Psychologist*, *32*, 187–194.

Sudman, S. (1976). *Applied sampling*. New York: Academic Press.

Sue, S., & Lam, A. G. (2002). Cultural and demographic diversity. In J. C. Norcross (Ed.), *Psychotherapy relationships that work: Therapist contributions and responsiveness to patients* (pp. 401–421). New York: Oxford University Press.

Tabachnick, B. G., & Fidell, L. S. (2007). *Using multivariate statistics* (5th ed.). Boston: Pearson.

Tashiro, T., & Mortensen, L. (2006). Translational research: How social psychology can improve psychotherapy. *American Psychologist*, *61*, 959–966.

Thompson, B. (1996). AERA editorial policies regarding statistical significance testing: Three suggested reforms. *Educational Researcher*, *25*(2), 26–30.

Thyer, B. A., & Wodarski, J. S. (Eds.). (2007). *Social work in mental health: An evidence-based approach*. New York: Wiley.

Toolkits for Evidence-Based Practices. Shaping mental health services toward recovery, mentalhealth.samhsa.gov/cmhs/communitysupport/toolkits/about.asp

Tryon, G. S., Collins, S., & Felleman, E. (2006, August). *Meta-analysis of the third session client-therapist working alliance*. Paper presented at the annual convention of the American Psychological Association, New Orleans, LA.

Tryon, G. S., & Winograd, G. (2002). Goal consensus and collaboration. In J. C. Norcross (Ed.), *Psychotherapy relationships that work* (pp. 109–125). New York: Oxford University Press.

Tukey, J. W. (1977). *Exploratory data analysis*. Reading, MA: Addison-Wesley.

Turk, D. C., & Salovey, P. (Eds.). (1988). *Reasoning, inference, and judgment in clinical psychology.* New York: Free Press.

Ullman, J. B. (2007). Structural equation modeling. In B. G. Tabachnick & L. S. Fidell (Eds.), *Using multivariate statistics* (5th ed., pp. 676–780). Boston: Allyn and Bacon.

University of Hertfordshire EBM Resources, www.herts.ac.uk/lis/subjects/ health/ebm.htm

University of Sheffield. Netting the evidence, www.shef.ac.uk/scharr/ir/ netting/

Villanueva, E. V., Burrows, E. A., Fennessy, P. A., Rajendran, M., & Anderson, J. N. (2001). Improving question formulation in evidence appraisal in a tertiary care setting: A randomized controlled trial. *BMC Informatics and Decision Making, 1,* article 4.

Walker, B. B., Seay, S. J., Solomon, A. C., & Spring, B. (2006). Treating chronic migraine headaches: An evidence-based practice approach. *Journal of Clinical Psychology: In Session, 62,* 1367–1378.

Wallerstein, R. S. (1986). *Forty-two lives in treatment.* New York: Guilford.

Walters, G. D. (2003). Predicting institutional adjustment and recidivism with the Psychopathy Checklist factor scores: A meta-analysis. *Law and Human Behavior, 27,* 541–558.

Wampold, B. E. (2001). *The great psychotherapy debate: Models, methods, and findings.* Mahwah, NJ: Erlbaum.

Weisz, J. R., Jensen-Doss, A., & Hawley, K. M. (2006). Evidence-based youth psychotherapies versus usual clinical care. *American Psychologist, 61,* 671–689.

Westen, D. I. (2006). Patients and treatments in clinical trials are not adequately representative of clinical practice. In J. C. Norcross, L. E. Beutler, & R. F. Levant (Eds.), *Evidence-based practices in mental health: Debate and dialogue on the fundamental questions* (pp. 161–171). Washington, DC: American Psychological Association.

Westen, D., & Morrison, K. (2001). A multidimensional meta-analysis of treatments for depression, panic, and generalized anxiety disorder: An empirical examination of the status of empirically supported therapies. *Journal of Consulting and Clinical Psychology, 69,* 875–899.

Westen, D., Novotny, C., & Thompson-Brenner, H. (2004). The empirical status of empirically supported therapies: Assumptions, methods, and findings. *Psychological Bulletin, 130,* 631–663.

Wilkinson, L., & APA Task Force on Statistical Inference. (1999). Statistical methods in psychology journals: Guidelines and explanations. *American Psychologist, 54*, 594–604.

Wilson, G. T. (1995). Empirically validated treatments as a basis for clinical practice: Problems and prospects. In S. C. Hayes, V. M. Follette, R. M. Dawes, & K. E. Grady (Eds.), *Scientific standards of psychological practice* (pp. 163–196). Reno, NV: Context Press.

Witkiewitz, K. A., & Marlatt, G. A. (Eds.). (2007). *Therapist's guide to evidence-based relapse prevention.* London: Elsevier.

Wolf, F. M. (1986). *Meta-analysis: Quantitative methods for research synthesis.* Newbury Park, CA: Sage.

Wyer, P. C., Keitz, S., Hatala, R., Hayward, R., Barratt, A., Montori, V., et al. (2004). Tips for learning and teaching evidence-based medicine: Introduction to the series. *Canadian Medical Journal Association, 171*, 77–81.

■■ INDEX ■■

Independent variables (*continued*)
  research report appraisal and,
    171–173, 178
Indexed databases, advantages of, 36
Information resources, 37–68. *See
    also* background information
    resources; filtered information
    resources; unfiltered information
    resources
  BMJ Clinical Evidence, 50–52
  Campbell Collaboration Reviews
    of Interventions and Policy
    Evaluations, 47–48
  Cochrane Database of Systematic
    Reviews, 43–47, 292
  Cork Database, 65–66
  Cumulative Index to Nursing and
    Allied Health Literature, 58–60
  Database of Abstracts of Reviews
    of Effects, 48–50
  eMedicine Clinical Knowledge
    Database, 38–39
  evidence-based journals, 52–54
  Google Scholar, 66–67
  LexisNexis, 63–65
  MEDLINE, 54–57
  Physicians' Information and
    Education Resource, 38
  practice guidelines, 42–43
  PsychINFO, 61–63
  PubMed, 57–58
  Social Services Abstracts, 60–61
  textbooks, 37–38
  Web sites, 39–42
Informed consent. *See* consent
Innovative treatments
  ethics of, 263–264
  liability of, 260–263
Insurers
  outcome measures used by,
    255–256
  probability of approval by, 217

Interaction, between independent
    variables, 98–99, 297
Internal consistency reliability, 131
Internet resources
  for background information, 39–42
  precautions for use of, 40–41
Interquartile range (IQR), 154, 297
Interventions. *See also* treatments
  acceptability of, 217
  adopt, adapt, or abandon options,
    232–236
  failure of, 218, 235–236
  IQR (interquartile range), 154, 297

Journals, evidence-based, 52–54

Keyword searches, limitations of, 36
Kumho Tire Co., Ltd. v. Carmichael, 263
Kurtosis, 126

Laboratory-validated treatments,
    11–12
Latent variables, 120
Legal liability, four Ds of, 259–260, 296
LexisNexis, 63–65
Liability, 259–263, 296
Librarians, as resource, 76
Lifetime prevalence rate, 144
Literature research, 29–77
  basic search concepts, 32–36
  evidence-based medicine search
    engines, 68–70
  expert assistance for, 76
  resources for. *See* information
    resources
  search process, 29–32
  on tests and measures, 70–76
Loading, 116, 297
Logistic regression, 114–115, 297

Main effect, 98, 297
Maintenance, 282–283, 298